CP1

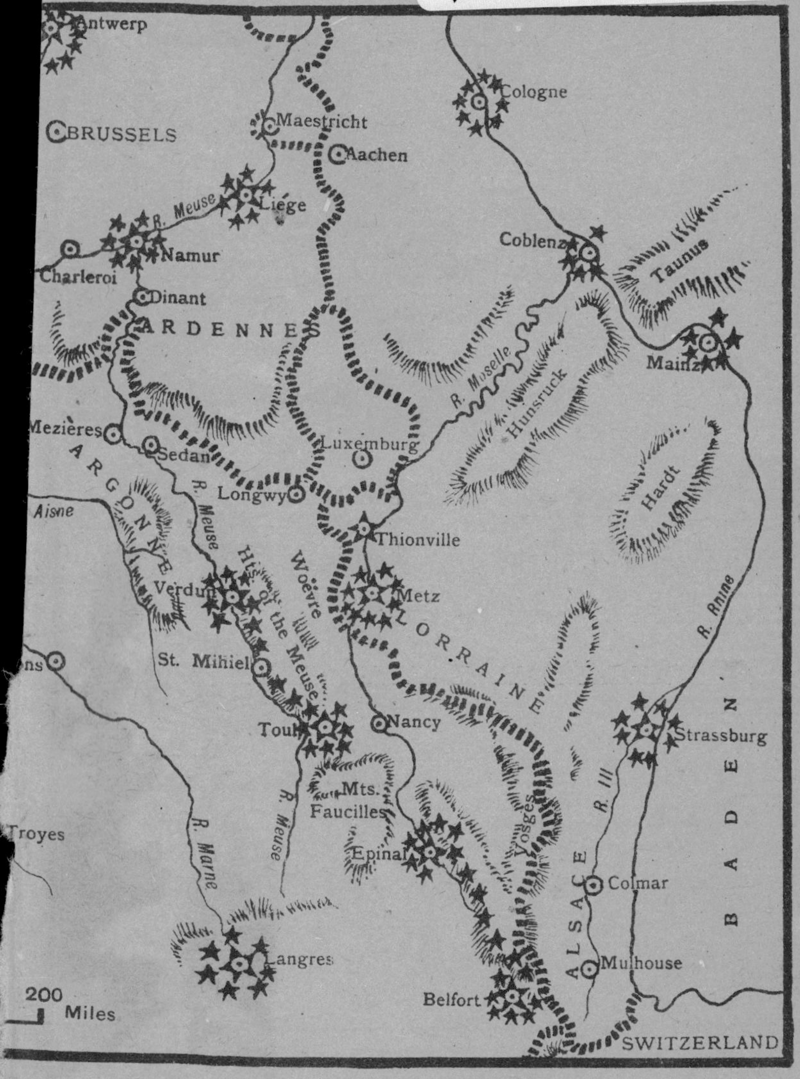

...stern Theatre of War.

NELSON'S HISTORY OF THE WAR

VOLUME XXIV.

NELSON'S HISTORY OF THE WAR. By

John Buchan.

Volume XXIV. Victory.

THOMAS NELSON AND SONS, LTD.
LONDON, EDINBURGH, AND NEW YORK

CONTENTS.

APPENDICES.

LIST OF MAPS.

LIST OF MAPS.

NELSON'S HISTORY OF THE WAR.

CHAPTER CLXIV.

THE LAST PHASE IN THE WEST.

The German High Command calls on Berlin for an Armistice—Change of Ministry—Prince Max of Baden Chancellor—His Record—His Note to Washington of 4th October—His Reichstag Speech—American Reply of 8th October—German Note of 12th October—American Reply of 14th October—Haig carries the Line of the Selle—Evacuation of Douai—King Albert advances—Fall of Roulers, Menin, and Thourout—Fall of Ostend—Fall of Lille—Mangin enters Laon—Germans retire to Hunding Line—Haig and Débeney attack on 17th October—The Sambre Canal crossed—The New German Water-line—British Attack of 23rd October—The Battle of the Rivers—Advance between Mormal Forest and the Scheldt—The Rhonelle crossed—Advance in the South—Desperate Position of German Armies—German Peace Note of 20th October—The Alleged Democratization of the German Government—American Reply of 23rd October—German Reply of 27th October—Ludendorff resigns—His Character and Career—The Twilight of the Gods.

THE destruction of the Siegfried defences broke the nerve of the German High Command, and when Ludendorff began to waver it was inevitable that the civilian statesmen should follow suit. The Western offensive had collapsed, and even a Western defensive was becoming doubtful.

Bulgaria and Turkey were on the verge of utter defeat. Austria was pleading for peace at any price. The German people were dumbly determined that somehow or other the war should end before the winter. If the army was to be saved, by hook or by crook a way must be found to suspend hostilities, for every day made it clearer that retreat to a line of assured defence was beyond its power. Accordingly the High Command bade the politicians quicken the pace of their negotiations, and, discarding their old line of argument, beg unequivocally for an armistice. They were well aware that such a step would go far to wreck the *moral* of the troops, but they had no other choice.

First, however, a Government must be set up which might find favour in the eyes of their enemies, for von Hertling and von Payer and von Hintze were fatally compromised. On 30th September the Emperor accepted the resignation of the Imperial Chancellor and the Foreign Secretary, and announced his desire that "the German people shall co-operate more effectively than hitherto in deciding the fate of the Fatherland." At the same time all the Secretaries of State placed their portfolios at the disposal of the Crown. The other posts mattered less at the moment, but a new Chancellor was urgently required, for with him it would lie to open negotiations with the enemy Powers.

Sept. 30.

The Emperor's choice fell upon Prince Maximilian of Baden, the cousin of the reigning Grand Duke and the President of the Upper House of the Baden Legislature. He was a man of fifty-one, a student of popular philosophy, and an amateur of liberal thought. His personal charm was considerable, he spoke fluently and well, and he had earned some reputation by his efforts on behalf of the unhappy Allied prisoners of war. He was fond of expounding a democracy of his own, which he sedulously distinguished from the molluscous type in vogue—as he said—in America, as well as from the class tyranny of Bolshevism. For the statesmen of the Allies—notably Lord Grey of Fallodon and Mr. Wilson—he professed small respect; but he preached a diluted version of their doctrines. For example, in December 1917 he warned the Baden Upper House that the German people were "too apt to maintain an indolent attitude of acquiescence towards the authorities without any longing to assume personal responsibility for the cause of the Fatherland;" and concluded: "The sword cannot break down the moral opposition that has reared itself against us. If the world is to be reconciled to the greatness of our power, it must feel that behind our power stands a world conscience."

The new Chancellor had therefore a fair record for amiable if somewhat vague liberalism. He lost no time in setting to work on the task for which he had been appointed. On 4th October he sent a Note to President Wilson, asking him to take in hand the restoration of peace, and to invite the Allies to send plenipotentiaries to open negotiations. He announced that Germany accepted the President's proposals set forth in his message to Congress of January 8, 1918 (the famous "Fourteen Points"), and in his later pronouncements, as a basis for the discussion of peace terms. In order to prevent further bloodshed he asked for the con-

Oct. 4.

clusion of an immediate armistice on land and water and in the air. That same day the Government of Vienna dispatched a message to Washington in similar terms.

These appeals marked a dramatic change in German policy, for they specifically accepted as their basis a speech which President Wilson had made in New York on 27th September on the eve of the opening of the fourth great American war loan. In that speech he had declared that the price of peace was "impartial justice in every item of the settlement, no matter whose interest is crossed," and had developed this thesis in five particulars.* Germany may well have believed that these principles would be unacceptable to certain classes among her opponents, especially in

Sept. 27.

* *First,* the impartial justice meted out must involve no discrimination between those to whom we wish to be just and those to whom we do not wish to be just. It must be a justice which plays no favourites and knows no standard but the equal rights of the several peoples concerned.

Second, no special or separate interest of any single nation or any group of nations can be made the basis of any part of the settlement which is not consistent with the common interest of all.

Third, there can be no leagues or alliances or special covenants and understandings within the general and common family of the League of Nations.

Fourth, and more specifically, there can be no special, selfish economic combinations within the League, and no employment of any form of economic boycott or exclusion, except as the power of economic penalty, by exclusion from the markets of the world, may be vested in the League of Nations itself as a means of discipline and control.

Fifth, all international agreements and treaties of every kind must be made known in their entirety to the rest of the world.

France, and hoped thereby to drive a wedge into the Alliance. But President Wilson had also dealt faithfully with the Governments of the Central Powers. "They have convinced us that they are without honour, and do not intend justice. They observe no covenants, accept no principle but force and their own interest. We cannot 'come to terms' with them. They have made it impossible. The German people must by this time be fully aware that we cannot accept the word of those who forced this war upon us. We do not think the same thoughts or speak the same language of agreement." Prince Max's acceptance of the speech of 27th September involved, therefore, a jettison of his predecessors.

Next day, 5th October, in the Reichstag, he elaborated his policy. He stood, he said, on the ground of Germany's reply to the Pope's Note of August 1, 1917, and of the Reichstag resolution of 19th July in the same year. He was an enthusiast for a League of Nations on the basis of equal rights for all, both weak and strong. He advocated the complete restoration of Belgium, and hoped that an understanding could be reached as to an indemnity. He would not permit the Russian treaties to stand in the way of a settlement. Finally he declared that in selecting the members of the new Government he had selected only those who stood "on the basis of a just peace, regardless of the war situation," and who had "openly declared this to be their standpoint at the time when we stood at the height of our military successes."

Oct. 5.

Among such could not be reckoned Prince Max himself, for in the preceding February, on the eve of the great Western attack, he had written a letter to Prince Alexander of Hohenlohe, in which this striking passage occurred: "As I reject parliamentary institutions for both Germany and Baden, I had to tell the German and the Baden people that I understand their need, but that I do not believe such institutions would bring them any help. As regards the question of peace, my line is exactly the same. Even I naturally wish to make as much as possible out of our successes. In contrast to the so-called Peace Resolution * (the hateful child of fright and the Berlin dog days), I want to get as much in the way of indemnities as we can in any shape or form, so that the end of the war will not leave us impoverished. On this point I do not quite agree with you. I still think that it is not necessary to say more about Belgium than has been said already. The enemy know enough already, and Belgium is the only commodity we have to barter with in dealing with an enemy as cunning and wide-awake as England." The publication of this letter did not improve Prince Max's prestige. The Whig aristocrat is an ancient type, and his wavering impulses and intermittent flirtations with democracy have made sport for the cynic in every age.

On 8th October President Wilson replied. In the first place, he asked the Imperial Chancellor what precisely he meant. Did Germany accept the terms he had laid down in his speeches, and was her object in entering upon discussions merely to decide the practical details of their application? In the second place, he

Oct. 8.

* The Reichstag Resolution of July 19, 1917.

announced that America could not propose to her Allies a cessation of hostilities so long as the armies of the Central Powers were upon Allied soil. As a guarantee of good faith there must first be withdrawal from invaded territory. In the third place, he asked if Prince Max spoke for the constituted authorities of the Empire who had so far conducted the war.

Germany made haste to answer, for by 12th October, the date of the reply, the last remnants of the Siegfried zone had gone, and Gouraud and Pershing had made dangerous progress towards Mezières. To President Wilson's first and third questions the answer was yes, on the understanding that the Governments of America's Allies also accepted the President's principles. As for the second, Germany and Austria were willing to evacuate invaded territory as a preliminary to an armistice, and suggested a mixed commission to make the necessary arrangements.

Oct. 12.

Small wonder that Germany assented. To get her troops back intact to her frontier was her dearest wish. She was in truth offering nothing and asking everything. Evacuation by consent would no doubt mean that the French and Belgian towns still in her power would suffer no further destruction ; but it was unlikely, with the shadow of defeat hanging over her, that she would persist in such destruction and so increase the indemnities to be exacted from her. It would mean, on the other hand, the immunity of her armies from a besetting danger, for Ludendorff was engaged in an impossible task. Her reply opened the eyes of the most innocent among the Allies to the snare spread before them. Peace negotiations were impossible without an armistice, for otherwise the currency of negotiations would be changing from day to day; but an armistice such as she suggested would rob Foch of that military advantage which he had so laboriously won. There was nothing to prevent Germany, once safe inside her frontiers, from breaking off negotiations and instituting war on a new plan. It was clear that if an armistice came it must be one which was equivalent to surrender.

On 14th October President Wilson made his rejoinder, and there was no dubiety about the terms.

Oct. 14.

Events of some significance had happened within the past days. On the morning of 10th October the Irish mail boat had been torpedoed, with the loss of nearly 500 lives. On 14th October the report of a British committee on the treatment by Germany of prisoners taken in the spring of 1918 was published, a hideous record of callousness and brutality. Moreover, the German armies in retreating were burning and looting in their old fashion. The Allies were not in the mood to be tender with their failing enemy. The President told Prince Max that no armistice could be considered while Germany continued her illegal and inhuman practices. He pointed out that one of his principal terms had been the destruction of every arbitrary Power which could disturb the peace of the world; the power which had hitherto controlled Germany was of this type: what guarantees were there that it had been changed? "It is indispensable that the Governments associated against Germany should know beyond a peradventure with whom they have been dealing."

Most important of all, he clinched in memorable

words the question of an armistice, and destroyed Germany's last hope on that score.

"It must be clearly understood that the process of evacuation and the conditions of an armistice are matters which must be left to the judgment and advice of the military advisers of the Government of the United States and the Allied Governments, and the President feels it his duty to say that no arrangement can be accepted by the Government of the United States which does not provide absolutely satisfactory safeguards and guarantees of the maintenance of the present military supremacy of the armies of the United States and of the Allies in the field."

This was final. Foch and Haig, Pétain and Pershing, were not likely to fling away the predominance which was now assured to them.*

The history of events runs now in two parallel streams, one of diplomacy and one of war. We turn to the campaign in the field.

Oct. 10.

By the evening of 10th October, as we have seen, Le Cateau was in Haig's possession, and our troops held the very slopes where in August 1914 Smith-Dorrien had fought his great battle against odds, and bluffed von Kluck at a moment when that General had victory in his hands. Pershing and Gouraud had cleared the Argonne

* On 15th October President Wilson informed Austria that the tenth of his original points must be modified, in view of the recognition by the U.S.A. of the Czecho-Slovaks as a *de facto* belligerent Government, and of the national aspirations of the Jugo-Slavs. "The President is no longer at liberty to accept a mere 'autonomy' of these peoples as a basis of peace, but is obliged to insist that they, and not he, shall be the judge of what action on the part of the Austro-Hungarian Government will satisfy their aspirations."

Forest, and were threatening the southern section of the vital lateral railway; Lille was in danger of envelopment; the two great salients—between the Lys and the Somme, and between the Selle and the Argonne—were becoming daily more precarious. Ludendorff had no further thought of holding what

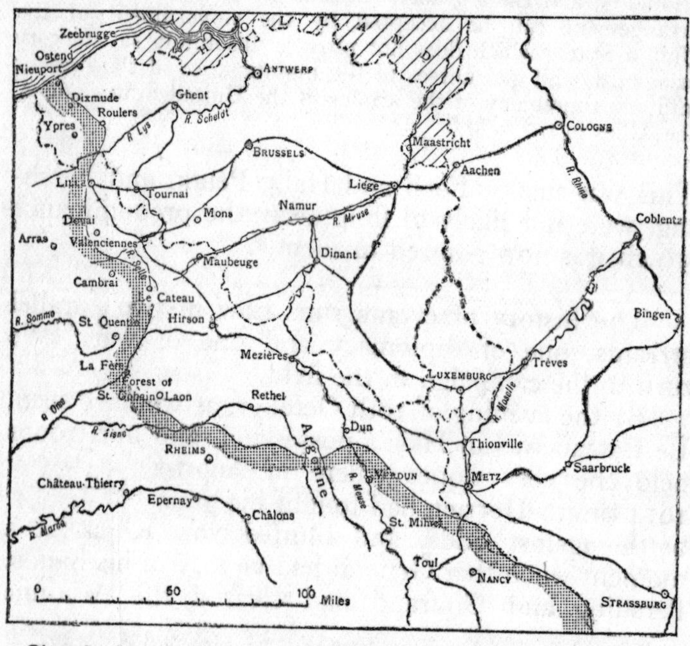

Sketch showing Situation on the Western Front, evening of October 10, 1918.

for two years he had regarded as his key positions—Lille and the St. Gobain *massif*—for the other keys, such as Cambrai and St. Quentin, had gone. His one object was to protect the railway, Lille-Valenciennes-Hirson-Mezières, long enough to ensure an orderly withdrawal; for if it fell too soon, large parts of his intricate front would be cut off. Accordingly he expedited the general retirement between the sea and the Meuse, and massed his chief resistance in the sections where the railway was most directly threatened—against Pershing and Gouraud in the south, and against Rawlinson, Byng, and Horne in the centre.

The Selle is a little stream which runs from the hilly ground around Bohain and Busigny northwards by Le Cateau and Solesmes to join the Scheldt. On its east bank the enemy had taken up position, and Haig's first business was to master the river line. By the 13th he had reached the Selle as far north as Haspres, and held strong bridgeheads on the east bank. On the 16th he took the village of Haussy well east of the river. Meantime Horne's left and Birdwood's right had been closing in on Douai from north and south. On the 12th the western side of the Sensée Canal between Arleux and Corbehem had been cleared, and the outskirts of Douai reached; and east of Lens we were in Montigny and Annay. On the 17th Douai was evacuated by the enemy.

Oct. 13.

Oct. 16.

Oct. 12.

Oct. 17.

The time had come for a forward movement in the north, where the difficulties of the countryside compelled long delays for the reorganization of traffic routes between each stage of the advance. At 5.35 on the morning of Monday, 14th October, King Albert attacked on the whole front between Dixmude and Comines on the Lys, with the Belgians on his left; the French

Oct. 14.

Third Army, under Humbert, and other Belgian troops in the centre ; and the British Second Army, under Plumer, on the right, between the Menin-Roulers road and the Lys. In spite of the difficulties of the Flanders autumn, the Allies moved fast, for they were beyond the area which had been tortured by four years of incessant war. The British 10th and

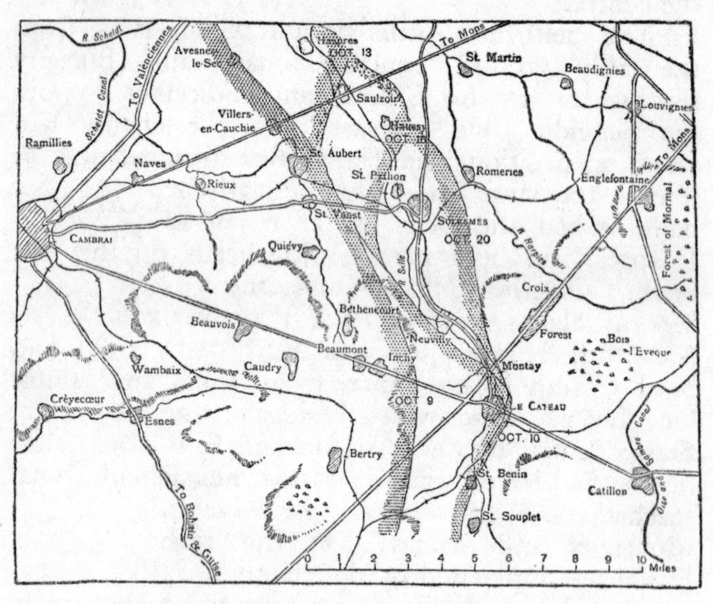

The Advance from Cambrai across the Selle.

19th Corps pushed forward to the heights overlooking Menin and Wervicq ; the 2nd Corps took Moorseele, and came close to Gulleghem and Steenbeek ; the French surrounded Roulers, and the Belgians took Iseghem and Cortemarck. Next day Menin and Wervicq fell, and Thou-

Oct. 15.

rout was surrounded. By the 16th Plumer held the north bank of the Lys from Frelinghien to Harlebeke, and had forced a passage at many points, while the French and the Belgians to the north had advanced eighteen miles since the morning of the 14th. Von Armin had no choice but to retreat. By the evening of the 16th the Allied front ran from the Lys at Harlebeke by Pitthem and the western skirts of Bruges to the neighbourhood of Ostend. Next day the British Navy had arranged to descend upon Ostend, but when Sir Roger Keyes arrived he found the place empty. The enemy had fled. Three days later the advance guards of the Allies were on the Dutch frontier. This was the end of the use of Belgium for German submarines and aircraft, and by the work of these six days Germany's sea-base had been flung back 250 miles, from Westende to Borkum.

Oct. 16.

Oct. 17.

King Albert's advance had made Lille untenable. With Plumer at Harlebeke and Horne at Douai its defence was outflanked, and von Quast fell back between the Lys and the Sensée, with Birdwood's Fifth Army at his heels. On the 15th we forced the Haute Deule Canal on a wide front north of Pont-à-Vendin. Early on the morning of Thursday, the 17th, our airmen reported that the enemy was retiring from Lille, and had sent out some thousands of civilians towards our lines. At noon a patrol of the Liverpools entered the city, to be received with frenzied joy by the inhabitants; and that night divisions of the British 8th and 11th Corps had reached the outskirts. Next day Lille was occupied by our

Oct. 15.

Oct. 17.

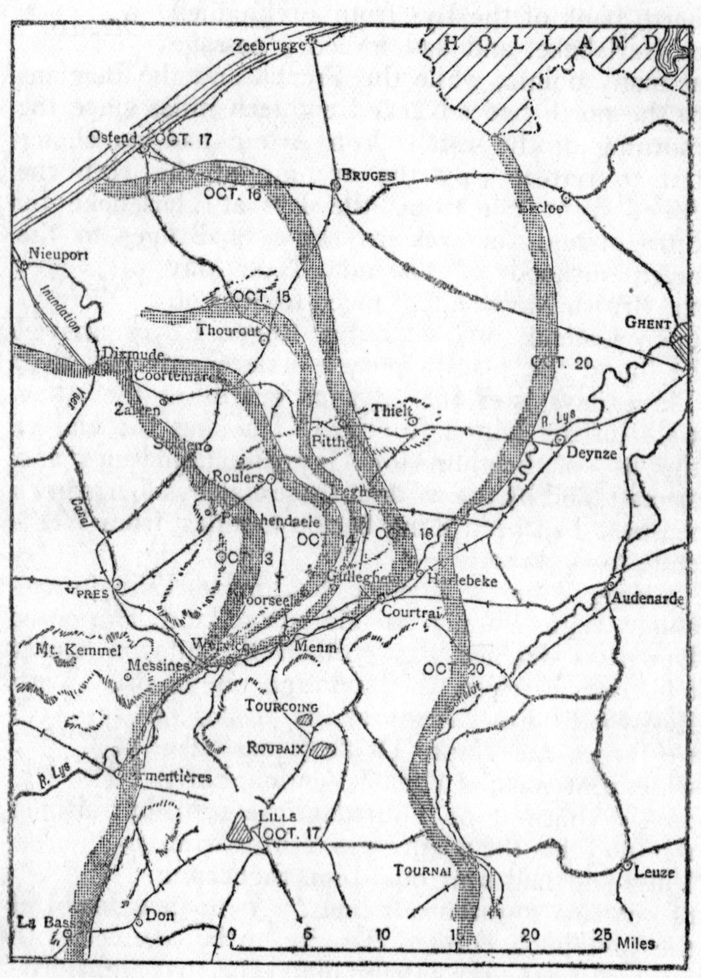

The Allied Advance in Flanders, October 14–20.

troops, and the 15th Corps pressed on to the east, taking Roubaix and Tourcoing. The capital of the north-east was restored to France, and its statue in the Place de la Concorde could once again be garlanded with flowers.

Oct. 18.

The progress of that week was not less conspicuous in the south, where the French First, Tenth, and Fifth Armies were directed towards the Hunding Line, the last German defence between the Oise and the Aisne. As early as the 11th there were signs of a withdrawal from the Laon salient. The St. Gobain *massif* was relinquished, and at ten in the morning of the 13th Mangin's vanguard entered Laon, and *Te Deum* was sung in the great cathedral. The VII. and I. German Armies were falling back on the Hunding Line, which ran along the Serre from its junction with the Oise, then along the Sissonne, and thence to the Aisne at Condé-lez-Herpy. Behind that line lay another along the Serre by Marle and Montcornet to the Ardennes Canal. The system was the protection of the lateral railway at Hirson, as the Siegfried zone had been its protection in the Valenciennes section. By the 15th Mangin and Guillaumat were in touch with the front Hunding position. On their left Débeney, with the French First Army, held the western bank of the Oise, from the mouth of the Serre to near Hauteville, whence he stretched north to the west of Mennevret till he linked up with Rawlinson at Vaux Andigny on the Selle.

Oct. 13.

Oct. 15.

The next move was with Haig. Already he was within eight miles of Valenciennes. It was his business to force the Selle positions, and reach a

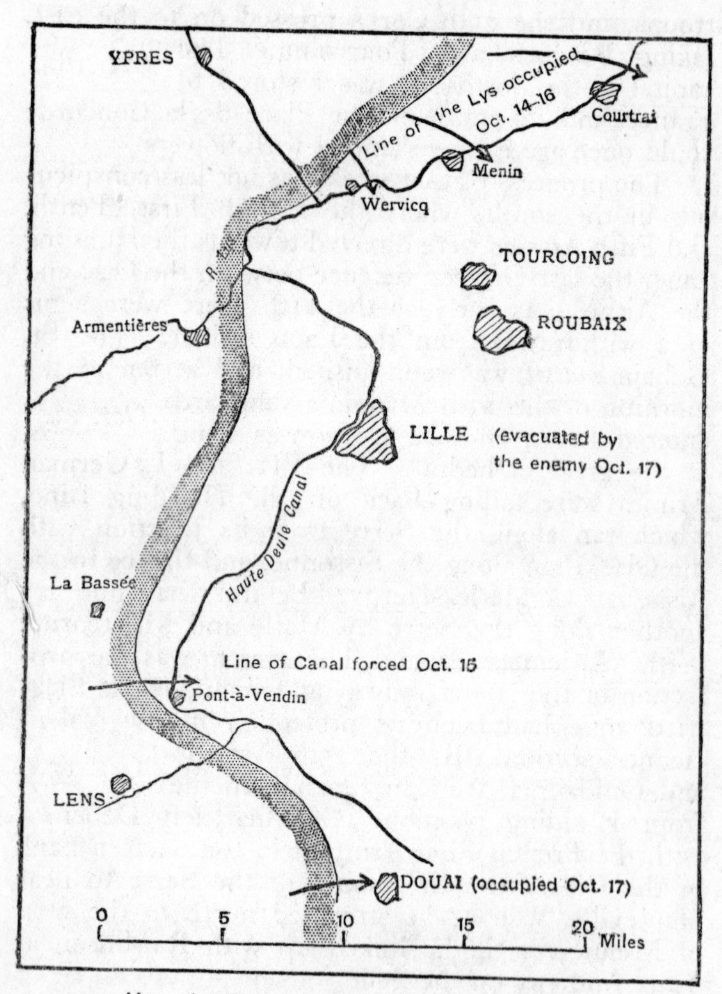

How the Germans were forced out of Lille.

front from the Sambre-et-Oise Canal by the western edge of the Forest of Mormal to Valenciennes, and

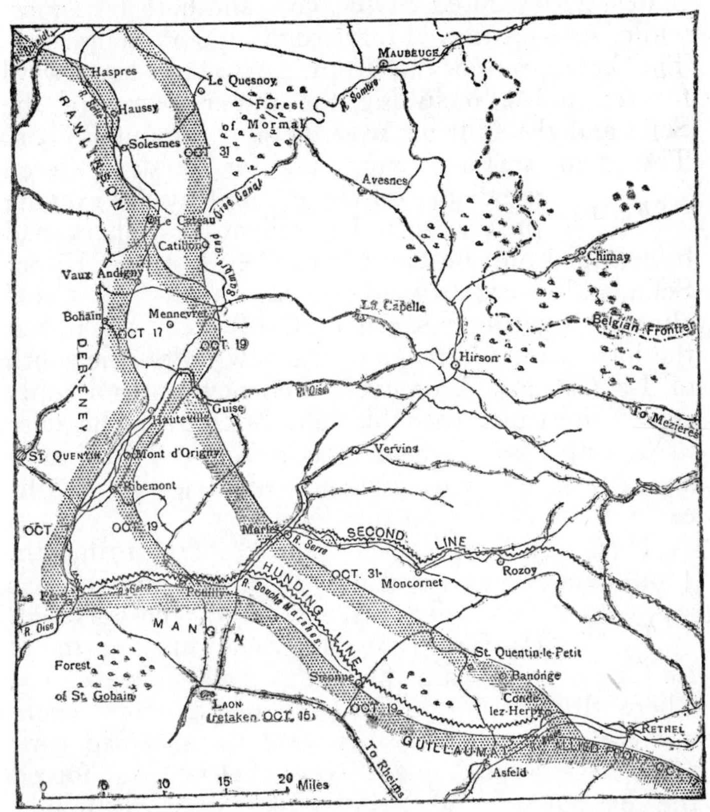

The French Advance against the Hunding Line, and over the Oise and the Sambre Canal on the right of the British.

so destroy the section of the main railway north of Avesnes. The advance began with an attack by Rawlinson at 5.20 on the morning of Thursday the 17th. He had in line from

Oct. 17.

right to left the 9th, 2nd United States, and 13th Corps, embracing the 46th, 1st, 6th, 30th United States, 27th United States, 50th and 66th Divisions, while Débeney moved forward in support on his right. The battleground ran from Le Cateau southward for ten miles, including the upper course of the Selle and the difficult wooded slopes about Bohain. The enemy was in strength, and for two days offered a gallant resistance. But by the evening of the 19th his salient at Bohain had been wiped out, he had been driven from the Upper Selle, and forced beyond the Sambre-et-Oise Canal almost everywhere south of Catillon. This meant the loss to the Germans of the new water-line south of Le Cateau. Moreover, Débeney was not only across the canal with his left, but across the Oise itself with his centre and right between Ribémont and Mont d'Origny, whence his line ran south-eastward to Pouilly on the Serre.

Oct. 19.

Next day Byng struck with the 38th, 17th, 5th, 42nd, 62nd, Guards and 19th Divisions, and Horne's right division, the 4th, co-operated. His aim was the Selle line north of Le Cateau to Denain, five miles from Valenciennes, where that stream joins the Scheldt. Here again the enemy resisted stoutly, and he had had time to wire his positions. Nevertheless, we forced the passage of the Selle, took Solesmes, fought our way, with the assistance of tanks, up the eastern slopes, and by the close of the rainy afternoon were looking down on the little valley of the Harpies. On the left, Horne reached the left bank of the Ecaillon River, and took Denain. All along the line there was a conspicuous advance.

Oct. 20.

Birdwood was now within two miles of Tournai, Plumer and Humbert were crossing the Lys on a wide front, and the Belgians, having taken Bruges and Zeebrugge, lay along the Lys Canal from Deynze to the Dutch frontier.

The Selle position had fallen, and Haig could now move towards his larger objective, the line from Valenciennes to the Sambre-et-Oise Canal along the west edge of the Mormal Forest. The enemy was seeking a new water-front, the Scheldt and the Sambre Canal, each broad and navigable, and therefore formidable barriers against tanks, but separated by a wide neck of land. He was about to lose another part of his lateral line, for the Valenciennes section was almost out of use ; but if he could hold the Mormal Forest, he had an alternative—the branch from Avesnes to Maubeuge and Mons, and thence to Ghent and Brussels. The position was a strong one—the Scheldt, the Sambre Canal, and the Mormal Wood—but it had one weak spot. Between the Scheldt and the northern end of the forest was a gap of ten miles. Across this gap ran two little streams, the Ecaillon and the Rhonelle, and on these the enemy proposed to stand. If Haig broke through that gap, the whole position must crumble.

Oct. 23.

Haig struck in force on Wednesday, 23rd October, on a front of fifteen miles from a point north-east of Haussy to Mazinghien, south of Catillon. On the first day Rawlinson, on the right, attacked at 1.20 in the morning, with the 9th and 13th Corps, embracing the 1st, 6th, 25th, and 18th Divisions, while Byng, on the left, brought into action the 5th, 4th, 6th, and 17th Corps, including the 33rd, 21st, 5th, 42nd, 37th, New Zealand, 3rd, 2nd, and 19th Divisions. Next day Horne's right, the 61st Division of the 17th Corps, and the 4th and 51st Divisions of the 22nd Corps, extended the battle five miles farther north to the Scheldt.

Oct. 24.

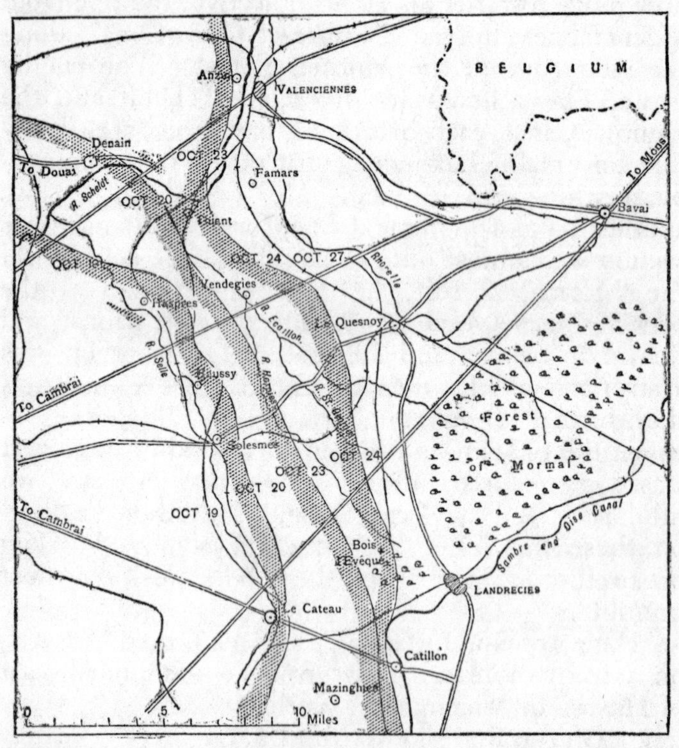

Haig's Advance between the Sambre Canal and the Scheldt.

The Battle of the Rivers—the Scheldt, the little streams in the gap, the Sambre-Oise Canal, and farther south the Serre and the Aisne—was now beginning: the last of the great conflicts in the West. Everywhere on the centre and left the Allies were now in open country, and facing hastily prepared field defences; but in the south Mangin and Guillaumat, Gouraud and Pershing, had still to carry the last system fortified on the old enemy plan. The resistance, as before, was most stubborn against Haig opposite the Mormal Forest, and against Pershing on the extreme right. Indeed, the First United States Army on the fifteen miles between the Meuse and the Argonne had not less than thirty German divisions crowded against them.* The weather was bad, and the misty air made it hard to locate enemy batteries, while the undevastated woods and hamlets gave endless chances for machine-gun resistance. The Mormal Forest, too, made a perfect screen for counter-attack.

Yet in two days the British Fourth, Third, and First Armies advanced six miles. The launching of the attack at different hours was a repetition in miniature of Foch's general strategy. We forced the outer defences formed by the Ecaillon and its tributaries, the Harpies and the St. George, taking Thiart on the Scheldt and the village of Vendegies-sur-Ecaillon. We did not attempt to enter the forest, nor to touch Landrecies at its south-western end, though we cleared the enemy out of the adjacent Bois l'Evêque; nor did we make any further assault on Valenciennes. Haig's aim was to take both this last town and the Mormal Wood by turning movements. On the evening of the 24th we were

* Gouraud's Fourth Army on a much wider front had engaged between 26th September and 12th October twenty-four German divisions.

on the western skirts of the forest, and within a mile of Le Quesnoy. For the next few days we advanced slowly, but by the 27th were east of the main railway from the skirts of Le Quesnoy to Famars, where the 51st Division were repeating their familiar exploits. In the operations in this area since 17th October twenty-four British and two American divisions had been opposed by thirty-one German, and had taken from them 20,000 prisoners and 475 guns.

Oct. 24.

Oct. 27.

By the last day of October Haig had established bridgeheads east of the Rhonelle, while Plumer and Humbert had made good progress between the Lys and the Scheldt. The British advance had had its effect on the line farther south, and the Germans had evacuated the angle between the Oise and the Serre. By the end of the month Débeney was in the outskirts of Guise, while Mangin was well north of the Souche, and Guillaumat had reached the line St. Quentin-le-Petit-Banogne-Condé-lez-Herpy. Each of the three was about twenty-three miles distant from Hirson. This area offered special opportunities for a great advance, for it was the old avenue by which the armies of France had been wont to move upon Namur and East Flanders. Though there were many little streams and woods, there were no broad rivers or continuous ranges to assist the defence. Pershing had also made progress, but slowly, and in the face of desperate counter-attacks. The American front now ran from the Meuse by Andevanne and Remonville to Champigneulles, and thence north of Grand Pré and Olizy. In the month's fighting on this

Oct. 31.

front they had taken 24,000 prisoners and over 150 guns.

The condition of Ludendorff's forces was be-

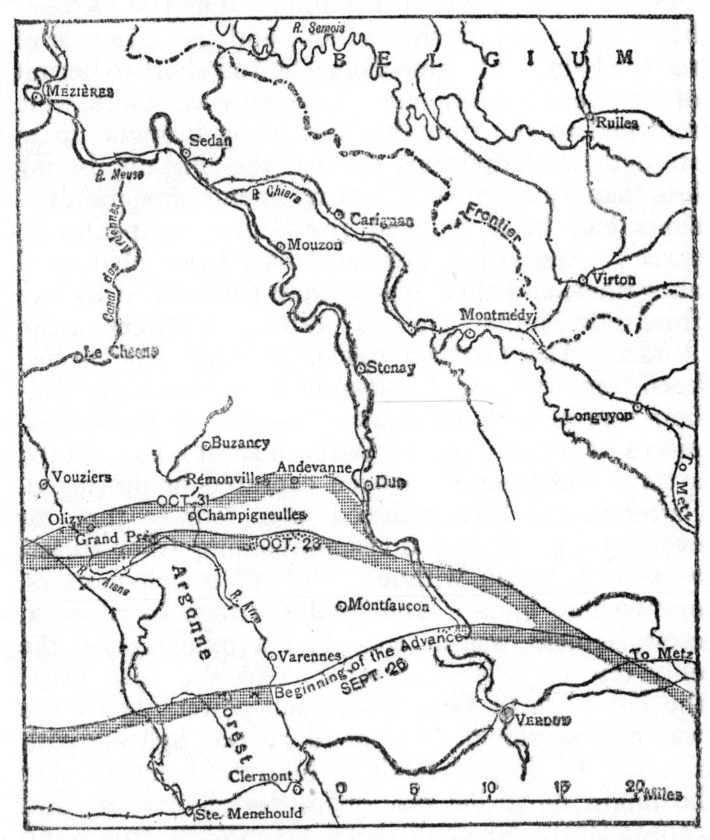

The American Advance between the Aisne and the Meuse towards the Belgian Frontier.

coming tragic. If those of the Allies were tired, his were in the last stages of fatigue. On 21st

March the enemy had possessed a reserve of eighty fresh divisions, and during April, May, and June divisions were not sent back to the line without at least a month of rest and training. On 31st October he had but one fresh division, and the intervals of rest had shrunk to nine days—far too short to permit of recovery. Moreover, these wearied units were returned to the front without being brought up to strength, and divisions entered the line numbering less than 1,000 rifles. The regiments in some divisions had been reduced from nine companies to three; twenty-five divisions had been disbanded altogether, and their places were badly filled by five third-rate units brought during October from Russia. The German casualties since March had been some two and a half million, of which one million represented permanent losses. Of the 18,000 pieces of artillery on the Western front on 15th July, a third had since then been captured or destroyed. Batteries had been reduced from four to three or even two guns, and divisions coming from Russia went into action without artillery, trench mortars, or machine guns. The total shortage of rifles on establishment was at least half a million, and the only reserves were the remains of the 1920 class, the last hope of Germany's man-power, which she was now sacrificing. Ludendorff was fighting with the fury of despair to delay his retirement, so that he might move his vast quantities of material, and consequently he could give his broken troops no rest. The result was that their discipline was breaking, and the whole enemy *moral* was on the brink of collapse.

To make matters worse, it was clear that there

was no city of refuge in the shape of a shorter line to which he could retreat and find a breathing space. There was indeed the theoretical line based on Antwerp, and running along the Lower Scheldt to Termonde, and thence by the Dendre, covering Brussels, and by Namur and the Meuse to Mezières. But this line had the glaring disadvantage that in the Central Meuse section it had no lateral communications, and that it would not be sufficiently shorter to enable him to save greatly in men. If he fell farther back he might get a line about half the length of his present front, from Liége, over the high moors of the Ardennes, covering Luxembourg, Thionville, and Metz. But that would bring him close to his own frontier, and expose Germany's chief industrial area to the perils of war ; to fall back upon that would be to admit defeat. As for the line of the Rhine, it had the same drawbacks intensified, and it was of an impossible length. But, indeed, the whole discussion of those remote positions was academic. Had the enemy reached them, he could not have stayed in them, and it was very certain that he would never reach them. The Meuse was already turned. It needed but a final bound to set the Americans astride the Metz railway. With Haig pressing fiercely in on the centre it was inevitable that the retreat would be shepherded northward, with appalling losses, into the gap of Liége, and there, on the scene of her worst infamies, Germany would meet her fate. The men who had outraged Belgium were for the most part dead in dishonoured graves, but justice would be done upon their haggard successors. The shadow of a far more terrible Sedan brooded over the proud German High Command.

In such circumstances it was small wonder that Germany strove feverishly for peace. She flung dignity to the winds, blasphemed her old gods, and recanted with indecent haste her former creeds—

The Allied Front at the end of October.

not as a penitent, indeed, but as a criminal who stands condemned and seeks to ingratiate himself with his judges. On 20th October she addressed a Note to President Wilson,

Oct. 20.

agreeing to leave the conditions of armistice to the military advisers of both sides, and to accept the present relative strength on the fronts as the basis of arrangement, trusting to the President to approve no demand " irreconcilable with the honour of the German people." She denied the charge of illegal and inhuman practices in war, but undertook, " in order to avoid anything that might impede the efforts to secure peace," to instruct the U-boat commanders for the future to refrain from torpedoing passenger ships. As for the President's condition about the removal of every arbitrary power, she urged that she had already set her house in order. The new Government in Germany was free from all arbitrary influence, and approved by an overwhelming majority of the people.

> " A fundamental change has come about in this regard. The new Government has been formed in complete accord with the desires of a Parliament which issued from equal, general, secret, and direct suffrage. The leaders of the great parties of the Reichstag are amongst its members. In the future, too, no Government can enter upon or carry on its office without possessing the confidence of the majority of the Reichstag. The responsibility of the Imperial Chancellor towards Parliament is being legally extended and safeguarded. The first act of the new Government was to submit a Bill to the Reichstag so amending the Constitution of the Empire that the approval of Parliament is requisite for a decision on war and peace."

The new German Ministers claimed that their Government had been democratized. But the claim was untrue. The sovereignty of the German Empire lay in the Bundesrat or Federal Council, of which Prussia, represented by the Imperial Chancellor, held the presidency and the majority of votes. The Secretaries of State were not Ministers of the Empire in the constitutional sense: they were subordinates of the Chancellor, who was the spokesman of the Federated Governments, with whom the power lay. The delegates to the Federal Council were not elected by any franchise, popular or otherwise; they were nominated by each Government without parliamentary control. The recent changes had in no way modified the prerogatives of the Bundesrat, or transferred the seat of power from it to a new Imperial Government. The Chancellor was not a member of the Reichstag, nor was there any constitutional guarantee that in the future he would not be appointed without the assent of the Reichstag majority. The German claim that responsible and representative government had been introduced was therefore false; the recent changes in no way touched the heart of the constitutional position. But that the claim should have been made was a proof of Germany's dire predicament. Only nine months before Prince Max had been declaring that he rejected the idea of parliamentary institutions for his country. Scarcely a German politician of note but had praised the existing constitution as the last word in human wisdom. It was not easy for the Allies to believe in the sincerity of this death-bed repentance. History has rarely shown a parallel to such a case of a political creed brazenly flaunted for decades, and then suddenly within a week or two as brazenly recanted.

On 23rd October President Wilson replied. *Oct. 23.* Germany sought to place him in an invidious position with respect to his Allies by addressing her communications only to him, but his cautious and measured answers were the authentic voice of the whole Alliance. He took note of the German asseverations, but repeated that the only armistice that he would feel justified in submitting to his colleagues was one which made impossible a renewal of hostilities on the part of Germany. Should such an armistice be accepted it would be the best proof of the *bona fides* of Germany's new professions. He solemnly warned Berlin that he found the boasted reforms far from adequate.

"It may be that future wars have been brought under the control of the German people; but the present war has not been; and it is with the present war that we are dealing. It is evident that the German people have no means of commanding the acquiescence of the military authorities of the Empire in the popular will; that the power of the King of Prussia to control the policy of the Empire is unimpaired; that the determining initiative still remains with those who have hitherto been the masters of Germany. . . . The President deems it his duty . . . to point out once more that, in concluding peace and attempting to undo the infinite injuries and injustices of this war, the Government of the United States cannot deal with any but veritable representatives of the German people, who have been assured of a genuine constitutional standing as the real rulers of Germany. If it must deal with the military masters and monarchial autocrats of Germany now, and if it is likely to have to deal with them later in regard to the international obligations of the German Empire, it must demand not peace negotiations but surrender."

This Note was the last main stage in the diplomatic conversations. It left no loophole of escape. In effect it demanded the abdication of the Emperor and the destruction of all for which he had stood; it asked that the great German Staff should be deposed from its autocracy and placed under civilian control; it declined to treat save with new men bearing a popular mandate. To accept these demands was tantamount to an admission of final defeat in the field. Germany accepted them on 27th October, declaring that peace negotiations would be conducted by a people's Government, to which the military powers were subject. The American President had distinguished between peace negotiations and surrender, but the two things were now for Germany the same.

Oct. 27.

On Saturday, 26th October, Ludendorff resigned; he had handed in his resignation some time before, but that day it was formally accepted. Few friends remained to him. The German people at large saw in his military dictatorship of the past two years the cause of all their misfortunes, and especially they blamed him for the rash optimism which had led to the March offensive; while the reactionaries reprobated him as the originator of the first armistice proposals, which had taken the heart out of the army. He had had an amazing career since, in August 1914, he first stood, a very junior and obscure general, by the side of Hindenburg in the Masurian battles. At the age of fifty-three he had been one of the triumvirate that ruled Germany; and now, almost on the anniversary of his "crowning mercy" of Caporetto, he had gone the way of von Moltke and von Falkenhayn. He was a soldier of great second-class ability, the resolute, indefatigable, long-headed type of German officer; but at the end it would seem that his nerve failed. He was accused by his countrymen of pro-

Oct. 26.

posing an armistice prematurely, and then attempting feverishly to go back on his policy and intrigue for a military *coup d'état*. But, whatever truth there may be in the second, the first accusation was only the plea of those who, to salve their pride, maintained that the German Army had been betrayed rather than defeated. Ludendorff judged correctly enough the situation of his troops, and sought to avert an utter disaster. He resigned when that disaster was imminent, because the direction of affairs had gone out of his hands. The Government of Berlin was treating for an armistice the terms of which must lie at Foch's discretion, and the High Command, from the Kaiser to the most junior staff officer, was now superseded by Prince Max and Erzberger, Solf and Scheidemann, and the other proselytes of democracy.

Upon Ludendorff and the old world the Twilight of the Gods was falling. In the wild legends of the Northern races, which Germany had so grievously vulgarized, the shades of the dead appeared to those on the brink of doom, and the heavens were filled with the Shield-maidens riding to choose the slain. The superstitious among Germany's rulers had in these days the spectacle of many portents to convince them of approaching calamity. Everywhere the wheel was coming full circle. The Belgians were approaching the dark land where each village spoke of German crimes. The British were almost within sight of the region where they had first met the enemy, swinging south, as he thought, to victory before the leaves fell. The French and the Americans had but a little way to go till their eyes beheld the wooded hills of Sedan. The alliance of which Germany had boasted was now utterly dissolved; Turkey and Bulgaria were prostrate, and Austria was pleading desperately for peace on any terms. More ominous still, that Eastern Europe, which had seen her most spectacular triumphs, was like to prove her worst undoing. The poison of Bolshevism, with which she had sought to inoculate her opponents, was beginning to creep into her own veins. Whatever crimes she had committed in the long war were now blossoming to her hurt.

> "The Gods alone
> Remember everlastingly; they strike
> Remorselessly and ever like for like.
> By their great memories the Gods are known."

CHAPTER CLXV.

AUSTRIA CAPITULATES.

Situation in Austria before 26th October—The Austrian Army—Why Diaz delayed his Attack—The Italian Dispositions—Diaz's Plan—Cavan seizes Grave di Papadopoli—The Grappa Battle begins—The Main Attack launched on the Piave—The River crossed—Cavan reaches the Monticano—Rout of Austrian Armies—The Livenza and Tagliamento crossed—Italians enter Trieste—Vienna's Note of 27th October—Austria capitulates—Trieste occupied—The Fleet at Pola—Break-up of Dual Monarchy—Murder of Count Tisza.

BY the beginning of the last week of October the Dual Monarchy as a state was dead. Count Andrassy, who had taken Burian's place as Foreign Minister, made an ineffective journey to Switzerland to attempt to negotiate with the Allies; but he found every door closed, and realized that Austria-Hungary had no choice but to place herself unreservedly at her enemies' disposal. The manifesto of the Emperor Charles, promising a separate state to each of the Austrian races, had been the last step in the process of disintegration. The Czecho-Slovaks had on 18th October, through their Provisional Government in Paris, declared their independence; the Southern Slavs were preparing to follow suit; on 24th October there was a mutiny of the Croat garrison at Fiume ; Hungary and German Austria alike were clamouring to be free of the encumbrance of antipathetic associates in the moribund Empire. But the Austrian Army in Italy was still alive, and till that army was destroyed in the field the Empire would not disappear. The army would remain till it was decisively beaten, and then the political and moral causes which had wrecked the Dual Monarchy would complete its ruin.

It is not the least strange of the ironies of the war that on 26th October the only forces of the Teutonic League which had not suffered military defeat were the despised levies of Austria. Bulgarians and Turks had been vanquished ; the Germans were staggering to their fall ; but the Austrians were still unconquered. Their part in the campaign had been constantly decried by their German masters ; but the sneer was not deserved. They had done more for Germany than Germany had done for them. Out of a museum of antagonistic races Austria had created an army which was of first-rate quality in many of its services, and showed a stamina under enormous handicaps at least as great as Germany's own. Marvellous is the power of a military machine and a long tradition of discipline. It was the army which had always been the one true force of unity in the Empire. In 1848, when the thing seemed to be dissolving, Radetsky's victory at Custozza had renewed its lease for another seventy years. Until the army was beaten the Hapsburg spectre would not finally disappear.

During the early autumn there was much speculation among the Allies as to why Diaz did not launch an attack in co-operation with the offensives in France and the East. But the Italian Commander-in-Chief had good reasons for his delay. He had lent troops to Foch, and since Austria had now but the one front, she mustered against him a superiority of twelve divisions and a 20 per cent. predominance in artillery. She had all the best positions, and, as we have seen in an earlier chapter, Italy was singularly ill-placed for attack. An abortive attempt would have strengthened Austrian *moral* and weakened the Italian, and Diaz was well aware that after the past year he could not take liberties with the delicate temper of his armies. The immense losses of Italy were not appreciated in Europe. It was not till the close of the war that figures were published, and then it appeared that out of a population of 34 million she had mobilized 5 million men, had lost nearly 470,000 killed and nearly 1,000,000 wounded, of whom more than half a million were permanently disabled. He accordingly waited till the process of internal decay in Austria had become accelerated, and she had no hope of assistance from any of her allies. Who shall say that his Fabian tactics were not justified? Fate so disposed it that the date of his final offensive should be the anniversary of Caporetto.

General Diaz's forces in October were in constitution a microcosm of the whole Alliance. He had fifty-one Italian divisions, three British, two French, one Czecho-Slovak, as well as one American regiment. He had altered his dispositions considerably since the June battle. On the Asiago plateau lay the Italian Sixth Army, containing one British division (the 48th). Between the Brenta and the

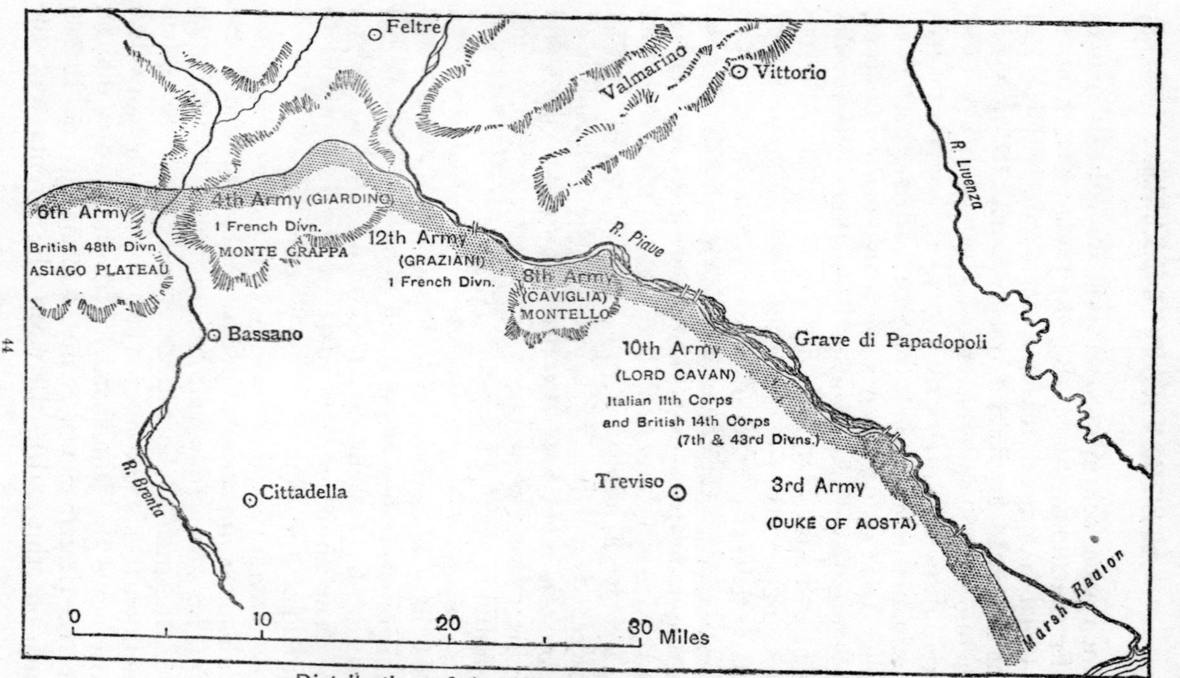

Distribution of the Allied Armies on the Piave Front.

Piave in the Grappa section was the Fourth Army, under General Giardino, including one French division. Along the Piave as far south as the Montello was the Twelfth Army, under the French general Graziani, with one French division. At the Montello lay General Caviglia's Eighth Army. South of it was the Tenth Army, the command of which Diaz had entrusted to Lord Cavan, consisting of the 11th Italian Corps and the British 14th Corps, which latter had two divisions (the 7th and the 23rd). South of Cavan to the Adriatic lay the Duke of Aosta's Third Army.

Diaz's strategy was simple but effective. The battle was to begin with a feint attack by the Fourth Army on the Grappa. Then the main blow was to be delivered by the Twelfth, Eighth, and Tenth Armies against the VI. and V. Austrian Armies, so as to drive a wedge between them and cut the communications connecting the Austrian forces in the mountains with those in the plains. He had not many advantages of position, but he had one; he held the interior lines, and if he could split the outer segment and capture the few precarious routes which linked the Trentino with Venetia, he could destroy the halves piecemeal. There were two points to aim for. One was Feltre, on the Piave, whence a road ran into the Trentino, another south to the plains, and a railway to Belluno; the second was Vittorio, through which ran the communications of the Austrian VI. Army by way of the low watershed of the Valmarino. The task of the Twelfth Army was to fight its way up the Piave to Feltre, of the Eighth Army to make good the Valmarino and Vittorio, and of the Tenth Army to move due east to the Livenza, protecting the flanks of the two armies on its left in their sweep northward.

The first step must be the crossing of the Piave. That was difficult everywhere, for there had been heavy rain, and the river was in flood. It was most difficult, perhaps, opposite the front of the Tenth Army, where it was a mile and a half broad, a hundred streams racing between a multitude of islands, with a current of ten miles an hour in the main channel. The largest island was that known as the Grave di Papadopoli, some three miles long by one broad. It occurred to Lieutenant-General Sir J. M. Babington, commanding the British 14th Corps, that it might be well to occupy this island previous to the general attack, and Cavan agreed. The British troops in the front line were all in the Italian *grigio-verde* uniform, and no British guns were permitted to fire, for had the Austrians discovered our presence in that area they would have guessed the scheme of the coming offensive.

On the night of Wednesday, 23rd October, two British battalions, the 2/1 H.A.C. and the 1st Welsh Fusiliers, embarked in strange little punts, each holding six men, and were ferried by *pontieri* of the Italian corps of Engineers from shingle bank to shingle bank, till they had crossed the main channel of the river, reached Grave di Papadopoli, surprised the garrison, and occupied the northern half of the island. There they hung on for two days, and on the night of the 25th were joined by other Italian and British troops, who mastered the rest of the place. All day on the 26th they were heavily bombarded, but they were able to begin the

Oct. 23.

Oct. 26.

bridging of the main Piave channel behind them, and make other preparations for the coming attack.

Meantime, on Monday, 24th, the Grappa battle had begun. It was such a holding fight as the British and Greeks had fought at Lake Doiran a month before during the Balkan advance, and, like most holding battles, it was costly to the attack. The Italian bombardment began at five in the morning, and at 7.15 the infantry advanced in wild weather between the Brenta and the Piave. The enemy resisted stoutly, and positions were lost and recaptured many times, especially in the Pertica area and in the Solarolo salient. This stubborn fighting endured through the 25th and 26th; and by the evening of the latter day, though Giardino had not advanced far, he had taken 4,000 prisoners. The action had the effect of misleading the Austrian command. This, it seemed, was the main offensive, and there was no danger on the Piave front, where the river ran in roaring spate. But by the morning of the 26th Cavan had the whole island of Grave di Papadopoli, and that night at 11.30 the artillery of the Twelfth, Eighth, and Tenth Armies began their "preparation." The firing of British guns warned the enemy that there had been a change in Diaz's old dispositions which his Intelligence Service had not foreseen.

Oct. 24–26.

With the bombardment the rain began, and all night it poured, so that it seemed as if the weather which had saved Italy the year before was now likely to save Austria. But with the dawn it changed, and the rest of the battle was fought under clear autumn skies. At 6.45 on Sunday, the 27th, the Tenth Army attacked from its position on the island of Grave across the eastern channel of the Piave. The current was very strong, and it was hard for heavily-laden troops to keep their feet; but

Oct. 27.

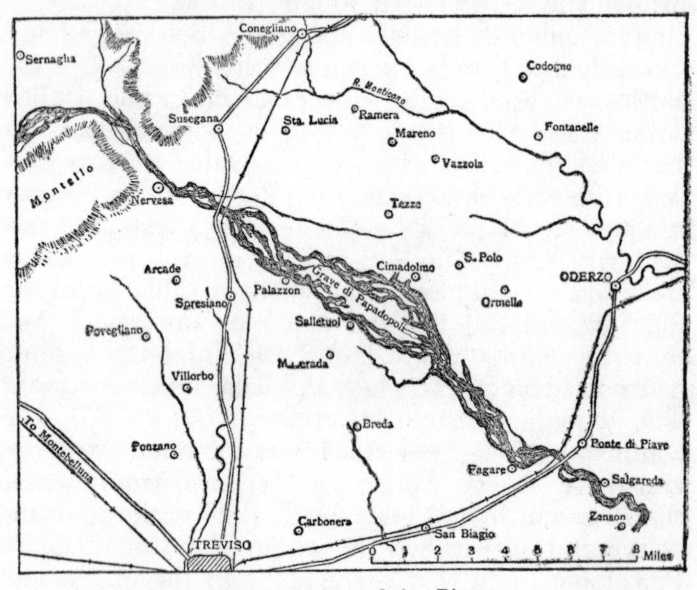

The Crossing of the Piave.
(Ground on which the Tenth Army (Lord Cavan) operated.)

by the evening the British 14th Corps on the left, and the Italian 11th Corps on the right, had won an extensive footing on the eastern shore, and bridges were being rapidly built behind them. On the left, in the Montello section, the Eighth Army, under Caviglia, got a division beyond the river, but it failed to cross at the junction with the British, and there was a gap of ten kilometres between the bridgeheads held by the two armies. Farther north the Twelfth Army, under Graziani, was fighting its way up the Piave gorge towards Feltre, to turn the flank of the Austrians on the Grappa. The Monte Cosen ridge above Feltre was the immediate object of Graziani's Alpini.

The difficulties of the Eighth Army bridgehead on the night of the 27th made the situation serious, and Diaz took a bold step. He withdrew the 18th Corps from Caviglia and allotted it to Cavan, so that it might be passed over the British bridges and clear the front of the Eighth Army. General Basso safely took two divisions of his corps across, but the weight of the traffic and the strength of the flood broke down the bridge behind him, so that he could not complete his deployment. Nevertheless, on the morning of the 28th, with such troops as he had on the east bank, Basso advanced in line with Cavan, and by the evening the Tenth Army had pushed its patrols up to the river Monticano. This broke the resistance opposite Caviglia, and that night the Eighth Army got its right over the Piave at Nervesa, and the 18th Corps was returned to it next morning. Meantime Graziani had pushed up the Piave as far as Alano.

Oct. 28.

That night the crisis of the battle was past. On the 29th Cavan moved steadily forward, and reached the Monticano between Fontanelle and Ramera. The fires which lit the eastern sky showed that the enemy was in full retreat. The Eighth Army was sweeping on to Vittorio, and had entered Conegliano. Early next morning the Twelfth Army was on Monte Cosen, and Feltre was under its fire. That day, Wednesday, the 30th,

Oct. 29.

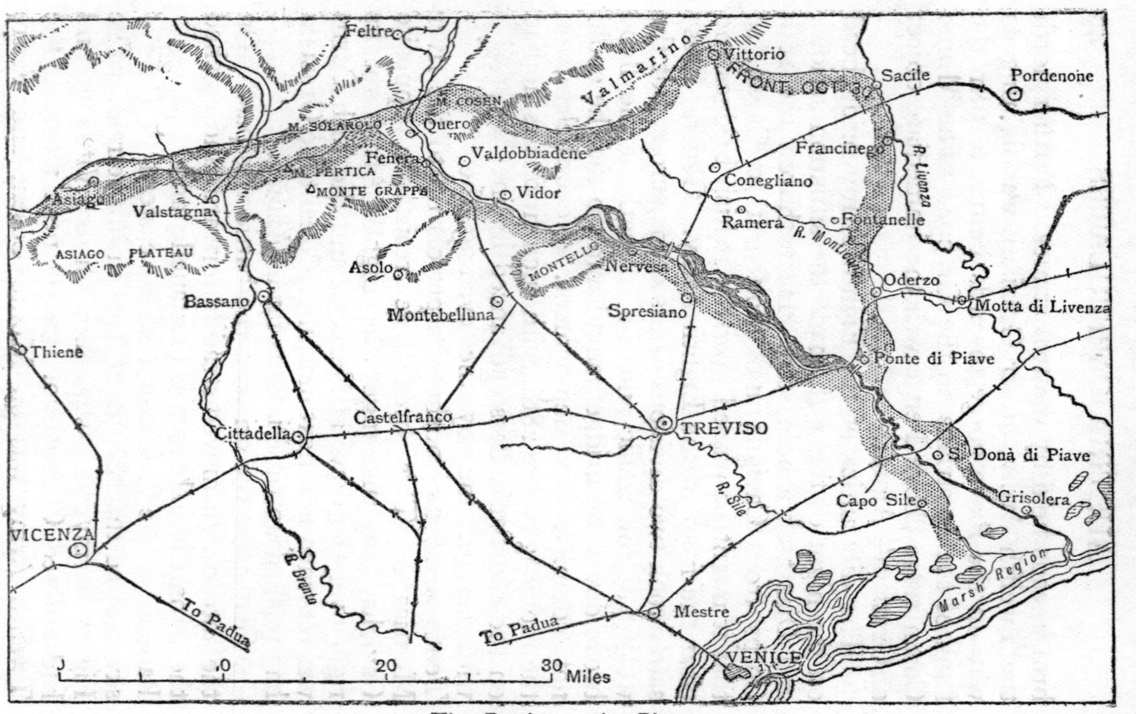

The Battle on the Piave.

Diaz had driven his wedge fairly and squarely between the two halves of the Austrian front. Caviglia took Vittorio, and Cavan, who had now received the 332nd United States Regiment, broke the improvised line of the Monticano and reached the Livenza at Francenigo and Sacile. In the words of the British Commander's dispatch: "From this moment the retreat became a rout." The retirement had also begun in the mountains. Giardino found the resistance weakening on the Grappa, and the Sixth Army reoccupied Asiago. That day, too, the Duke of Aosta's Third Army entered the battle, and crossed the Piave everywhere between Cavan and the sea.

Oct. 30.

On the 31st the rout grew like an avalanche with its own movement, for, the enemy having once suffered defeat in the field, all the political and economic decay of the past year combined to hasten his *débâcle*. The Czech and Polish battalions surrendered wholesale; even the Magyars showed themselves weary of war; only a few picked German-Austrian units kept their discipline and vigour. That day Cavan was across the Livenza, and the Duke of Aosta, on his right, was advancing swiftly to the lower reaches of that stream. The Sixth and Fourth Armies were moving forward in the hills, the Twelfth was fighting in the gorge of Quero, the Eighth was pressing on Consiglio and Pordenone. "The hostile masses," said the Italian *communiqué*, "are thronging into the mountain valleys or struggling to reach the crossings of the Tagliamento. Prisoners, guns, material, stores, and depôts almost intact are being left in our hands."

Oct. 31.

On 1st November the Grappa front collapsed.

Graziani was past the Quero gorge and close on Feltre, Caviglia's left wing was nearing Belluno, Cavan was beyond the Livenza, and the Italian cavalry were far to the east, riding down the retreat. On the 3rd Cavan was on the Tagliamento ; on the 4th he was across it. On the evening of the 2nd the British 48th Division, on the Asiago plateau, having carried Monte Catz and Monte Mosciagh, bivouacked on Austrian soil. By the afternoon of the 4th the Sixth Army was far over the watershed, and in the eastern outskirts of Trent itself. The Austrian armies had collapsed, and left in the conqueror's hands more than 300,000 prisoners and 5,000 guns. Caporetto had been amply avenged.

Nov. 1.

Nov. 2–4.

Those were strange days for the triumphant soldiers of Italy. When they crossed the enemy's lines they passed into a land like a wild dream. Roads were in ruins ; material stood rusting by the wayside, as if there had been insufficient labour to use it ; the neglected hospitals were in chaos. Everywhere was the proof that Austria had long been dying at the heart. The countryside was bare of food, and the wretched villagers were starving. Long lines of broken men, Italian prisoners taken the year before, were stumbling westward to their homes, but already 100,000 of these prisoners had perished of want. Austria's military adventure had ended not in a tragic cataclysm but in a nightmare of senile weakness.

On the night of 2nd November there was a continuous murmur of shouting to be heard all along the Italian front. It was the news of the first step of the enemy towards capitulation. On 27th

October, in reply to the American Note of the 18th, the Government of Vienna accepted all President Wilson's conditions, and "declared itself ready, without awaiting the results of other negotiations, to commence negotiations for peace between Austria-Hungary and the opposing States, and for immediate armistice on all Austro-Hungarian fronts." On the first day of November the Vatican, mindful of the interests of that unhappy daughter of the Church, appealed to Britain in support of Austria's plea for a separate peace. "After a request of this nature, the cessation of the sanguinary conflict appears to be imperiously called for by every principle of humanity."

Oct. 27.

Nov. 1.

There was no need for the Allies to do as they had done with Germany, and refer Austria to the Italian military command. Her bitter necessities did not allow her to waste time in *pourparlers*. On the evening of 29th October an Austrian officer appeared with a white flag near Ala in the Adige valley. He had no proper authority, and was sent back with a message that only a duly accredited mission would be received. On Wednesday, the 30th, the white flag appeared again, and an Austrian corps commander, General von Weber, with seven other plenipotentiaries, crossed the Italian lines. Next day they were taken to a villa near Diaz's headquarters, and on Sunday, 3rd November, the Italian Chief of Staff, General Badoglio, interviewed the mission and presented them with the Allied terms. These were promptly accepted, and at three o'clock on the afternoon of Monday, 4th November, the armistice came into effect, and hostilities ceased.

Oct. 29.

Nov. 4.

The events of that week were like the mad changes of a kaleidoscope. On the last day of October two Italian sailors entered the inner roadstead at Pola and blew up the Austrian Dreadnought *Viribus Unitis*.* It was a theatrical climax, for in that vessel, in June 1914, the Archduke Francis Ferdinand had travelled to the Dalmatian coast on the way to his death at Serajevo. On the evening of 3rd November a detachment of Bersaglieri landed at Trieste, and the city passed under the control of Italy. Meantime the Fleet at Pola was seized by the Jugo-Slavs, and everywhere throughout the Dual Monarchy there was revolution. New transient Premiers—Lammasch at Vienna, Michael Karolyi at Budapest—flitted across the scene, to give place to councils of soldiers and republican committees. Agram, Laibach, and Prague became suddenly the capitals of new states and the seats of new *de facto* governments. To crown all, on 1st November Tisza was murdered. He had been the last stalwart of the old *régime*, the last buttress of autocracy, and the last support of that unhallowed union between Magyar and Prussian which had made the war. Narrow and fanatical both in his religious and political creeds, he was in many respects the strongest man in Central Europe, and his life was not without its stormy grandeur. He had played for high stakes and greatly failed, and it was of a piece with his character and career that he should go down with the sinking ship.

Nov. 1.

The terms of the armistice † put an end to

* The vessel was already in the hands of the Jugo-Slavs, who protested with some bitterness.

† See Appendix III.

Austria's army and navy, and placed all her territories at the disposal of the Allies for military operations. The vast straggling fortress of the Teutonic League had now been shorn of every outwork, and only the central keep of Germany remained. But that keep was already in desperate case, and was on the eve of hoisting the flag of surrender.

CHAPTER CLXVI.

THE SURRENDER OF GERMANY.

Foch's Last Step—Capture of Valenciennes—Advance of Gouraud and Pershing—Americans reach Buzancy—The Metz Railway under Fire—Haig's Advance—The Mormal Forest cleared—Gouraud crosses the Ardennes Canal—Situation in Germany—Naval Mutiny—Revolution in the Northern Ports—The Allies' Last Word—Germany chooses her Delegates—They leave Berlin—Nature of Last German Resistance—Byng reaches Bavai—Rawlinson enters Maubeuge—The Old British Campaigning Ground—The Line of the Scheldt broken—Fall of Tournai—Débeney enters Vervins—Gouraud takes Rethel—Pershing at Sedan—Gouraud enters Mezières—Débeney enters Hirson—Position of Allied Line on 10th November—Revolution in Germany—The Thrones fall—Ebert proclaimed Chancellor—The Emperor and Crown Prince flee to Holland—The German Delegates meet Foch—The Armistice Terms accepted—Nature of Terms—The Last Day—The Canadians enter Mons—Hostilities cease.

LUDENDORFF had gone, and the Supreme Command was in commission. His nominal successor was von Groener, the Würtemberg general; but von Groener was an administrator rather than a strategist, and such strategical direction as was still possible seems to have been in the hands of von Lossberg, formerly Chief of Staff to von Armin's IV. Army in Flanders. Hindenburg contented himself with appeals for German unity; and the Emperor, who on 29th

Oct. 29.

October sought refuge with Army Headquarters at Spa from the troubles of the capital, was in no position to interfere. He was occupied with adapting democratic tunes to the damaged trumpets of absolutism.

Foch was now on the eve of his last step in the West. He had to get Gouraud and Pershing forward so as to cut the Metz-Montmédy-Mezières line, and limit the avenues of retreat for the army groups of the Bavarian and Imperial Crown Princes to the gap of Liége, and at the same time to push his British centre down the Sambre towards Namur, so as to make the retirement of the latter impossible. Then would come the final operation—the swinging of his American right north-eastward between Metz and Longuyon so as to cut the Metz-Arlon-Namur railway, and shepherd into captivity the whole of the southern German armies. In such an event only a few beaten divisions would escape by the pass between Dutch Limburg and the Ardennes, and the most complete catastrophe in all history would have overtaken the German command.

Haig, having crossed the little streams between the Forest of Mormal and the Scheldt, was ready for his final movement. He was in the position of Wellington on the evening of Waterloo, when he raised his hat as a signal for "everything to go in." For three months the British armies had been locked in a continuous battle; for nearly ten months they had been in the forefront of the struggle. From 21st March to 27th October no United Kingdom division had been on an average more than 69 days out of the line, while the Australian average was 79 days, and the Canadian 102 days. During the same period the percentage of casualties to strength in the British divisions was 118 for officers and 121 for men.* The strain had been colossal, but the reward was very near, and however great the weariness of the Allied troops, it was a small thing compared to the exhaustion of the enemy. The boys of the 1921 class, who had been called up for "national auxiliary service" in occupied territory, were being transferred to the fighting line, so that the ranks of Germany were becoming like the levies of France when in 1814 they fell back before Blücher and Schwarzenberg. But in this case the defeated armies had no Napoleon.

As a preliminary to the British advance, Valenciennes must fall. At 5.15 on the morning of 1st November, the Canadians and the 22nd Corps of Horne's First Army and the 17th Corps of Byng's Third Army attacked on a six-mile front south of the town. The struggle was sharp, and the enemy resisted strongly on the flooded banks of the river; but his defences had been constructed to meet an attack coming from the west, and the Canadians struck upward from the south. That afternoon four companies of Canadians entered Valenciennes from the west, and the 49th and 4th Divisions of the 22nd Corps crossed the Rhonelle. Next day, 2nd November, the 4th Canadians completed the capture of the city of Sir John Froissart, and the 22nd Corps were well beyond the Rhonelle, taking Maresches and Préseau, and the high ground two miles to the east. On the 3rd the Germans fell

Nov. 1.

Nov. 2.

* The Canadian figures were 97 per cent. and 84 per cent., the Australian 83 per cent. and 85 per cent.

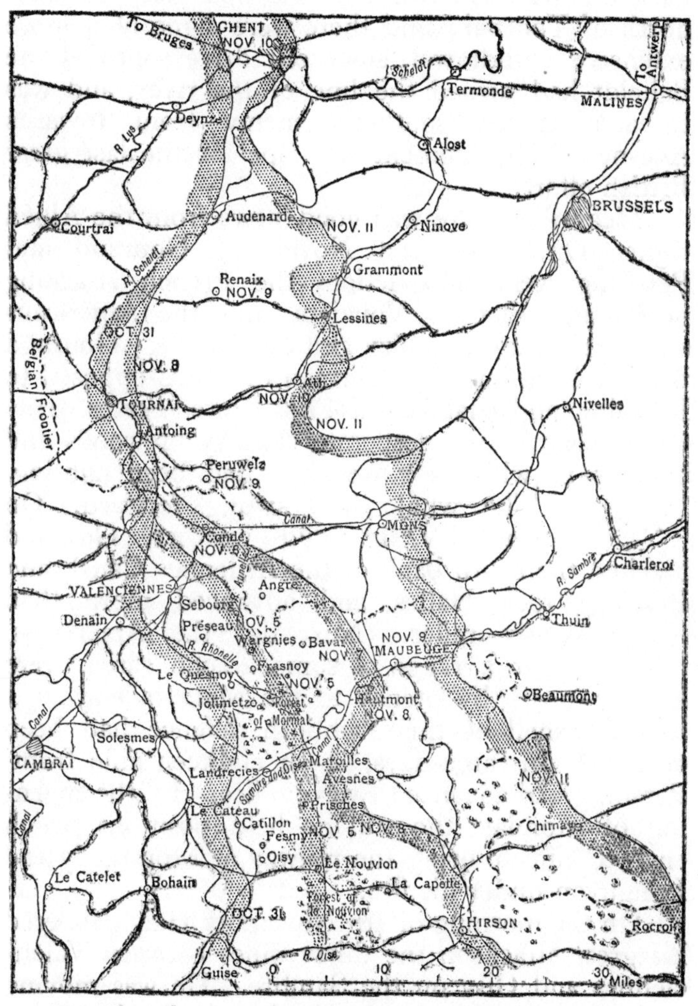

The Final Stage of the Allied Advance (November 1–11)—
Left and Left Centre.

back on the front south of Valenciennes, and also north of Tournai; and there were signs of a more extensive withdrawal, since our drive south of the Scheldt had turned the line of the river, and was threatening the southern enemy front towards Avesnes. The moment was ripe for the last great British effort.

Meantime there was good news from the Allied right. On Friday, 1st November, Gouraud and Pershing went into action, the French attacking north and east of Vouziers, and the Americans advancing between Olizy and the Meuse. Gouraud thus took in flank the German divisions opposed to Pershing, and enabled the First United States Army to get clear of the desperate country of woods and pockets in which for weeks it had been fighting.

Nov. 2. The whole line swung forward. On Saturday, in wild weather, Gouraud reached the south bank of the Ardennes Canal, and Pershing took Halles, and advanced more than six miles. *Nov. 3.* Next day the Americans, at a range of some 20,000 yards, were looking north by Stenay to the Metz railway. At last the shell of this stubborn defence had been cracked. In three days, on an eighteen-mile front, Pershing had advanced twelve miles. By the morning of Monday, the 4th, he held positions which enabled him to bring the railway at Montmédy and Longuyon under his fire.

On the morning of 4th November Haig delivered his great attack on the thirty miles between Valenciennes and Oisy on the Sambre. He was moving against formidable defences—the canalized channel of the Sambre in the south; the great Mormal Forest in the centre; and on his left the fortifications of the town of Le Quesnoy, and the broken woody country

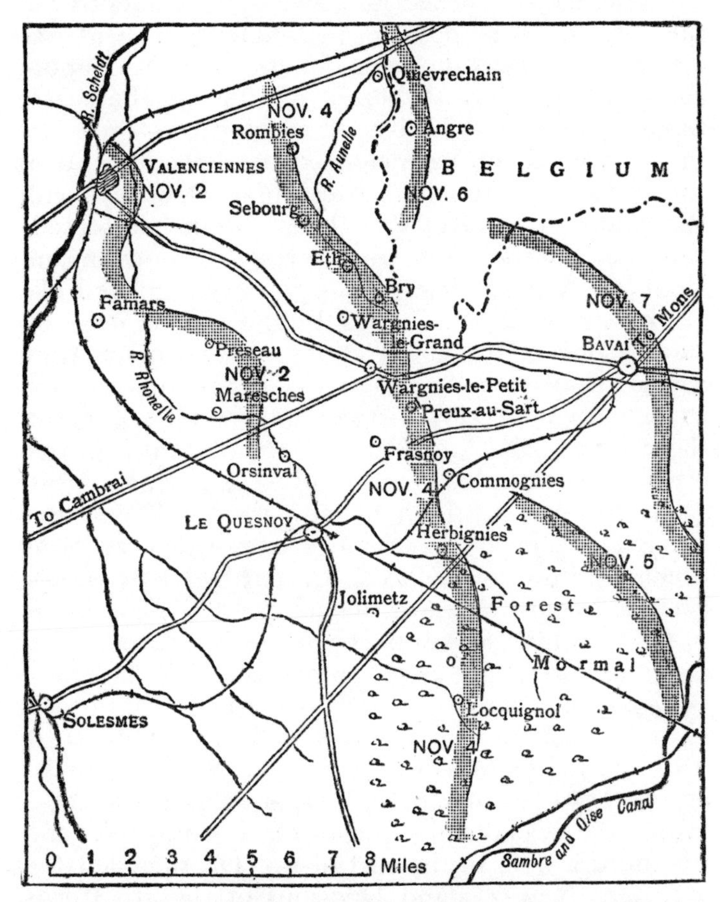

The Advance across the Rhonelle (November 2–7).

intersected by many streams which lay northward towards the Condé Canal. But his troops knew they were on the eve of victory, and were not to be checked by any defences.

The battle opened at dawn, and presently all the German first position had fallen. It was the task of Rawlinson on the right to cross the Sambre south of the Mormal Forest, of Byng in the centre to clear the Forest itself, and of Horne to cross the marshes north of Valenciennes and advance east of the little river Aunelle. Meantime, Débeney, with the First French Army on Haig's right, was to advance to conform into the Forest of Nouvion and along the Upper Oise. The whole plan moved like clockwork. Sir W. P. Braithwaite's 9th Corps, on Rawlinson's right, took Catillon, in two hours were across the Sambre, and by the afternoon were well to the east of Fesmy in the south and La Folie in the north. Sir T. L. N. Morland's 13th Corps, attacking a little later with the 25th, 50th, and 18th Divisions, had a stiff fight with the 1st Guard Reserve Division at the Sambre crossings near Landrecies. But ere nightfall the 25th Division had occupied the little town, where in the August dusk in the first month of war Haig's 1st Corps had faced and checked the great sweep of the enemy from the Belgian frontier. In the Third Army area the 5th Corps, under Lieutenant-General Shute, fought their way into the pathless thickets of the Mormal Forest, and by dawn on the 5th had reached its eastern edge, taken the woodland village of Locquignol, and advanced a mile to the east of it. On their left the 37th and New Zealand Divisions of the 4th Corps swept through the northern part of the Forest, taking Jolimetz and Herbignies; and at four in the afternoon the garrison of Le Quesnoy, now hopelessly cut off, made its surrender. On their left, the 62nd Division took Orsinval and, advancing along with the Guards, carried Frasnoy and Preux-au-Sart, and reached the edge of Gommegnies. The left corps of the Third Army, the 17th, met with less opposition, and by the evening were east of Bry and Eth and the two Wargnies, and so beyond the upper streams of the Aunelle. That day Horne, moving forward to conform, had his right well east of the Aunelle at Sebourg, while his Canadians were in the streets of Rombies.

It was a day of almost bewildering success. Twenty British divisions had scattered thirty-two German divisions, taking 19,000 prisoners and more than 450 guns. Nor was the success only in the central area. Débeney crossed the Sambre Canal on his whole front, and on the 5th was in Guise. The Belgians had driven von Armin behind the Ghent-Terneuzen Canal and were closing in on Ghent. Plumer and Humbert were fording the Scheldt. Mangin and Guillaumat had breached the Hunding Line between Sissonne and Condé-lez-Herpy, Gouraud had crossed the Ardennes Canal between Montgon and Le Chesne, and the Aisne farther west towards Rethel. Pershing was continuing his brilliant advance, and his Second Army under Liggett was now moving forward on the right bank of the Meuse with a view to thrusting the enemy off the last of the heights into the plain. His van was at Pouilly, where he was only six miles from the bend north of Montmédy on the Metz railway.

On Tuesday, 5th November, the enemy's resistance was finally broken. Henceforth he was not in retreat but in flight. The two wings of his armies were separated for ever. The Hunding and Brynhild zones had gone the way of the Siegfried. The opening of the pocket was now the fifty miles between Avesnes and Mezières, and through this gut the whole remaining German forces in the south must squeeze if they would make good their escape. But that gut was hourly narrowing. Gouraud and Pershing were approaching Mezières; Mangin and Guillaumat were pressing towards Hirson, with nothing to bar the road; while Haig, now east of the Mormal Forest, had the Sambre valley as an avenue to Namur. Moreover, Foch had still his trump card to play, the encircling swing of his right, north of Metz, to close the last bolt-hole. If a negotiated armistice did not come within a week there would be a *de facto* armistice of complete collapse and universal surrender.

Nov. 5.

During that week in Germany the mutterings of the storm of revolution were growing louder. Some issued heated appeals for a patriotic closing up of ranks in a last stand against the coming disaster; others attempted to make a scapegoat of the unhappy Ludendorff; but everywhere was apparent a rising anger against the Emperor and the Imperial House. He had fled to the army, but the army was in no case to protect him. The Social Democrats in the Government, led by Scheidemann, were clamouring for his instant abdication, and they had the support of the great mass of the people. Everywhere there reigned a frantic fear of invasion, especially in Bavaria, where the collapse of Austria made the populace

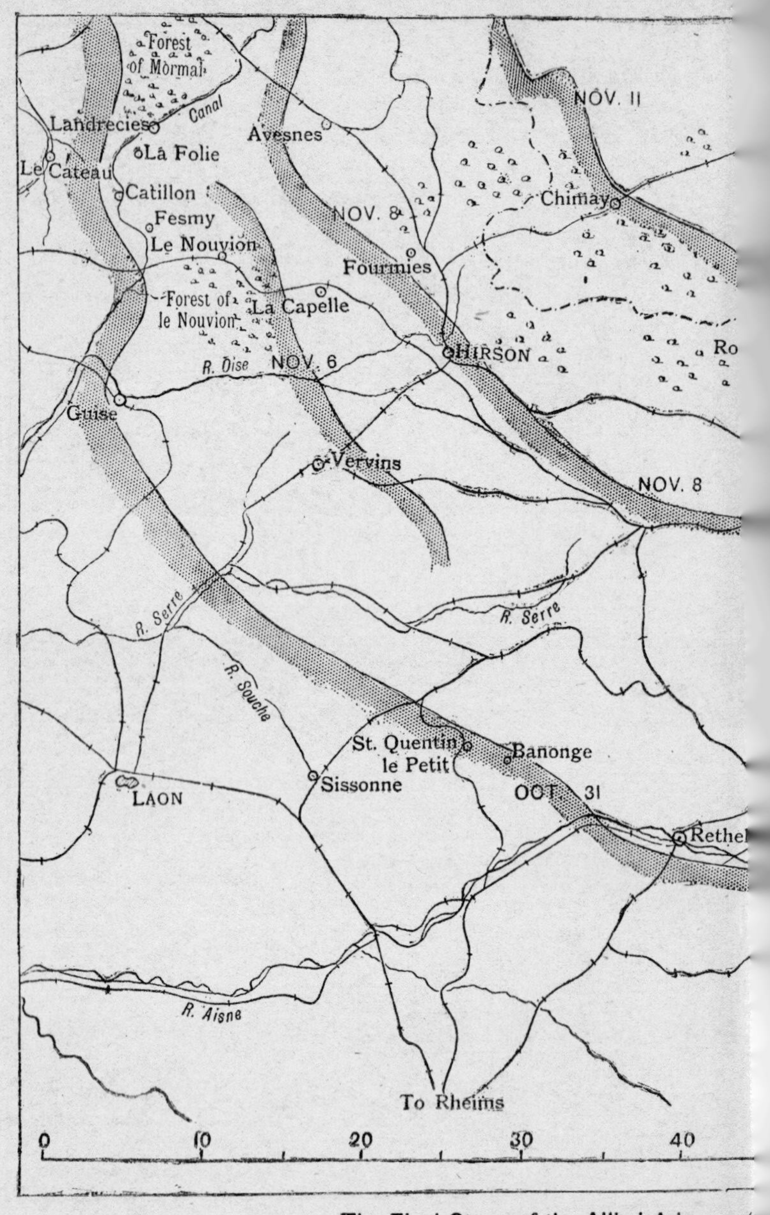

The Final Stage of the Allied Advance (

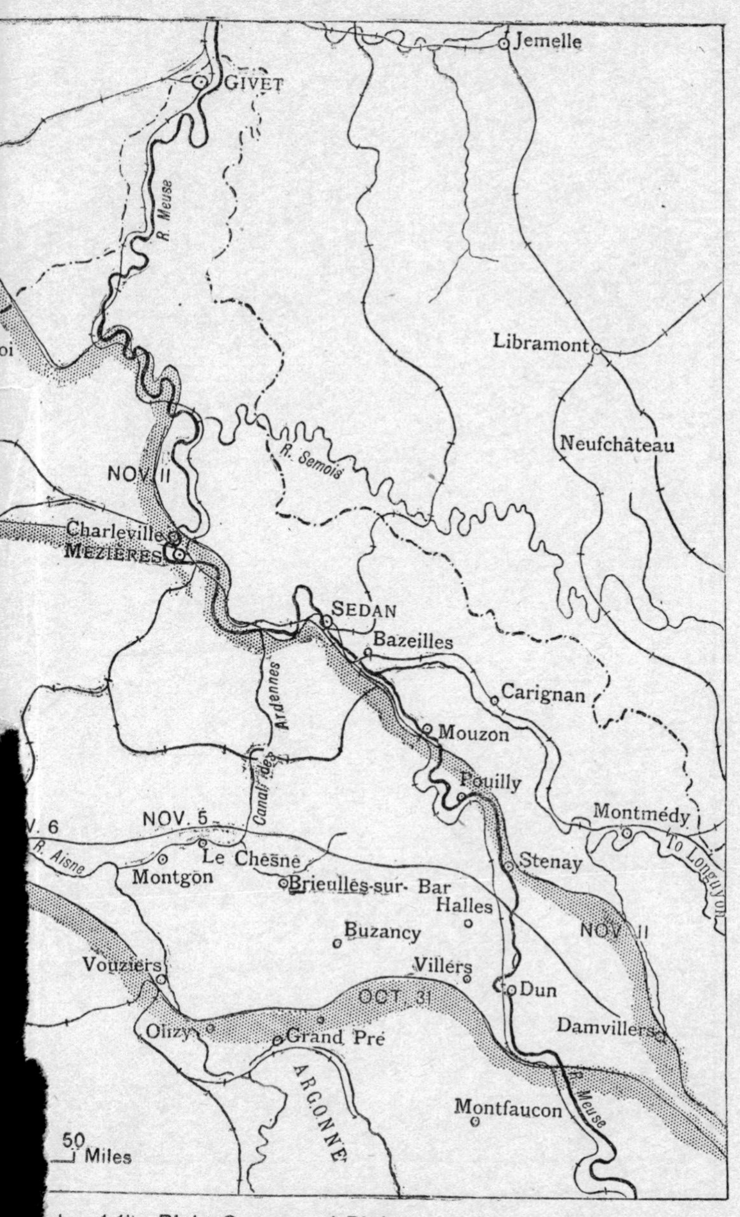

...nber 1-11)—Right Centre and Right.

expect to see at any moment the victorious Italians in their streets; and invasion was no cheerful prospect to Germany when she remembered her own method of conducting it, and reflected that for four years she had been devastating the lands and torturing the peoples of the Powers now marching to her borders.

Strange things, too, were happening within her own confines. In the first days of November the stage had been set for a great sea battle. Her High Seas Fleet was ordered out, but it would not move. The dry-rot, which had been growing during the four years' inaction, had crumbled all its discipline. "Der Tag" had come, but not that joyous day which her naval officers had toasted. She had broken the unwritten laws of the deep sea, and she was now to have her reward. On 4th November the red flag was hoisted on the battleship *Kaiser*. The mutiny spread to the Kiel shipyards and workshops, where there had always been a strong Socialist element; a Council of soldiers, sailors, and workmen was formed; and the mutineers captured the barracks, and took possession of the town. The trouble spread like wildfire to Hamburg, Bremen, Lubeck, and adjacent ports, and it was significant that in every case the soldiers and sailors took the lead. Deputations of Social Democrats were sent down post-haste by the Government, and succeeded in temporarily restoring order, but the terms on which peace was made were the ruin of the old *régime*. In Cologne, in Essen, and in other industrial centres there were grave disturbances, and everywhere the chief outcry was against the Emperor and the Hohenzollerns.

Nov. 4.

He who had been worshipped as a god, because he was the embodiment of a greater Germany, was now reviled by a nation disillusioned of dreams of greatness. At the same time the Empire was dissolving in its periphery. The Polish deputies from Posen and Silesia seceded from the Reichstag, and Schleswig demanded liberation.

It was hard to tell where in Germany the seat of power now lay. On the 5th the Army Command invited to Headquarters representatives of the majority parties in the Reichstag to discuss the next step, and search was made for military officers who might be least inacceptable to the Allies. On that day the Government at Washington transmitted to Germany, through Switzerland, the last word on the matter of negotiations. This Note gave the reply of America's Allies to the correspondence which had been formally submitted to them. They had accepted the President's Fourteen Points as a basis of peace with two provisos: first, they reserved their own liberty of action on the question of the freedom of the seas, since that phrase was open to so many interpretations; second, by the word " restoration " in the case of invaded territories, they declared that they understood " compensation by Germany for all damage done to the civilian population of the Allies, and to their property by the aggression of Germany by land, by sea, and from the air." President Wilson signified his assent to these provisos, and announced that Marshal Foch had been authorized by all the Allies to receive properly accredited representatives of the German Government, and to communicate to them the terms of an armistice.

Nov. 5.

Germany made haste to choose her delegates. They were Erzberger, now a Secretary of State; General von Gündell, an old associate of Marshal von Bieberstein, and the German military delegate to the Hague Conference of 1907; Count Oberndorff, sometime German Minister in Sofia; and General von Winterfeld, who had once been military attaché in Paris, and had recently acted as von Falkenhausen's Chief of Staff at Brussels. The Allied plenipotentiary was Foch, who had associated with him Sir Rosslyn Wemyss, the British First Sea Lord, to represent the British Navy. On the afternoon of Wednesday, the 6th, the German delegates left Berlin, Foch having directed them by wireless to approach the French outposts by the Chimay-Fourmies-La Capelle-Guise road. That day Prince Max of Baden, as Imperial Chancellor, issued an appeal to his people that negotiations might not be endangered by indiscipline. "For more than four years the German nation, united and calm, has endured the severest sufferings and sacrifices of war. If at the decisive hour, when only absolute unity can avert from the whole German people the greatest dangers for its future, our internal strength gives way, then the consequences cannot be foreseen. The indispensable demand which must be made in this crisis by any people's Government is the maintenance of the calm which has hitherto prevailed under voluntary discipline."

Nov. 6.

We leave the delegates on their embarrassed journey, while we review the last days of the Allied advance.

Let us look first at the British centre. Before Haig, if anywhere, the Germans must attempt a stand, for he was marching straight for Namur and the one narrow door still open to their frontiers. No soldier will withhold his tribute of admiration to the gallantry of his foe, and during those desperate days the German armies still made forlorn attempts at resistance to gain for other parts of the line a little respite.* But it was like the efforts of a mop to stay the advance of the ocean. The great

Nov. 5.

victory of 4th–5th November had opened the roads of the Condé Canal and the Sambre valley. On the 5th Rawlinson advanced

* Some idea of the straits to which the Germans were reduced and their stubborn efforts to hold back the advance may be gathered from a study of the enemy divisions engaged by the British in the operations of our First, Third, and Fourth Armies between 27th September and 11th November. For example, the 25th Reserve, which had been relieved in the beginning of October, came into action again on 5th October. The 20th and the Jaeger Divisions appeared for a second time on 8th October, and that day the 25th Reserve fought stubbornly at Sequehart. The 6th and 185th Divisions appeared for the second time on 9th October, the 1st Guard Reserve for the second time on 20th October. On 24th October the Jaeger, 113th, 18th Reserve, and 21st Divisions appeared for the third time; on 1st November the 6th and 34th; on 2nd November the 54th, and on 4th November the 1st Guard Reserve—all for the third time. That day this last division fought stoutly at Landrecies. The Jaeger Division on 4th November, and the 18th Reserve on 5th November, appeared for the fourth time. During this battle the British had sixty-one divisions to face, and these divisions had the following record :—

30	divisions	engaged	once.
21	,,	,,	twice.
8	,,	,,	thrice.
2	,,	,,	four times.

four miles beyond Prisches and Maroilles, while that evening Byng was approaching Bavai, which had been French's headquarters at the start of the Battle of Mons. Horne had a harder day. His 22nd Corps crossed the Belgian frontier, but was held up for some time in front of the village of Angre and the line of the Honnelle stream. Next day, Wednesday, 6th November, Horne broke down the resistance, took Angre and crossed the Honnelle, while the Canadians captured Quievrechain. That night came another enemy landslide, and early on the morning of the 7th the Guards Division of Byng's army entered Bavai. On the 8th Rawlinson occupied Avesnes, and Byng took Hautmont, and reached the outskirts of Maubeuge.

Nov. 6.

Nov. 7.

Nov. 8.

In these days the weather was wet and chilly, very different from the bright August when British troops had last fought in that region. The old regular forces which had then taken the shock of Germany's first fury had mostly disappeared. Many were dead or prisoners or crippled for life, and the rest had been dispersed through the whole British Army. The famous first five divisions of the Retreat from Mons were in the main new men. But some were there who had fought steadily from the Sambre to the Marne, and back again to the Aisne, and then for four years in bitter trench battles, and who now returned after our patient fashion to their old campaigning ground. Even the slow imagination of the British soldier must have been stirred by that strange revisiting. He was approaching places which in 1914 had been no more than names to him, half-understood names heard dimly in the confusion of the great retreat. But some stood out in his memory—the fortress of Maubeuge, on which France had set such store; above all, the smoky coal pits of Mons, which had become linked for ever in the world's mind with the old "Contemptibles." Then he had been marching south in stout-hearted bewilderment, with the German cavalry pricking at his flanks. Now he was sweeping to the north-east on the road to Germany, and far ahead his own cavalry and cyclists were harassing the enemy rout, while on all the packed roads his airmen were scattering death.

On the night of the 7th the thrust of the Fourth, Third, and First Armies bore fruit in the north. The line of the Scheldt broke. Horne's left corps, the 8th, and Birdwood's right corps, the 1st, crossed the river south of Antoing on the 8th, and took Condé. This was the end of the Tournai bridgehead, and that evening Birdwood occupied the western part of the ancient city. On the 9th the Guards entered Maubeuge, while the Canadians with Horne were sweeping along the Condé Canal towards Mons. Birdwood cleared Tournai and took Peruwelz, and Plumer crossed the Scheldt on his whole front and reached Renaix. Next day the Belgians had Ghent.

Nov. 8.

Nov. 9.

Nov. 10.

In the south the advance of the Allies was still more rapid, for Débeney and Mangin, Guillaumat and Gouraud had little before them, and Pershing's gallant Americans were at last reaping the fruits of their fierce October struggle. On the 6th Débeney advanced six miles, passed

Nov. 6.

the Forest of Nouvion, and entered Vervins, while Gouraud took Rethel, and Pershing's two armies crept down both sides of the Meuse nearer to the Metz railway. It was a race for the three points of

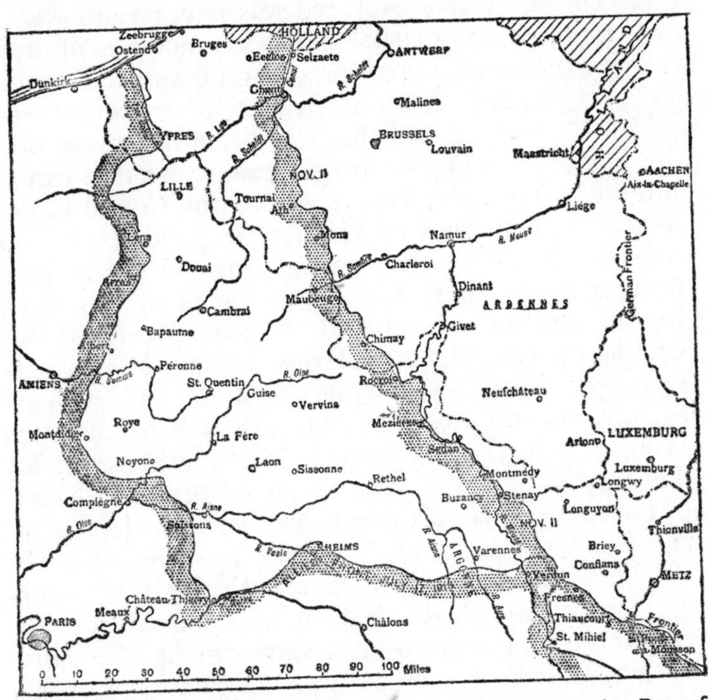

Allied Front from the Dutch Frontier to Lorraine on the Day of the Armistice, November 11, 1918, and the Front in July on the Eve of the Allied Offensive.

Hirson, Mezières, and Sedan. On the afternoon of the 7th the vanguard of the First United States Army took that part of the town of Sedan which lies in the meadows on the west bank of the Meuse. On the 8th Gouraud reached

Nov. 7.

Mezières, and held the Meuse shore as far east as Bazeilles; the Second United States Army completed its conquest of the Heights of the Meuse; and Débeney entered Hirson. But indeed the record of places captured was now meaningless; over much of the battlefield the advance was limited only by the weariness of marching infantry. On the 10th—from north to south—Plumer was far beyond the Scheldt, and approaching the Dendre Canal; Birdwood was across that canal, and had taken Ath; Horne was on the Condé Canal west and north-west of Mons; Byng and Rawlinson were far down the Sambre and close on the Belgian frontier; Débeney was on the edge of Chimay; Rocroi had been occupied, as had Mezières and Charleville (the old seat of the German High Command in the West); while Pershing had reached Stenay, and his Second Army was well through the Woëvre Forest. This was on Sunday, the 10th; for Thursday, the 14th, Foch had fixed the great sweep of the Americans north-eastward between the Meuse and the Moselle.

Nov. 8.

Nov. 10.

These were feverish days both for the victors and the vanquished. Surrender hung in the air, and there was a generous rivalry among the Allies to get as far forward as possible before it came. This was specially noted among the British troops, who wished to finish the war on the ground where they had started. Take as an instance the 8th Division in Horne's First Army. It had spent the winter in the Ypres salient; it had done gloriously in the retreat from St. Quentin; it had fought in the Third Battle of the Aisne; and from the early days of August it had been hotly engaged in the

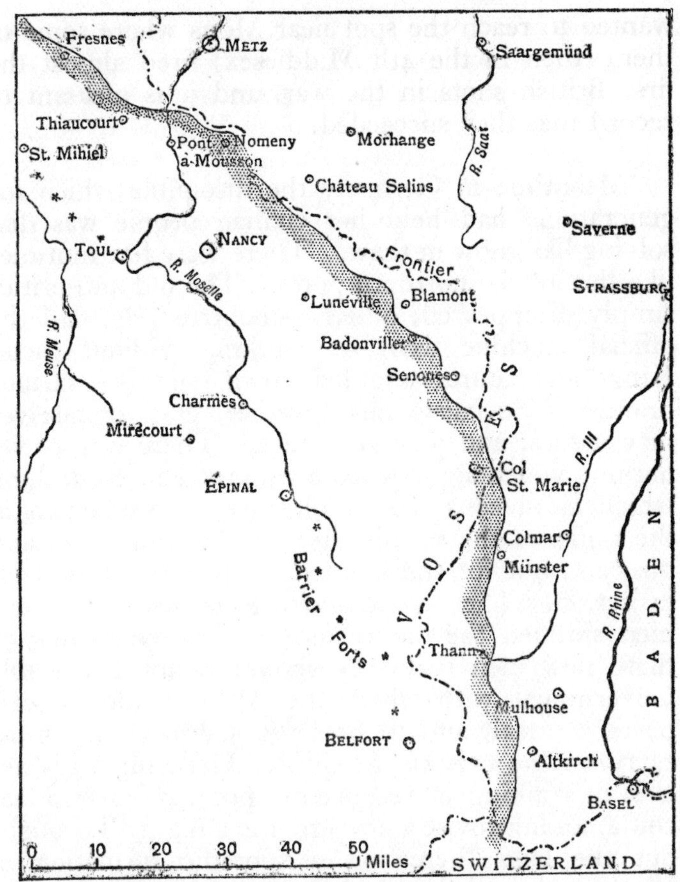

Line of the French Front in Alsace-Lorraine on the Day of the Armistice, November 11, 1918.

British advance. Yet now it had the vigour of the first month of war. On the 10th of November one of its battalions, the 2nd Middlesex, travelled for seven hours in 'buses, and then marched twenty-seven miles, pushing the enemy before them. They wanted to reach the spot near Mons where some of them (then in the 4th Middlesex) fired almost the first British shots in the war, and it is pleasant to record that they succeeded.

Meantime in Germany the discipline which for generations had held her civilian people was dissolving like snow in thaw. There were few mutinies like that of the northern ports. The old authorities simply disappeared, quietly, unobtrusively, and the official machine went on working without them. Kings and courts tumbled down, and the various brands of Socialists met together, gave themselves new names, and assumed office. There was as yet nothing which approached a true revolution, nothing which involved a change of spirit. Deep down in the ranks of the people there was a dull anger and disquiet, but for the moment it did not show itself in action. They stood looking on while the new men shuffled the old cards. It was everything to these new men that they should establish a stable Government with which the Allies would be disposed to deal, and to preserve stability they must carry on the existing machine. Germany with her lack of training in responsible popular government could not improvise a new order in a night. Throughout the land there was a sporadic formation of Workmen's and Soldiers' Councils, but as yet these meant little, and were well under control.

But it was essential for Germany to get rid of the signposts of the old *régime*. Bavaria took the lead, and on Friday, the 8th, a meeting of the Workmen's and Soldiers' Council, under the leadership of a Polish Jew, Kurt Eisner, decreed

Nov. 8.

the abolition of the Wittelsbach dynasty. In Frankfort, Cologne, Leipzig, Bremen, Hanover, Augsburg, and elsewhere, similar councils were formed, who took upon themselves the preservation of order, and declared that they held their power in trust for the coming German Socialist Republic. So far there had been few signs of despotic class demands on the Russian model; in most places the change was made decently and smoothly. Saturday, the 9th, saw the crowning act in the capital. Bands of soldiers and enormous assemblies of workmen patrolled the streets, singing republican songs. There was a little shooting, and a certain number of windows were broken. Troops flung away their badges and iron crosses. Everywhere the royal arms were torn down, and the Red Flag fluttered from the balcony of the Imperial Palace, where, in the first week of August 1914, the Emperor had addressed his loyal people. The day before most of the civil Ministers like Solf and Delbrück had gone to Army Headquarters. Berlin was in the hands of the Workmen's and Soldiers' Council; but, contrary to expectation, there was no friction with the soldiers. The latter had been brought into the city in great numbers with many machine guns; but by the early afternoon they were fraternizing with the workmen's processions, and Liebknecht was making an oration from the Castle balcony. General von Linsingen, the officer commanding in the Mark of Brandenburg, resigned, and Prince Max issued a decree announcing the appointment as Chancellor of Fritz Ebert, the Majority Socialist, who, like Cleon, was in private life a merchant of leather.

Nov. 9.

The two Socialist groups had come together, and a Council of National Plenipotentiaries was formed, consisting of three from the Majority and three from the Minority. For the moment the extremists of the Spartacus group, led by Liebknecht and Rosa Luxemburg, were quiet and biding their time. The revolution had been largely made by reservists, the older men in the home garrisons, who were imbued with the wilder doctrine of Socialism. Some kind of "soviets" had been necessary to give impetus to the change, but the new "People's Government" hoped to absorb them in an orderly democracy. They appealed to all the stable elements in the people to safeguard the transition, and announced to the world that Bolshevism had no partisans in their nation. At the moment it looked as if they might succeed. Berlin took the revolution with complete placidity. Before nightfall on the Saturday the normal life of the city had been resumed, and on the Sunday crowds as usual visited the Karlshorst racecourse.

Yet, orderly as was the first stage in Germany's revolution, and strenuous as were the efforts made to provide administrative continuity, on one side the revulsion was complete. The old absolutism was gone, and monarchy within the confines of Germany had become a farce—hated in some regions, in all despised as an empty survival. For centuries the pretensions of German kinglets had made sport for Europe. Now these kinglets disappeared, leaving no trace behind them. In Bavaria, Saxony, Würtemberg, the Mecklenburgs, Hesse, Brunswick, Baden, the dynasties fell with scarcely a protesting voice. And with them fell the men who had been the pillars of the thrones, the great nobles and the industrial magnates who had risen to power by courtiership. On the Sunday morning came the news of the death of Ballin, the advocate of unrestricted submarine warfare, and one of the main abettors of German megalomania. He chose not to outlive the fabric which he had given his life to build.

Nov. 10.

With the lesser fell the greater. In Prince Max's decree of Saturday, the 9th, it was announced that the Emperor had decided to abdicate, and that the Imperial Crown Prince renounced the succession. With a revolution behind him and his conquerors before him, there was no place left for him in the world. He did not stay upon the order of his going. On Sunday, the 10th, he left Main Headquarters at Spa, crossed the Dutch frontier, and sought refuge in the house of Count Bentinck at Amerongen. Prince Rupprecht retired to Brussels to await the victors, and the Imperial Crown Prince fled from his armies, and, like his father, found sanctuary in Holland.

History has not often recorded a more ignominious end to a vain-glorious career. The man who had claimed to be the vicegerent of God on earth, and had arrogated to himself a power little short of the divine, now showed less hardihood than the humblest of his soldiers. Other kings and leaders who have failed have been content to go down in the ruin they made, but this actor of many parts had not the nerve for a dramatic exit. His light, emotional mind and his perverse vanity had plagued the world for a generation, and had now undone the patient work of the builders of Germany. Tragic, indeed, was the cataclysm of German hopes, but there was no tragedy in the fall of William the Second, King of Prussia, Margrave of Brandenburg, and Count of Hohenzollern. He who had sought to rule the world stole from the stage like a discredited player, leaving his dupes to pay the penalty. Like Lucian's Peregrinus, his life had been dominated by a passion for notoriety; but, unlike that ancient charlatan, he lacked the heart to round off his antics on a public pyre. His ὕβρις had received the most terrible of retributions, for its end was squalor.

The German delegates, who left Berlin on the afternoon of Wednesday, the 6th, arrived in the French lines at ten o'clock on the Thursday night, and were given quarters in the château of the Marquis de Laigle at Francport, near Choisy-au-Bac. On Friday morning they presented themselves at the train in the Forest of Compiègne which contained Marshal Foch and Sir Rosslyn Wemyss. The French Marshal asked, "Qu'est-ce que vous désirez, Messieurs?" and they replied that they had come to receive the Allied proposals for an armistice. To this Foch answered that the Allies were not seeking any armistice, but were content to finish the war in the field. The Germans looked nonplussed, and stammered something about the urgent need for the cessation of hostilities. "Ah," said Foch, "I understand—you have come to *beg for an armistice*." Von Gündell and his colleague admitted the correction, and explicitly begged for an armistice. They were then presented with the Allied terms, and withdrew to

Nov. 8.

consider them, after being informed that they must be accepted or refused within seventy-two hours—that is to say, before eleven o'clock on the morning of Monday, the 11th. They asked for a provisional suspension of hostilities, a request which Foch curtly refused.

The delegates declared that they were astonished at the severity of the terms, and sought permission to communicate with Berlin. A courier bearing the text of the armistice was dispatched to Main Headquarters at Spa, and the German Command was informed by wireless of his coming. He was to cross the French lines that night between six and eight o'clock. The French fire ceased according to arrangement, but the unfortunate messenger had to wait long before the German barrage stopped. It was not till the afternoon of the following day that he could enter the German zone. Once there, he found everything in chaos. The retreating armies had made such havoc of roads and bridges that his car could not proceed, and he did not reach Spa till ten o'clock on the Sunday morning.

Nov. 9.

Nov. 10.

The terms were immediately telephoned to Berlin, and a conference of the new Government was held that morning. The hours of grace were fast slipping away, and Foch was adamant about the time limit. The delegates were instructed to accept, and after a protest they submitted to the inevitable. At five o'clock on the morning of Monday, 11th November, the armistice was signed, and Foch telegraphed to his generals: "Hostilities will cease on the whole front as from 11th November, at eleven o'clock. The Allied troops

Nov. 11.

will not, until a further order, go beyond the line reached on that date and at that hour."

The terms were so framed as to give full effect to the victory on land and sea which the Allies had won.* All invaded territory, including Alsace-Lorraine, was to be immediately evacuated, and the inhabitants repatriated. Germany was to surrender a large amount of war material, specified under different classes. The Allies were to take control of the left bank of the Rhine and of three bridge-heads on the right bank in the Cologne, Coblenz, and Mainz districts, and a neutral zone was to be established all along that bank between Switzer-land and the Dutch frontier. A great number of locomotives and other forms of transport were to be immediately delivered to the Allies. All Allied prisoners of war were to be repatriated forthwith, but not so German prisoners in Allied hands. German troops in Russia, Rumania, and Turkey were to withdraw within the frontiers of Germany as these existed before the war. The treaties of Brest-Litovsk and Bucharest were cancelled. German troops operating in East Africa were to evacuate the country within one month. All submarines were to repair to certain specified ports and be surren-dered ; certain units of the German Fleet were to be handed over to the charge of the Allies, and the rest to be concentrated in specified German ports, disarmed, and placed under Allied surveillance, the Allies reserving the right to occupy Heligoland to enforce these terms. The existing blockade was to be maintained. . . . Such were the main provi-sions, and the duration of the armistice was fixed at

* See Appendix V.

thirty-six days, with an option to extend. If Germany failed to carry out any of the clauses, the agreement could be annulled on forty-eight hours' notice.

The acceptance of such terms meant the surrender of Germany to the will of the Allies, for they stripped from her the power of continuing or of renewing the war.

The morning of Monday, 11th November, was cold and foggy, such weather as a year before had been seen at Cambrai. The front was for the most part quiet, only cavalry patrols moving eastwards in touch with the retreat. But at two points there was some activity. The Americans on the Meuse were advancing, and the day opened for them with all the accompaniments of a field action. At Mons, on the Sunday night, the Canadians of Horne's First Army were in position round the place. Fighting continued during the night, and at dawn the 3rd Canadian Division entered the streets and established a line east of the town, while the carillons of the belfries played "Tipperary." For Britain the circle was now complete. In three months her armies had gained seven victories, each greater than any in her old wars; they had taken some 190,000 prisoners and 3,000 guns; and they had broken the heart of their enemy. To their great sweep from Amiens to Mons was due especially the triumph which Foch had won, and on that grey November morning their worn ranks could await the final hour with thankfulness and pride.*

* See the maps on pp. 71 and 73 for the line of the Allies at the armistice.

The minutes passed slowly along the front. An occasional shell, an occasional burst of firing, told that peace was not yet, but there were long spells of quiet, save in the American area. Officers had their watches in their hands, and the troops waited with the same grave composure with which they had fought. Men were too weary and deadened for their imaginations to rise to the great moment, for it is not at the time, but long afterwards, that the human mind grasps the drama of a crisis. Suddenly, as the watch-hands touched eleven, there came a second of expectant silence, and then a curious rippling sound which observers far behind the front likened to the noise of a great wind. It was the sound of men cheering from the Vosges to the sea.

After that peace descended on the long battlefield. A new era had dawned and the old world had passed away.

CHAPTER CLXVII.

THE AFTERMATH.

Demonstrations after Victory—The Monarchy in Britain—The King's Reply to the Address of Parliament—The German Retirement—Beginning of the Allied Advance—The Rhine Bridgeheads—King Albert in Antwerp—Pétain in Metz—Pétain and Gouraud in Strasbourg—The French Proclamation—Plumer crosses the Cologne Bridges—Mackensen interned in Hungary—The Naval Surrender—Conference between Beatty and von Meurer—Tyrwhitt receives the First German Submarines—Beatty receives the Battleships and Cruisers—His Message to the Grand Fleet—The Voyage of the *Hercules* to Kiel—Internal Condition of Germany—Problems of Settlement before the Allies—The Congress of Vienna and the Conference of Paris.

VICTORY had been won, as complete and final as any that history has recorded. The common sense of the world recognized that, though the war had ended formally in an armistice, that armistice was, in fact, surrender. The Allies had been throughout the campaign conspicuously reticent, and had not tempted Fate by jubilation over partial successes. Now the flood-gates were loosed, but the rejoicings were curiously restrained. They seemed to spring from relief rather than triumph, as if the memory of the desperate strain and uncountable loss was too keen to permit of extravagance. Youth, indeed, will always be served, and during the nights of that week, when the streets of London and Paris once again shone with unfamiliar light, there was much harmless exuberance on the part of boys and girls and young soldiers. In the dripping November weather there was a perpetual dancing on the causeways, the blowing of every instrument musical and unmusical, and the promenading of crowds in every form of conveyance. There were demonstrations before the houses of Ministers, and solemn scenes of rejoicing in the different legislatures. But the note everywhere was relief and thankfulness and sober joy, rather than exuberant triumph. In Paris men would greet each other in the streets : " C'est bien. Mon fils reviendra " ; and in London the churches were thronged by thanksgivers.

These days provided a dramatic illustration of the significance of monarchy in a free land. While elsewhere thrones had disappeared and their occupants were in exile, in Britain, Italy, and Belgium it was to their kings that the peoples turned as the representatives of the liberties they had fought for. On Monday, the 11th, great crowds assembled outside Buckingham Palace, moving thither from all quarters by a common impulse. The King and Queen appeared on the balcony to receive such an ovation as has rarely greeted the monarch of an unemotional people. Next day they went in solemn procession to St. Paul's to return thanks to the Giver of Victory. But the most impressive spectacle had taken place the evening before, when in the wet November twilight, almost unattended and wholly unheralded, they drove in a simple open carriage

Nov. 11–12.

through the city. The merrymakers left their own occupations to cheer, and a crowd accompanied the carriage, running beside it and shouting friendly greetings. It was an incident which interpreted better than any formula the meaning of a people's king.

On Tuesday, 19th November, in the Royal Gallery of the Palace of Westminster, the King replied to the addresses of the two Houses of Parliament. There, in the presence of political leaders and the great officers of State, and representatives of India and all the Britains overseas, he expressed in simple words the gratitude of the nation to its fleets and armies for their superb achievement; the pride of Britain in her Allies; the unspectacular toil of the millions at home who had made victory possible; and the great task still before the nation if a new and a better world was to be built out of the wreckage of the old. The losses of war could be repaired only by a wiser and juster organization of industry, and machinery must be devised to avert the risk of international strife and to reduce the crushing burden of armaments. "In what spirit should we approach these great problems? How shall we seek to achieve the victories of Peace? Can we do better than remember the lessons which the years of war have taught, and retain the spirit which they instilled? In these years Britain and her traditions have come to mean more to us than they had ever meant before. It became a pleasure to serve her in whatever way we could, and we were all drawn by the sacredness of the cause into a comradeship which fired our zeal and nerved our efforts. This

Nov. 19.

is the spirit we must try to preserve. It is on a sense of brotherhood and mutual goodwill, on a common devotion to the common interests of the nation as a whole, that its future prosperity and strength must be built up. The sacrifices made, the sufferings endured, the memory of the heroes who have died that Britain may live, ought surely to ennoble our thoughts and attune our hearts to a higher sense of individual and national duty, and to a fuller realization of what the English-speaking race, dwelling upon the shores of all the oceans, may yet accomplish for mankind."

The military terms of the armistice were intended to prevent any German army again taking the field. The two main means to this end were the surrender of military equipment, and the occupation of three great bridgeheads on the Rhine. The first proceeded slowly and laboriously, as such things must, for the German machine was in dire disorder. The second, which lay with the Allied troops, advanced with steady precision. At first the German retirement beyond the Rhine was chaos—confused columns, a hundred miles long, of stragglers of every arm. Then discipline reasserted itself, and the last part of the retreat was conducted in good order. The defeated armies of Germany marched into their cities with bands playing and flags flying, and there was some attempt made to prepare for them a popular reception. No one will grudge the effort of a conquered enemy to "save his face"; and those troops deserved a welcome, for they had fought with a courage and resolution worthy of a better cause. But with the Allies following at their heels, it was hard to build up the legend that Germany had not suffered defeat in the field. If proof were needed, it was to be found in the condition of the hinterland of the old German front. Every road was littered with abandoned tractors, lorries, and tanks; every line was blocked with loaded trucks, and every canal with barges; everywhere there were huge dumps of war material, which could neither be used nor removed. Not the war material surrendered under the terms of the armistice, but material already derelict before the armistice was signed. On all sides was the proof that the German war-machine had gone to pieces, and that it would not have needed Foch's projected encirclement of 14th November to complete the ruin.

The meaning of a bridgehead on a river is that the army occupying it commands the crossings, and has room to deploy on the farther bank. Of the three great bridgeheads, the northern—that of Cologne and Bonn—was to be occupied by the British troops; the central, at Coblenz, by the Americans; and the southern, at Mainz, by the French. The full meaning of victory was scarcely realized by the Allied armies during the week in which they waited quietly in their lines. They only knew that fighting had ceased, and that a great space now separated them from the enemy. It was cold, rimy weather, and the quiet under the grey skies seemed fantastic to those whose ears were accustomed to the unending din of battle. But when early on the morning of Sunday, 17th November, the advance began, there came a sudden awakening of all ranks to the tremendous thing that had been achieved. Names

Nov. 17.

long heard of as German headquarters took concrete form as towns and villages; rivers, which once seemed as remote as the moon, were left behind them; and daily they came nearer that mysterious land from which their enemy had issued. For four years they had fought him on their own soil; they were now to visit his home as conquerors. The advance was slow, for the Germans had made a wonderful destruction of roads, bridges, and railways. It was a grim business, for the joy of the liberated inhabitants could not disguise the horrors of the enemy occupation, and everywhere our advancing troops met strings of returning prisoners, dazed and emaciated men cast loose by the enemy to find their way home, and now staggering blindly westward. Yet pride was the dominant note, and the troops swung out on the long road to the Rhine with well-groomed horses, polished harness-chains, spick-and-span guns and limbers, and every man smart and trim.

To the French was reserved the chief romance of the march, for they were entering their own lands of Lorraine and Alsace, which after forty-eight years they had freed. On the 17th the Moroccan Division passed through Château Salins; at noon the Second Army, under General Hirschauer, was in Mulhouse; and farther north, French troops, with what feelings may be guessed, crossed the battlefields of Gravelotte and Morhange. That day the Third American Army, under Major-General Dickman, left the tormented uplands of the Meuse behind them, passed through Longuyon and Conflans, and entered the frontier fortress of Longwy and the mining town of Briey. The 19th was an historic

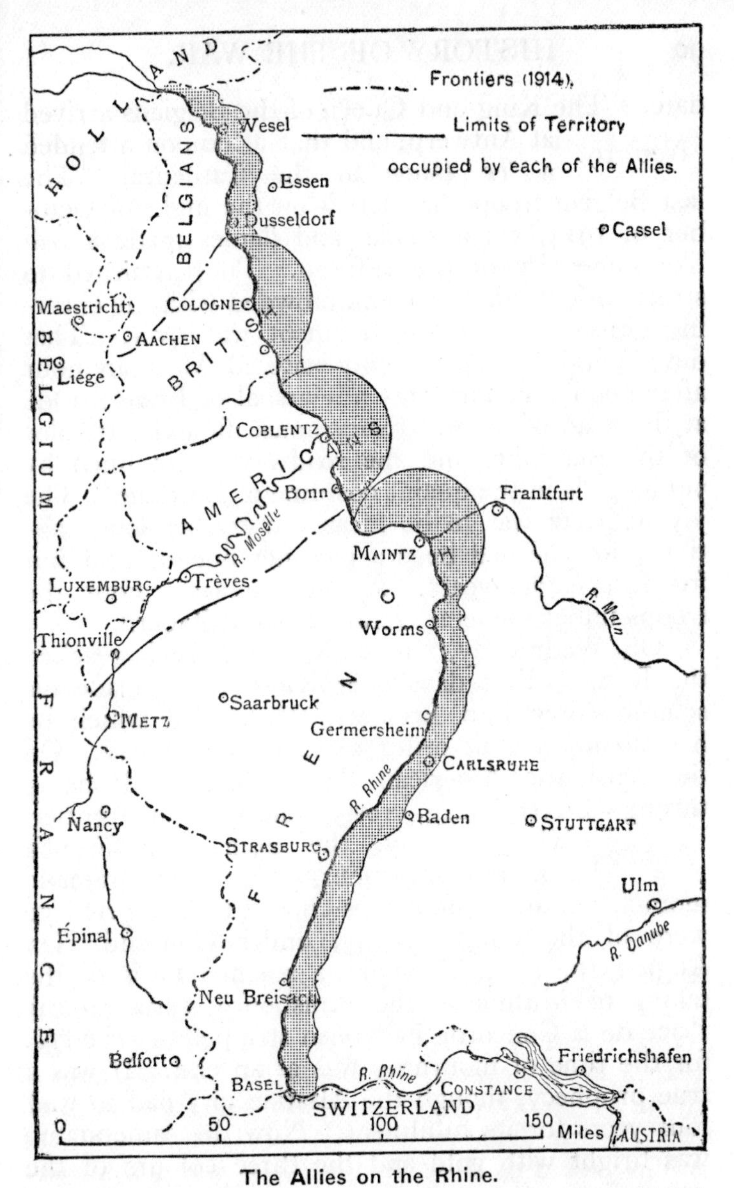

The Allies on the Rhine.

(Map showing the neutral zone and the three bridgeheads on the right bank, and the extent of German territory occupied by each of the Allied Armies.)

date. The King and Queen of the Belgians arrived at Antwerp, and that afternoon attended a *Te Deum* in the Cathedral. The last Belgian troops had left it on the night of October 9, 1914, when smoke and flames made a pall like some city of the Inferno. They returned to streets bright with flags and crowded with the cheering citizens whose long torment was over. That day Mangin's Tenth Army entered Metz an hour after noon. Pétain, now a Marshal of France, rode at the head of them. Every house flew the tricolor of the Republic, and the roadways were lined by young girls in the quaint costume of Lorraine. The joy of Metz was to be measured by her long captivity, for she had been a prisoner not for four but for forty-eight years. About the same hour the troops under General Gerard entered Zabern.

Nov. 19.

On Wednesday, the 20th, the French reached the Rhine. Five days later King Albert made his solemn entry into Brussels, the capital which he had abandoned in order to save his country. On the 23rd the American Third Army, advancing through Luxembourg, crossed the German frontier.

Nov. 25.

On Monday, the 25th, the French entered Strasbourg, the most dramatic moment of all. The troops chosen for the privilege were of the Fourth Army, under Gouraud. On August 10, 1914, when news reached Paris of the taking of Mulhouse, the Strasbourg statue in the Place de la Concorde had been stripped of its *crèpe*, for the time of mourning was at an end. It was a true prophecy, though the Alsatian city had to wait four years for its fulfilment. Now the same statue was bright with gold and the three colours of the

Republic, for the march of the deliverers was ended. Early in the afternoon came Pétain, in his long cavalry cloak, since the day was chilly, and took his stand in front of the Imperial Palace in the Kaiserplatz. Beside him stood Gouraud, with his empty right sleeve, the most romantic figure among the great captains of France; and the three group commanders, de Castelnau, Fayolle, and Maistre. Then through the streets, where nearly every name was German and every flag was French, moved the men and guns of the Fourth Army. The hour was too solemn for cheering, and there was little sound save from the drums and clarions of the regiments. That day there was posted up on the walls not the least finely inspired of the many great proclamations of France :—

"To the inhabitants of Strasbourg,
"To the soldiers of the Fourth Army—

"The day of glory has arrived. After forty-eight years of tragic separation, after fifty-one months of war, the sons of Great France, our brothers, are united once more. This miracle has been wrought by you, people of Strasbourg and men of Alsace, because you have kept in your faithful hearts the sacred love of the Mother Country through all the trials and indignities of the hated yoke. History will scarce furnish a like instance of such noble fidelity.

"This miracle has been wrought by you, soldiers, who have fought heroically the hardest battles ever known, and issued from them with immortal glory. The redoubtable barrier has fallen. The eagles of the frontier posts have been laid low for ever.

"France comes to you, people of Strasbourg, as a mother to her darling child who has been lost and is found again. . . . At this solemn and magnificent hour, which proclaims the triumph of right, justice, and liberty, let us unite, liberated Alsatians and liberating soldiers, in the same love."

By the middle of December the armies of the Allies had reached their goals; the tricolor guarded the mouth of the Main, and the stars and stripes flew above the city where the Moselle joins the Rhine, and the dumb fortress of Ehrenbreitstein. If we seek for a parallel in drama to the French entry into Strasbourg, we may find it in the passage of the great river by Plumer's Second Army. *Dec. 13.* It took place on 13th December in heavy rain, the weather in which most of their battles had been fought. Six months before the British forces had been cooped up in a space of forty-five miles, between the enemy trenches and the Channel; now they were 250 miles east of Boulogne. The cavalry had already gone ahead, and on that morning it was the turn of the infantry. General Plumer took his stand at the great Hohenzollern Bridge at Cologne, and past him filed the 29th Division, the men of the Gallipoli landing and Cambrai. At the Nord Bridge, where Sir Charles Fergusson, the new Military Governor of Cologne, took the salute, the 9th Division crossed, the division which at Loos and Delville Wood, at Arras and Passchendaele, in the retreat from St. Quentin and in the desperate stand on the Lys, had won imperishable glory. Farther up stream, at the iron suspension bridge, the 1st Canadian Division were crossing; and the 2nd Canadians made the passage by the bridge of Bonn, in presence of General Currie. All the marching tunes of the British Empire were heard in the rain—the "Maple Leaf" and the "Men of Harlech," "John Peel" and "Blue Bonnets." There was no parade, no gaudy triumph, but in the lean efficiency of the men there was for the watching crowd a grim lesson of power. They recognized their conquerors. The handful of British soldiers who had been present at the start of the contest against odds in 1914, and who now witnessed the end of the long road, may well have wavered in their minds between thankfulness and awe. For they were watching the consummation of a miracle, a miracle of patience, courage, and resolution. The little Expeditionary Force, small in numbers and small in the esteem of its opponents, had grown to almost the most formidable army that the world has seen. They might have said, in the words of Jacob, "With my staff I passed over this Jordan, and now I am become two bands."

It was on the Western Front that the consequences of victory were most patent, but it was the same on every battlefield. Turkey and Bulgaria were in Allied occupation; Allied troops were in Vienna and Innsbruck and Budapest. The German divisions were returning from Russia as best they could, with Poland and the Baltic provinces ablaze behind them, and Trotski's new levies speeding the parting guests. Fantastic was the fate of von Mackensen's Rumanian Army. It was travelling homeward by way of Hungary, but when the Field Marshal arrived at Budapest he found the station guarded by Hungarian troops, and was informed that Franchet d'Esperey, in terms of the treaty between Hungary and the Allies, proposed to intern him and his command. So closed the career of the General whose name throughout the campaign had been used as a bogey to awake, in turn, the fears of each little nation. There was irony in the fact that the man who had led the great German advance on the Donajetz, and had thereby saved the Hungarian plains from invasion, should be held captive in the land and by the men he had protected.

We turn to the surrender at sea. On Tuesday, 12th November, the Allied fleets, under Admiral Calthorpe, passed through the Dardanelles, and on the morning of the 13th arrived off Constantinople. It was the fourth time in a century that a British fleet had entered the Sea of Marmora. Behind them British and Indian troops garrisoned the Gallipoli forts, where so much good blood had been spilled in an enterprise now at long last concluded. The Black Sea lay open to the Allies, and they could control the south coasts of Russia, establish direct relations with Denikin and his army, and dominate the Caucasus and the Caspian.

Nov. 12–13.

At 2.30 in the afternoon of Friday, 15th November, the German light cruiser *Königsberg* arrived at Rosyth, bringing Admiral Hugo von Meurer to arrange for the carrying out of the armistice conditions. Von Meurer bore a good reputation as a sailor; he had been in command of the Dreadnought *König*, and had had charge of the last naval operations in the Gulf of Riga. He brought with him three delegates from the Sailors' and Soldiers' Council, and three from the People's Council. Under the terms of surrender all submarines were to be handed over, ten battleships, six battle cruisers, eight light cruisers, and fifty destroyers. These were to be disarmed and interned in neutral ports, or, failing that, in Allied ports; but the neutral Powers would have nothing

Nov. 15–16.

to do with the business, so it fell to the Allies to receive them. The remaining surface warships left to Germany were to be concentrated in certain German ports, paid off and disarmed, and placed under the supervision of an Allied commission. The terms meant nothing less than the total disappearance of German sea-power.

The conference between Admiral Beatty and Admiral von Meurer came to an end at ten o'clock in the evening of the 16th. The affair was conducted with all the punctilios of naval etiquette, and the German admiral departed into the fog which clouded the Firth of Forth with such formal salutes as might have attended a visit of officers of one great fleet to another. The humiliation of Germany was too dire to need expression by word or ceremony; the fact shouted itself throughout all the world. The nation which had sought to conquer the sea had smirched the honour of a great service, and was now surrendering tamely and ignobly without having dared to bring its boasting to the test of deeds.

On Wednesday, the 20th, the handing over of the submarines began. The truth about them was now known from German admissions. For the past year their numbers had been steadily shrinking, new constructions had not covered losses, the best commanders had all been killed, and the crews were weak and mutinous. At a point thirty-five miles from the Essex coast Admiral Sir Reginald Tyrwhitt with five British light cruisers received the surrender of the first twenty U-boats. It was a fine morning, with a quiet sea and the sun shining through the mist, when the British seamen

Nov. 20.

saw the low grey hulls, escorted by German transports, coming from the east. Only one submarine flew the German ensign, and all had their numbers painted out. They were navigated by their own crews till close to Harwich, when British officers took charge, the white ensign was run up above the solitary German flag, and the German sailors embarked on their transports to go home. A scene of grimmer humiliation could scarcely be conceived. The enemy craft were received in utter silence by the British cruisers, who had their men at action stations and their guns trained on the newcomers. There was no hint of fraternization, scarcely a word was spoken, and the British sailors looked stolidly and contemptuously at the men who had disgraced their calling. A hiss or a taunt would have been less insulting than that deadly stillness.

Next day, Thursday, the 21st, in the same ominous quiet, the German battleships and battle cruisers were handed over to the custody of the British Grand Fleet, accompanied by detachments of the French and American Navies. The event took place in the waters east of the mouth of the Firth of Forth. The four battle cruisers, which—with the *Seydlitz* now under repair—were all that remained to Germany, were the *Von der Tann*, *Derfflinger*, *Hindenburg*, and *Moltke*, and these were escorted to their place of internment by our First and Second Battle Squadrons. The battleships were the *König Albert*, *Kaiser*, *Kronprinz Wilhelm*, *Kaiserin*, *Bayern*, *Markgraf*, *Prinz Regent Luitpold*, *Grosser Kurfürst*, and *Friedrich der Grosse*, escorted by the Fourth and Fifth Battle Squadrons and the American Sixth Battle Squadron. The

Nov. 21.

seven light cruisers were the *Karlsruhe*, *Frankfurt*, *Emden*, *Nürnberg*, *Brummer*, *Köln*, and *Bremse*,* escorted by the 1st, 2nd, 3rd, and 6th Light Cruiser Squadrons and the 1st Cruiser Squadron. The rear of the procession was formed by the First and Second Battle Cruiser Squadrons and the 4th and 7th Light Cruiser Squadrons. In a few hours the main units of Germany's Fleet had passed out of her hands, and she, who had been the second Sea Power in the world in 1914, had sunk to the state of a sixth or seventh rate Power, while of what was left to her she had no longer the free use. Sir David Beatty ordered the surrendered vessels to haul down their flags at 3.37 that afternoon, and not to hoist them again without permission. Admiral von Reuter protested, on the ground that this was contrary to international custom and the "idea of chivalry between honourable opponents." To this Admiral Beatty replied: "I would draw your attention to the fact that an armistice suspends hostilities, and that a state of war still exists between Germany and the Allies. Under the circumstances no enemy vessel can be permitted to fly the national ensign in British ports whilst under custody." The incident sums up the situation more eloquently than any comment.

That day Sir David Beatty issued a message to his Fleet, which may well be quoted as a summary of the part of the British Navy in the war :—

* For various reasons the full complement of ships due under the terms of the armistice could not be handed over on the 21st. It should be noted that of the light cruisers most were new constructions to take the place of ships of the same name sunk during the war.

"I wish to express to the flag officers, captains, officers, and men of the Grand Fleet my congratulations on the victory which has been gained over the sea-power of our enemy. The greatness of this achievement is in no way lessened by the fact that the final episode did not take the form of a fleet action. Although deprived of this opportunity which we had so long and eagerly awaited of striking the final blow for the freedom of the world, we may derive satisfaction from the singular tribute which the enemy has accorded to the Grand Fleet. Without joining us in action, he has given testimony to the prestige and efficiency of the Fleet without parallel in history, and it is to be remembered that this testimony has been accorded to us by those who were in the best position to judge. I desire to express my thanks and appreciation to all who have assisted me in maintaining the Fleet in instant readiness for action, and who have borne the arduous and exacting labours which have been necessary for the perfecting of the efficiency which has accomplished so much."

The armistice gave to the Allies free access to the Baltic, and this involved mine-sweeping in German territorial waters, and the control of the enemy forts which protected the entrance to that sea. A flotilla of British minesweepers at once set out to clear the Kattegat; a British squadron followed them, and by 3rd December lay off Libau, where its presence was urgently needed owing to the Bolshevik advance. But if we seek for drama we will find it at its highest in the visit of the British warships, under Vice-Admiral Sir Montague Browning, to the German naval bases. Accompanied by naval representatives of the Allies, he set out on 3rd December in the *Hercules*, attended by four destroyers. A German pilot party took them through the minefields, and they anchored off Wilhelmshaven after midday. There the German ships were inspected, and air stations, such as

Dec. 3.

Borkum, Heligoland, Norderney, and Sylt, visited. The *Hercules* then passed through the Kiel Canal, and returning British prisoners on its banks had a glimpse of the white ensign. At Kiel the final details were settled, and on 18th December the *Hercules* left the Canal on her return voyage. In June 1914 a British squadron had been in Kiel Bay, and British guns had acclaimed the final deepening of the great waterway. The Emperor had visited our flagship, and the flag at her masthead had proclaimed the presence on board of an Admiral of the British Fleet. At a subsequent banquet a German admiral had declared that his Navy sought to model itself upon the great example of Nelson! Such is the mutability of mortal things. The German sea kings—von Ingenohl, von Scheer, von Hipper—had all disappeared into the darkness, and in a Dutch manor their master was waiting anxiously while the Allies decreed his fate. Only the words of Æschylus are adequate as an epitaph on so great a fall :—

> Ὕβρις γὰρ ἐξανθοῦσ' ἐκάρπωσε στάχυν
> Ἄτης ὅθεν πάγκλαυτον ἐξαμᾷ θέρος.*

The cessation of hostilities left Germany a seething cauldron of rival factions and immature theories, and it was hard to tell from the froth and bubbles of incipient revolution what might be the outcome. Some facts were clear. Monarchical Germany had gone. On 28th November, from his refuge in Holland, the Emperor issued his signed abdication.

* "Pride comes to flower and bears a sheaf of doom, whence is garnered a harvest all of tears."—ÆSCHYLUS, *Persæ*.

Fourteen days earlier the Emperor Charles of Austria had bidden farewell to his uneasy throne. The German Crown Prince, now dwelling in a cottage in the isle of Wieringen, and still consistent in folly, protested his innocence to the world in a newspaper interview, declared that he had always disapproved of things like air raids, and for Germany's military failure blamed every one but himself. The old *régime* had disappeared in vapour ; the old military chiefs had gone ; and the decomposing armies were no longer in charge of princelets.

The great work of Bismarck and his successors was all undone. It was not merely that Germany was about to lose her illicit territorial gains ; she had lost also her subtly organized spheres of influence. Turkey, the Balkans, the neighbouring Slav peoples, had passed out of her power. Her naval ambitions, her colonies, her schemes in the Near, Middle, and Far East, her dreams of Berlin-to-Bagdad, of Mittel-Afrika and Mittel-Europa, her hold over Belgium and Holland and Luxembourg, her far-flung commercial privileges, her fiscal domination of Europe—all had gone. More, the unity of her own territory seemed to be dissolving. The states which Bismarck had welded together in one Empire were breaking apart. Germany had been unified under Prussian domination, and the downfall of Prussia destroyed the solder. Union, provided it be a true one, is better for the world than disintegration, and the Allies had no wish to see Germany in fragments. But was it possible to devise in the chaos of defeat an honest principle of confederation to replace the false?

For the belief in the State, having for long been

pressed so far that it had become an idolatry, was for the moment fatally weakened in German minds. They were satiated with government, and the impulse to anarchy was everywhere. The extremists, who taught that political institutions were redundant or vicious, and that society must be brigaded by economic classes, now found a ready hearing. Could the respectable social-democrats and the middle-class leaders now in power provide a policy to counteract this impulse? Would the ordinary collectivist programme satisfy a palate which craved stronger meat? Moreover, the whole land—and all Central and Eastern Europe—was on the edge of famine, and famine is the mother of anarchy. In a country which had been despotically governed the first change is apt to be to a counter-despotism, and in the kennels of the German slums were many who looked to Russia for their example.

Nor could it be said that defeat had banished from Germany's creed all its old follies. Remnants of the former *régime* were still at work, and through neutral countries endeavoured to sow disputes among the Allies. The more thoughtful men like Delbrück admitted their blunders, but as blunders rather than crimes. Maximilian Harden rubbed in the humiliation, and jeered at the new democrats as he had jeered at the old bureaucrats; but the man who, in August 1914, had exulted in the professed immorality of Germany's aims, had no honest cure to offer for his country's ills. Leadership, policy, in Germany there was none—there could be none, for the shock was still too recent, and men's minds were giddy. It lay with the Allies to raise her out of the slough into which she had inveigled half the globe.

Such a task might well seem too great for human wisdom, such a burden too heavy for shoulders weary and bowed with the load of four years' war. Germany was the first problem, and it was not a mere question of the rectification of frontiers, but of direct assistance in building up a politically and economically broken people. Had that task stood alone it would have been sufficiently great, but it was but one of many; for the war, like a chemical change, had altered the constituents of all the world. Next in magnitude came the problem of Russia, where the social dissolution was now complete. Bolshevism was growing and spreading like a rank fungus in its unwholesome gloom, and daylight must be let into the darkness, for the settlements of Russia and Germany were mutually dependent. There, again, the solution was complicated by the intricate matter of the Baltic provinces and of Poland, which must be reconstituted as a Power in spite of the difficulties which had made her for two centuries the despair of European statesmen. There was the matter of Austria, now dissolved into her original racial elements. Last, in Europe, there was the eternal problem of the Balkans, where races were inextricably mixed, and of European Turkey, which must now pass from Ottoman hands.

In Africa were the German colonies, which could not be restored to their former owners, and for which a new *régime* must be devised under the trusteeship of the Allies. In Asia there were other German colonies, and the *débris* of the Turkish Empire, which must find new guardians. No one of these matters was simple, and all were clogged with old historical rivalries among the Allies themselves.

With the best will in the world it would be hard to judge these questions purely from the standpoint of the interests of their inhabitants and the future well-being of the world. The war had been fought largely for the cause of nationality; but nationality is not a term of art, and its interpretation would not be easy. Pressed too far, it might mean the splitting up of historic states into atoms, for which in the modern world there could be no hopeful future.

Nor did territorial adjustments exhaust the problem. There was the complex business of the details of Germany's reparation, of fixing indemnities and devising a means of exacting them from a bankrupt country, and of determining the guilt of the German leaders and decreeing their punishment. These were matters on which wide differences of opinion might appear among the Allies. Moreover, there was the whole question of the future economic relations of an exhausted world. The conquerors of Germany had to settle not only the fate of the conquered but their own.

When after Waterloo the soldiers laid down their task, the civilian statesmen who took it up had before them a comparatively simple problem. They were still dealing with the world in the form in which it had been handed down from the Middle Ages—with tangible things like dynasties and frontiers; not with a world closely linked in its every interest and with the *imponderabilia* of democracy. The Congress of Vienna was child's play to the coming Congress of Paris. But in one respect their successors had a shining advantage. They were pledged to do their work in the light of a great ideal, far richer and more true than any which inspired the labours of Castlereagh and Metternich and Talleyrand. It was right that the League of Nations should be set up in the forefront of the programme of the new Peace Conference, for on its establishment depended the settlement of every problem with which they were confronted. With such an ideal as a touchstone of policy and as an incentive to breadth and tolerance of spirit, the statesmen of the Allies, who in the last days of the year began to assemble in the French capital, could look forward to their labours with a reasonable hope: the hope that the Palace of Versailles, which had seen in 1783 the signature of the armistice which brought to an end the strife between America and Britain, and in 1871 the proclamation of that German Empire that had now crumbled, might witness the creation of an enduring peace of justice for mankind.

CHAPTER CLXVIII.

CONCLUSION.

The Untamed North—The Consequences of War—The Far-flung Battle Lines—The Character of the War—Germany's Problem and her Failure to solve it—Her Achievement—Blunders in Statesmanship and the Higher Command—Her Best Soldiers—The Allies' Problem—Their Failures—The Reason of their Success—Britain's Part—Foch and his Colleagues—Sir Douglas Haig—The Allied Civilian Leaders—The True Hero of the War—Conclusion.

IF a man stands on the left bank of the Rhine and looks towards the Taunus hills, he is looking away from Roman Germany to a land which was never settled by Rome. The eagles marched through the forests beyond the river, but they did not remain there, and that strong civilization which is the fibre of the Western world never took root and flourished. The thickets and plains running east and north to the frozen seas remained the home of aboriginal gods. It is long since the woods were thinned and the plains were tilled, but the healing and illuminating and formative forces of the great Mediterranean culture, though their aspect might be counterfeited, were never reborn in the hearts of the people. The North remained a thing incalculable and unreclaimed, and its ancient deities might sleep, but did not die. Some day, as

Heine in 1834 told France, they would rise from their graves to the undoing of Europe.

The prophecy had come true. Savagery and slavery had come out of the north to undo the liberating work of the centuries. It may be read in Tacitus how into the sombre grove of the High God of the Germans none might enter save with a chain round his neck to show his subjection to the divinity. Let the old legend stand as a parable. These gods were tyrants, and their mandate was to enslave. Their votaries, whether they were called Junkers or Bolsheviks, whether they spoke the rhetoric of a mad racialism or the chatter of a bastard science, were serfs themselves, and would reduce mankind to their own ignominy, though they called it by noble names. They had challenged the world, as Attila and Timour had challenged it, and once again the free men had proved themselves stronger than the slaves.

This book, begun in the early months of war, has followed the campaign as a chronicle, and it stands as a chronicle of events whose results at the time of writing could not be foreseen, and of the transient phases of contemporary opinion. While, therefore, it has reproduced the perplexities of the stages, it cannot reproduce the bold lines of the whole conflict, as history will see it in the retrospect. The matter is still too vast for our peeping eyes to behold, the changes have been so violent that we are still giddy from the shock of them. When Michelet after the writing of his history fell ill and sought rest, he excused himself on the plea, "J'ai abattu tant de rois." For his many shortcomings the present writer may proffer in all humility the same apology.

But since this work is the history of a war, it is right, before taking leave of the reader, that some attempt should be made to gather together the threads and present the struggle as it appeared to a contemporary looking back upon it after its close. All comparative tests fail us. It was so much the hugest war ever fought that it is idle to set it beside earlier conflicts. During its four years it depleted the world of life and wealth to a far greater degree than a century of the old Barbarian invasions. More than eight million men died in battle, and the casualties on all fronts were over thirty million. If we add deaths from disease and famine it cannot have cost the population of the globe less than twenty million dead, and as many more maimed and weakened for life. At least forty thousand millions sterling of money were spent by the nations in the direct business of war. The losses in property were incalculable; over fifteen million tons of the world's shipping had been destroyed, and the appurtenances of civilized life over millions of square miles of the globe's surface. And let it be remembered that this devastation has been wrought not in the loose and embryonic society of an elder world, but in one where each state was a highly-developed organism, where the economic fabric was intricate and far-extending, and where myriads of human souls depended for their existence on the mechanism of civilization performing its functions smoothly and in security.

No figures can bring before us the magnitude of the struggle, for the figures pass far beyond the stage where they can be visualized by the human mind. That visualization can best be got by recalling the geographical immensity of the battle-ground—a task which is for the imagination, since the soldier saw only his little area, and no man's first-hand experience could cover all the many fields. Only to the Celestial Intelligences of Mr. Hardy's "Dynasts" was a bird's-eye view possible. An observer on some altitude in the north, like the Hill of Cassel, on some evening in September 1918, could look east, and note the great arc from the dunes at Nieuport to the coal-fields about Lens lit with the flashes of guns and the glare of star-shells, and loud with the mutter of battle. That was a line of fifty miles—far greater than any battle-field in the old wars. But it was the tiniest fragment of the whole. Had he moved south to the ridge of Vimy he would have looked on another fifty miles of an intenser strife. South, again, to Bapaume, and he would have marked the wicked glow from Cambrai to the Oise. Still journeying, from some little height between the Oise and the Aisne he would have scanned the long front which was now creeping round the shattered woods of St. Gobain to where Laon sat on its hill. From the mounts about Rheims he might have seen Gouraud's battle-line among the bleak Champagne downs, and from a point in the Argonne the trenches of the Americans on both sides the Meuse, running into the dim woody country where the Moselle flowed towards Metz. Past the Gap of Nancy and down the long scarp of the Vosges went the flicker of fire and the murmur of combat, till the French lines stretched into the plain of Alsace, and exchanged greetings with the sentinels on the Swiss frontier. Such a battle-ground might well have seemed beyond the dream of mortals, and yet it was but a part of the whole.

A Celestial Intelligence, with sight unlimited by space, would have looked eastward and, beyond the tangle of the Alps, witnessed a strange sight. From the Stelvio to the Adriatic ran another front, continuous through glacier-camps and rock-eyries and trenches on the edge of the eternal snows to the gracious foothills of the Lombard plain, and thence, by the gravel beds of the Piave, to the lagoons of Venice. Beyond the Adriatic it ran, through the sombre hills of Albania, past the great lakes where the wild-fowl wheeled at the unfamiliar sound of guns, beyond the Tcherna and Vardar and Struma valleys to the Ægean shores. It began again, when the Anatolian peninsula was left behind, and curved from the Palestine coast in a great loop north of Jerusalem across Jordan to the hills of Moab. Gazing over the deserts, he would have marked the flicker which told of mortal war passing beyond the ancient valleys of Euphrates and Tigris, up into the wild Persian ranges. And scattered flickers to the north would have led him to the Caspian shores, and beyond them to that tableland running to the Hindu Kush which was the cradle of all the warring races. Passing north, his eyes would have seen the lights of the Allies from the Pacific coast westward to the Urals and the Volga, and little clusters far away on the shore of the Arctic Sea.

Had the vision of our celestial spectator been unhindered by time as well as by space, it would have embraced still stranger sights. It would have beheld the old Allied front from the Baltic to the Danube, pressing westward, checking, and falling east; breaking in parts, gathering strength, and again advancing; and at last dying like a lingering sunset into darkness. Behind would have appeared a murderous glow, which was the flame of revolution. Turning to Africa, it would have noted the slow movement of little armies in West and East and South—handfuls of men creeping in wide circles among the Cameroons forests till the land was theirs; converging lines of mounted troopers among the barrens of the German South-West territory, closing in upon the tin shanties of Windhoek; troops of all races advancing through the mountain glens and dark green forests of German East Africa, till after months and years the enemy strength had become a batch of exiles beyond the southern frontier. And farther off still, among the isles of the Pacific and on the Chinese coast, it would have seen men toiling under the same lash of war.

Had the spectator looked seaward, the sight would have been not less marvellous. On every ocean of the world he would have observed the merchantmen of the Allies bringing supplies for battle. But in the North Atlantic, in the Mediterranean, and in the Channel and North Sea he would have seen uncanny things. Vessels would disappear as if by magic, and little warships would hurry about like some fishing fleet when shoals are moving. The merchantmen would huddle into packs with destroyers like lean dogs at their sides. He would have seen in the Scottish firths and among the isles of the Orkneys a mighty navy waiting, and ships from it scouring the waters of the North Sea, while inside the fences of Heligoland lay the decaying monsters of the German Fleet. And in the air over land and sea would have been a perpetual coming and going of aircraft like flies above the pot of war.

The observer, wherever on the globe his eyes were turned, would have found no area immune from the effects of the contest. Every factory in Europe and America was humming by night and day to prepare the material of strife. The economic problems of five continents had been transformed. The life of the remotest villages had suffered a strange metamorphosis. Far-away English hamlets were darkened because of air raids ; little farms in Touraine, in the Scottish highlands, in the Apennines, were untilled because there were no men ; Armenia had lost half her people ; the folk of North Syria were dying of famine ; Indian villages and African tribes had been blotted out by plague ; whole countries had ceased for the moment to exist, except as geographical names. Such were but a few of the consequences of the kindling of war in a world grown too expert in destruction, a world where all nations were part one of another.

We may well leave to posterity the task of envisaging this colossal turmoil, in the sure confidence that posterity will not underrate it, for with every year the infinite ramifications of suffering will be more clearly seen. Let us attempt to set down briefly the character of the war itself, the objects of the combatants, the methods which led the Allies to victory, and the nature of that victory. We have watched the slow process, and we may now venture to summarize its salient features and results.

Germany began with the odds in her favour. She was superior to any combination of her enemies in the number of trained men she could put straightway into the field; she had a smooth and powerful military machine built up patiently during a generation; she had a centralized command, and her colleagues were subject in all matters to her will. She was aware that her opponents had great potential strength, but it would take time to become actual, and she hoped to win victory long before that day dawned. Unlike her enemies, she realized the fundamental weakness of Russia, and knew that if she could deal a crushing blow in the West she might safely leave the East to be dealt with at leisure. So, outraging every law of God and man in her methods, she sought to win in France that "battle without a morrow" of which her General Staff had always dreamed.

The dream was shattered at the Marne, but with praiseworthy courage she revised her plans. She fell back inside impregnable defences, and being, as she thought, self-subsistent and wholly disciplined, set herself to wear down the spirit of her foes. For three years the war became the siege of a fortress. There were sallies by the besieged, as when von Mackensen swept Russia out of Poland, when the same General overran Serbia, and when von Falkenhayn pushed Rumania behind the Sereth; there was the sally of Austria, first to the edge of the Lombard plain, and then to the Piave; there was the great and disastrous sally of the Imperial Crown Prince at Verdun. There were attacks, too, by the besiegers: by the Russians in the East; by the British at Gallipoli, on the borders of Palestine, and in Mesopotamia; by Italy across the Isonzo; by the British and French at Festubert and in Artois, at Loos and Champagne, in the long-drawn First Battle of the Somme, at Arras, Messines, Ypres, and Cambrai. These attacks gravely weakened the garrison of the fortress, and the blockade of the Allied navies lowered the resisting power of the vast population inside the defences. Early in the year 1917 it seemed as if the fortress might fall from an enveloping attack.

The downfall of Russia changed the prospect. Thenceforth there were no beleaguering armies in the East, and the garrison could be thinned on that side and supplies gathered from the huge undefended territories stretching to the Pacific. A new policy was revealed to the besieged. America had entered the war against them, but America would be slow in mustering her armies, and they had the chance of annihilating the weary levies of France and Britain while they were yet unreinforced. Germany still gambled upon her superior military prowess and disciplined *moral*. So far the offensive was in discredit, for the assaults of her enemies had not breached her fortifications, but she might devise a tactical method which would succeed where they had failed. Accordingly on March 21, 1918, she gathered all her strength for a final effort, the trench campaign ceased, and the day of the open battle began.

The plan, if it were to win, must win at once. For the Allies had begun to set their house in order, they had tightened the strings of the blockade and given authority into skilled hands. Moreover, ever nearer from the West crept the ominous cloud of America's battle-power. The German stroke miscarried, and its failure meant the certainty of Germany's defeat. She had staked everything on the venture, and her flagging vitality could not compass a second. Further, the peril had compelled her enemies to take the final step in reform, and they had entrusted the supreme command to their greatest soldier. We have seen the masterly strategy of Foch. Waiting patiently on the appointed time, he struck a blow which put the German machine out of gear. Carrying his enemy's tactics to their logical conclusion, he kept the battle "nourished" and mobile, till on 26th September he dealt those hammer strokes which turned a great machine into *débris*. The victory in the field, which faint-hearts among the Allies had despaired of, came in the most shattering and cataclysmic form. At last had been fought the "battle without a morrow," for it broke not only the German armies but the German people, and the creed for which they had contended.

History will not deny to Germany the credit of boldness in conception, and vigour and tenacity in execution. Her national trade had long been war, and for the first years of the campaign she was the professional arrayed against amateurs. Her disciplined people suffered great hardships patiently, and did not break till they were assured of defeat. Her armies showed, both individually and in the mass, the utmost valour and resolution. It was no contemptible foe that yielded on 11th November. She had the elasticity of spirit to be able to revise her plans in the face of failure, and to carry out the new as methodically and vigorously as the old. She showed beyond doubt a higher average of talent in subordinate commands than any of the nations allied against her.

Her blunders lay in statesmanship and in the supreme military direction. United herself and with complaisant colleagues, she had to face a loose alliance of proud and independent democracies. A little skill might have increased the looseness of its bonds till it dissolved, but Germany by her maladroitness welded it together. Her calculated barbarities sickened the world and turned neutrals into enemies; her clumsy propaganda weakened the impression of power which her victories had created; she lit revolutions to destroy her opponents, and scorched her hands in their flame; above all, she forced America, unwilling and unready, into the conflict. The mingled bluster and whine which had become her public voice ended by making her a laughing-stock. The policy of Germany throughout the war was of a piece with her diplomacy before 1914, an invitation to the hostility of mankind, and defensible only on the assumption that her soldiers were so great that fatuity in her statesmen did not matter.

But she produced no single great soldier, though many competent ones. Von Hindenburg had some of the indefinable magnetism that makes a great leader, and von Mackensen had remarkable driving power. But her best were von Falkenhayn and von Ludendorff, for they alone had some inkling of the art as opposed to the mere science of war. Again and again throughout the campaigns success was frustrated, not by patent blunders, but by a certain narrowness of outlook and scientific woodenness of method. The instances are endless: von Kluck's rigid adherence to his encircling plan during the retreat from Mons; the tripartite attack at First Ypres; the attack on the Lys in April 1918, which drifted from a minor to a major operation, and thereby defeated the general strategy; the Second Battle of the Marne, which cannot be justified on any military ground. Ludendorff was a great organizer and a master of detail, but he had not that synoptic view of a battlefield and that insight into the heart of a situation which has belonged to the great captains of history. It may be argued that the preoccupation of Germany with her machine and her meticulous industry made it impossible for her to produce the highest kind of military genius. She was too busy with the trees to see the wood, and in the long run it is the wood that counts.

The Allies entered upon the struggle against heavy odds; their strength lay in the fact that every day that disaster was evaded the odds would lessen, till presently they would be on their side. It is for this reason that the First Marne is to be reckoned one of the decisive battles of the world; it definitely shut the door on complete defeat, and gave them a breathing-space. They needed leisure to train their manhood and prepare a machine the equivalent of Germany's, and Russia's heroic battles during 1915 were vital as a distraction for the enemy. The Allies made countless blunders, but, while it is easy enough to detect them now, it is hard to see how at the time they could have been avoided. There was no central command, no single mind envisaging the whole world as one battleground, and the clumsy device of occasional conferences could not atone for the lack of executive unity. They suffered, too, from several profound misconceptions of fact. They exaggerated the strength of Russia, and did not foresee the underground forces which were destined to overthrow her. They underestimated the possibilities of their command of the sea, and were too slow to declare the blockade and, when it was declared, to make it effective. They underestimated the strength of the German war-machine, and the power of the defensive in modern war. Their various attacks in the West during 1915 were, as is now clear, mistaken; they were not prepared either in men or material for ambitious objectives. Again, while the necessities of their position forced them to undertake divergent operations, it may fairly be argued that these operations were too divergent. They lacked purpose and a definite place in a strategical scheme; for minor operations they were too costly, and for major operations too weak. In the long run they bore ample fruit, but only after victory was assured in the main theatre of the West. Finally, the Allies were slow to read the lessons of the new war, and for years followed unsuitable methods in the field. That was inevitable, and it is to their credit that in the end they read these lessons more correctly than their enemy. Remember that for long they were improvisers, and had to learn a new art and perfect their machine through many experiments.

Let it not be said that they "muddled through" to victory. Success was never yet won by such a road. While they muddled they stuck fast. Their problem was the same as that of the North in the American Civil War—to stave off immediate defeat and to make actual their potential human and economic superiority. When their material strength was so organized that it surpassed that of their opponents, and when it was so used that no part of it was wasted, victory followed like the conclusion of a mathematical demonstration. The war proved once again the supreme value of training and intellect. The Allies were victorious in the end because they used their brains better than Germany and outgeneralled their opponents.

It would be a task both futile and invidious to discuss the relative contributions of the different Allies to this achievement. All had in it a full and noble share. But since this book is a British history, it is permissible to emphasize the magnitude of our country's part. The British Fleet nullified Germany on the high seas in the first month of war, and conducted the blockade which sapped her internal strength. It alone made possible the co-operation in the field of allies separated by leagues of sea, and the conduct of campaigns in distant battle-grounds. The wealth of Britain bore for years the main financial burden of the Alliance, and her factories produced the greater part of that mighty reserve of material which ended by far surpassing Germany's long-prepared stores. Her armies, beginning from the smallest numbers, grew to be the equal of any in the world, alike in training, discipline, and leadership. Moreover, her steady resolution was a bulwark to all her confederates in the darkest hours. Such has always been her record in European wars. At the beginning she is underrated as a soft and pacific

Power already on the decline. Such in the eighteenth century was the view of the Continental monarchs, Frederick the Great, Joseph II. of Austria, Catherine of Russia; such in 1914 was the view of the German Government. She comes slowly to a decision, enters upon war unwillingly, but wages it with all her heart and does not slacken till her purpose is attained. It was so in the days of Philip of Spain, of Louis Quatorze, and of Napoleon. The "island Poland" ends by finding the future of the world in her hands. The few wise men in Germany were amply justified who on the news that Britain had entered the conflict cried Ichabod to the hopes of German victory.

The war was one of nations rather than of Governments, of the rank and file rather than of generals. Without the sustained endurance of every class in the community there could have been no success, and the battles were dependent upon the fighting vigour and endurance of the average soldier rather than upon any peculiar brilliance and subtlety in leadership. This was inevitable, partly because the struggle was so vast and desperate, reaching to the roots of human life; partly because it was a new kind of war, and generals as well as privates had their business to learn. One figure alone among the commanders in the field on any side stands out in the full heroic proportions. By whatever standard we judge him, Ferdinand Foch must take rank among the dozen greatest of the world's captains. Long before the outbreak of war he had made himself a master of his art, and a happy fate gave him the chance of putting into practice in the field the wisdom he had learned at leisure. He had studied closely the work of Napoleon, and had brought his mind into tune with that mighty intellect so that he absorbed his methods like a collaborator rather than a pupil. Discarding the pedantic cobwebs which the too laborious German Staff had woven round the Napoleonic campaigns, he mastered those principles which to the great Emperor were like "flashes of white light" to illuminate his path. Few soldiers have been more learned in their profession, and few have worn their learning more lightly. His broad, sane intelligence was without prejudice or prepossession. He turned a clear eye to the instant need of things, and read the facts of the case with a brave candour. But he did not forget that the maxims of strategy are eternal things, and he brought his profound knowledge of the past to elucidate the present. No aspect was neglected; he knew how to inspire men by the *beau geste* as well as how to labour at the minutiæ of preparation. He was both artist and man of science; he worked at a problem by the light of reason and knowledge; but when these failed he was content to trust that instinct which is an extra sense in great commanders. His character was a marvellous compound of patience and ardour; he could follow Fabian tactics when these were called for, and he could risk anything on the sudden stroke. He was not infallible, any more than Cæsar, or Napoleon, or Lee, but he could rise from his mistakes to a higher wisdom. In a word, he had a genius for war, that rarest of human talents. In the splendid company of the historic French captains he will stand among the foremost, behind, but not far behind, the greatest of all.

He was well served by his colleagues. Joffre and de Castelnau through the first difficult years laid the foundations of victory. Pétain showed a supreme talent for defensive warfare and for the organization of armies. Army and group commanders like Mangin and Gouraud, Fayolle and Franchet d'Esperey, Plumer and Cavan, were in all likelihood superior to any generals of the same rank on the enemy side; though men like von Armin, von Boehn, and von Einem were most capable soldiers. But if we are to seek for the first lieutenant of the Commander-in-Chief, the choice must fall on Sir Douglas Haig. He more than any other man made the final conception of Foch possible. He had not the great Frenchman's gift for strategy, but he had the scarcely less valuable power of creating the weapons for the strategist to use. He was a master in the art of training troops, the greatest Britain had seen since Sir John Moore. Under his guidance the British Army produced most of the main tactical developments of the campaign. He had his failures, as Foch had, but no failures or disappointments could shake his confidence in the ultimate issue. Drawing comfort from deep springs, he bore in the face of difficulties a gentle and unshakable resolution. The campaign—nay, the history of war—has produced no finer figure: great in patience, courtesy, unselfishness, serenity, and iron courage amid reverses and delays. He showed high military talent, but he showed a character which was above talent, and, since war is in the main a conflict of spirit, the finer spirit prevailed. Britain was fortunate indeed in the leader to whom she entrusted her manhood.

> " Here had been, mark, the General-in-Chief,
> Thro' a whole campaign of the world's life and death,
> Doing the King's work all the dim day long."

In a history of war the soldier must take first place, and in no campaign, it may fairly be said, did the soldier suffer less from civilian interference. The several Governments co-operated most loyally to meet the necessities of the field. Among statesmen no one figure towered above his fellows as did Lincoln's in the American Civil War. Cabinets passed through rapid changes ; politicians did their part and made way for others, leaving their contributions to the common stock. The struggle closed with three men directing the councils of the Allies, and standing forth as the representatives of their peoples. In each case the leader was not wholly typical of the nation he led. M. Clemenceau had much of the essential Gallic genius, but his inspired audacity was perhaps less characteristic of the France of 1918 than was the patient caution of Pétain. President Wilson guided his country without being in temperament a representative American, and Mr. Lloyd George irritated and puzzled millions who accepted his inspiration. That is no new thing in history. Cromwell was far removed in spirit from the tolerant and laughter-loving England which he ruled ; Burke, who more than any other man laid down the fundamentals of British policy, was as exotic as Disraeli. In these three men the Allies found their ultimate leaders, who controlled the spirit as well as the form of the final stages. It was a formidable combination, for they blended courage and tenacity with imaginative fervour, and with that rarer thing, a far-sighted gaze into the intricacies of the future.

Yet, when all due praise has been given to famous leaders, it remains true that the hero of the war was the ordinary man. Victory was won less by genius in the few than by faithfulness in the many. Freedom had undergone its supreme test, and had been abundantly justified. In this we may find matter for humble confidence. A war does not solve any problems but the one—which side is the stronger; but it clears the ground of encumbrances, and enables men to judge more truly of their duties and their needs. A great arrogance, which was the foe of humanity, had been overthrown. Of this arrogance Germany had been the extreme instance and the most truculent champion, but the thing had corrupted the whole world. In 1914 no nation was free from an inhumane pride, whether of race, or wealth, or culture. A senseless complacency, a perilous satisfaction had blinded mankind. With the outbreak of war the eyes of the honest were unsealed; they saw the thing which had betrayed them, and fought against it. Their victory was won not only over their enemies but over themselves, and in the long contest the grossest and dullest had the chance of purification, for every class and type were drawn into the battle.

The world had suffered a purgation by pity and terror. It had made solemn sacrifice, and the sacrifice was mainly of the innocent and the young. This was true of every side. Most men who fell died for honourable things. Perversities of national policy were changed in the case of the rank and file, both of the Allies and their opponents, into the eternal sanctities—love of country and home, comradeship, loyalty to manly virtues, the indomitable questing of youth. Against such a spirit the gates of death cannot prevail. Innocence does not perish in vain. We may dare to hope that the seed sown in sacrifice and pain will yet quicken and bear fruit to the amelioration of the world, and in this confidence await the decrees of that Omnipotence to whom a thousand years are as one day.

APPENDICES

APPENDIX I.

DOCUMENTS DEALING WITH GERMAN AND AUSTRIAN PEACE OVERTURES DURING OCTOBER 1918.

I.—The German Note to President Wilson of 4th October.

The German Government requests the President of the United States of America to take in hand the restoration of peace, acquaint all belligerent States with this request, and invite them to send plenipotentiaries for the purpose of opening negotiations. The German Government accepts the programme set forth by the President of the United States in his message to Congress of January 8, 1918, and in his later pronouncements, especially his speech of the 27th September, as a basis for peace negotiations.

With a view to avoiding further bloodshed, the German Government requests the immediate conclusion of an armistice on land and water and in the air.

Max, Prince of Baden,
Imperial Chancellor.

II.—The Austro-Hungarian Note to President Wilson of 4th October.

The Austro-Hungarian Monarchy, which has always waged the war solely as a defensive war, and has repeatedly announced its readiness to put an end to the bloodshed and to attain a just and honourable peace, approaches herewith the President of the United States of America with a proposal to conclude with him and his Allies an immediate armistice on land and sea and in the air, and immediately, therefore, to enter into negotiations for the conclusion of peace, for which the Fourteen Points of President Wilson's message to Congress of January 8, 1918, and the Four Points in his speech of February 12,* 1918, should serve as a basis, while attention will likewise be paid to the declarations by President Wilson on September 27, 1918.

III.—Extract from President Wilson's address in New York, September 27, 1918.

We are all agreed that there can be no peace obtained by any kind of bargain or compromise with the Governments of the Central Empires, because we have dealt with them already, and have seen them deal with other Governments that were parties to this struggle, at Brest-Litovsk and Bukharest. They have convinced us that they are without honour and do not intend justice. They observe no covenants, accept no principle but force and their own interest. We cannot "come to terms" with them. They have made it impossible. The German people must by this time be fully aware that we cannot accept the word of those who forced this war upon us. We do not think the same thoughts or speak the same language of agreement.

It is of capital importance that we should also be explicitly agreed that no peace shall be obtained by any kind of compromise or abatement of the principles we have avowed as the principles for which we are fighting. There should exist no doubt about that. I am, therefore, going to take the liberty of speaking with the utmost frankness about the practical implications that are involved in it.

* Query: 11th.

If it be, in deed and in truth, the common object of the Governments associated against Germany and of the nations whom they govern, as I believe it to be, to achieve by the coming settlements a secure and lasting peace, it will be necessary that all who sit down at the peace table shall come ready and willing to pay the price, the only price, that will procure it ; and ready and willing also to create in some virile fashion the only instrumentality by which it can be made certain that the agreements of the peace will be honoured and fulfilled. That price is impartial justice in every item of the settlement, no matter whose interest is crossed ; and not only impartial justice, but also the satisfaction of the several peoples whose fortunes are dealt with. That indispensable instrumentality is a League of Nations, formed under covenants that will be efficacious. Without such an instrumentality, by which the peace of the world can be guaranteed, peace will rest in part upon the word of outlaws, and only upon that word. For Germany will have to redeem her character, not by what happens at the peace table but by what follows.

And as I see it, the constitution of that League of Nations and the clear definition of its objects must be a part, is in a sense the most essential part, of the peace settlement itself. It cannot be formed now. If formed now it would be merely a new alliance confined to the nations associated against a common enemy. It is not likely that it could be formed after the settlement. It is necessary to guarantee the peace ; and the peace cannot be guaranteed as an afterthought. The reason, to speak in plain terms again, why it must be guaranteed is that there will be parties to the peace whose promises have proved untrustworthy, and means must be found in connection with the peace settlement itself to remove that source of insecurity. It would be folly to leave the guarantee to the subsequent voluntary action of the Governments we have seen destroy Russia and deceive Rumania.

But these general terms do not disclose the whole matter. Some details are needed to make them sound less like a thesis and more like a practical programme. These, then, are some of the particulars, and I state them with the greater confidence because I can state them authoritatively as representing this Government's interpretation of its own duty with regard to peace :—

First, the impartial justice meted out must involve no discrimination between those to whom we wish to be just and those to whom we do not wish to be just. It must be a justice which plays no favourites and knows no standard but the equal rights of the several peoples concerned.

Second, no special or separate interest of any single nation or any group of nations can be made the basis of any part of the settlement which is not consistent with the common interest of all.

Third, there can be no leagues or alliances or special covenants and understandings within the general and common family of the League of Nations.

Fourth, and more specifically, there can be no special, selfish economic combinations within the League, and no employment of any form of economic boycott or exclusion, except as the power of economic penalty, by exclusion from the markets of the world, may be vested in the League of Nations itself as a means of discipline and control.

Fifth, all international agreements and treaties of every kind must be made known in their entirety to the rest of the world.

Special alliances and economic rivalries and hostilities have been the prolific source in the modern world of the plans and passions that produce war. It would be an insincere as well as an insecure peace that did not exclude them in definite and binding terms.

IV.—President Wilson's Note to the German Chancellor of 8th October.

Before making reply to the request of the Imperial German Government, and in order that that reply shall be as candid and straightforward as the momentous interests involved require, the President of the United States deems it necessary to assure himself of the exact meaning of the Note of the Imperial Chancellor. Does the Imperial Chancellor mean that the Imperial German Government accepts the terms laid down by the President in his address to the Congress of the United States on the 8th January last, and in subsequent addresses, and that its object in entering into discussions would be only to agree upon the practical details of their application?

The President feels bound to say, with regard to the suggestion of an armistice, that he would not feel at liberty to propose a cessation of arms to the Governments with which the Government of the United States is associated against the Central Powers so long as the armies of those Powers are upon their soil. The good faith of any discussion would manifestly depend upon the consent of the Central Powers immediately to withdraw their forces everywhere from invaded territory.

The President also feels that he is justified in asking whether the Imperial Chancellor is speaking merely for the constituted authorities of the Empire who have so far conducted the war. He deems the answers to these questions vital from every point of view.

V.—German Note to President Wilson, October 12, 1918.

The German Government has accepted the terms laid down by President Wilson in his Address of the 8th January and in his subsequent addresses as the foundation for a permanent peace of justice. Consequently, the object of the proposed discussions would be only to come to an understanding upon practical details of the application of these terms.

The German Government assumes that the Governments of the Powers associated with the Government of the United States also adopt the position taken by President Wilson in his public declarations.

The German Government declares itself ready, in agreement with the Austro-Hungarian Government, with a view to bringing about an armistice to comply with the proposals of the President in regard to evacuation. The German Government suggests that the President should bring about the meeting of a mixed Commission, whose duty it would be to concert the necessary arrangements concerning the evacuation.

The present German Government, which takes the responsibility for this step towards peace, has been formed by negotiations and in agreement with the great majority of the Reichstag. The Chancellor, supported in all his actions by the will of this majority, speaks in the name of the German Government and of the German people.

SOLF,
State Secretary of Foreign Office.

VI.—President Wilson's Note to Germany of October 14, 1918.

The unqualified acceptance by the present German Government and by a large majority of the German Reichstag of the terms laid down by the President of the United States of America in his address to the Congress of the United States on January 8, 1918, and in his subsequent addresses justifies the President in making a frank and direct statement of his decision with regard to the communications of the German Government of October 8 * and 12, 1918.

It must be clearly understood that the process of evacuation and the conditions of an armistice are matters which must

* Query: 4th October.

be left to the judgment and advice of the military advisers of the Government of the United States and the Allied Governments, and the President feels it his duty to say that no arrangement can be accepted by the Government of the United States which does not provide absolutely satisfactory safeguards and guarantees of the maintenance of the present military supremacy of the armies of the United States and of the Allies in the Field. He feels confident that he can safely assume that this will also be the judgment and decision of the Allied Governments.

The President feels that it is also his duty to add that neither the Government of the United States nor, he is quite sure, the Governments with which the Government of the United States is associated as a belligerent will consent to consider an armistice so long as the armed forces of Germany continue the illegal and inhuman practices which they still persist in. At the very time that the German Government approaches the Government of the United States with proposals of peace its submarines are engaged in sinking passenger ships at sea,—and not the ships alone, but the very boats in which their passengers and crews seek to make their way to safety; and in their present enforced withdrawal from Flanders and France the German armies are pursuing a course of wanton destruction which has always been regarded as in direct violation of the rules and practices of civilized warfare. Cities and villages, if not destroyed, are being stripped not only of all they contain, but often of their very inhabitants. The Nations associated against Germany cannot be expected to agree to a cessation of arms while acts of inhumanity, spoliation and desolation are being continued which they justly look upon with horror and with burning hearts.

It is necessary also, in order that there may be no possibility of misunderstanding, that the President should very solemnly call the attention of the Government of Germany to the language and plain intent of one of the terms of peace which the German Government has now accepted. It is contained in the address of the President delivered at Mount Vernon on 4th July last. It is as follows:—

> "The destruction of every arbitrary power anywhere that can separately, secretly and of its single choice disturb the peace of the world; or, if it cannot be presently destroyed, at the least its reduction to virtual impotency."

The power which has hitherto controlled the German nation is of the sort here described. It is within the choice of the German nation to alter it. The President's words just quoted naturally constitute a condition precedent to peace, if peace is to come by the action of the German people themselves. The President feels bound to say that the whole process of peace will, in his judgment, depend upon the definiteness and satisfactory character of the guarantees which can be given in this fundamental matter. It is indispensable that the Governments associated against Germany should know beyond a peradventure with whom they are dealing.

The President will make a separate reply to the Royal and Imperial Government of Austria-Hungary.

VII.—President Wilson's Note to Austria of October 18, 1918.

The President deems it his duty to say to the Austro-Hungarian Government that he cannot entertain the present suggestions of that Government because of certain events of the utmost importance which, occurring since the delivery of his address of the 8th January last, have necessarily altered the attitude and responsibility of the Government of the United States.

Among the fourteen terms of peace which the President formulated at that time occurred the following:—

X. "The peoples of Austria-Hungary, whose place among

the nations we wish to see safeguarded and assured, should be accorded the freest opportunity of autonomous development."

Since that sentence was written and uttered to the Congress of the United States, the Government of the United States has recognized that a state of belligerency exists between the Czecho-Slovaks and the German and Austro-Hungarian Empires, and that the Czecho-Slovak National Council is a *de facto* belligerent Government, clothed with proper authority to direct the military and political affairs of the Czecho-Slovaks. It has also recognized in the fullest manner the justice of the nationalistic aspirations of the Jugo-Slavs for freedom.

The President is therefore no longer at liberty to accept a mere " autonomy " of these peoples as a basis of peace, but is obliged to insist that they, and not he, shall be the judges of what action on the part of the Austro-Hungarian Government will satisfy their aspirations and their conception of their rights and destiny as members of the family of nations.

VIII.—The German Note to President Wilson of October 20, 1918.

In complying with the proposal to evacuate occupied territories the German Government adopted the position that the procedure in this evacuation and the conditions of armistice are to be left to the judgment of military advisers, and that the present relative strength on the fronts must be made the basis of arrangements that will safeguard and guarantee it. The German Government leaves it to the President to create an opportunity to settle the details. It trusts that the President of the United States will approve no demand that would be irreconcilable with the honour of the German people and with paving the way to a peace of justice.

The German Government protests against the charge of illegal and inhuman practices that is made against the German land and sea forces, and thereby against the German people.

Destructions will always be necessary to cover a retreat, and are in so far permitted under international law. The German troops have the strictest instructions to respect private property and to make provision for the population according to their ability. Where, notwithstanding this, excesses occur, the guilty are punished.

The German Government also denies that in sinking ships the German Navy has purposely destroyed lifeboats together with their occupants. The German Government suggests that in all these points the facts shall be cleared up by neutral commissions.

In order to avoid everything that might impede the efforts to secure peace, orders have, at the direction of the German Government, been sent out to all U-boat commanders that will exclude the torpedoing of passenger ships. At the same time, however, for technical reasons, no guarantee can be undertaken that this order will reach every submarine at sea before its return.

President Wilson describes as a fundamental condition for peace the removal of every arbitrary power that can separately, uncontrolled, and of its own single choice disturb the peace of the world. To this the German Government replies :—In the German Empire the representatives of the people have hitherto had no right to influence the formation of the Government. The Constitution did not provide for the co-operation of Parliament in decisions on war and peace. A fundamental change has come about in this regard. The new Government has been formed in complete accord with the desires of a Parliament which issued from equal, general, secret, and direct suffrage. The leaders of the great parties of the Reichstag are amongst its members.

In the future, too, no Government can enter upon or carry on its office without possessing the confidence of the majority of the Reichstag. The responsibility of the Imperial Chancellor towards Parliament is being legally extended and safeguarded. The first act of the new Government was to submit a Bill to the Reichstag so amending the Constitution of the Empire that the approval of Parliament is requisite for a decision on war and peace. The pledge for the duration of the new system, however, does not lie only in legal guarantees, but also in the unshakable will of the German people, the great majority of which is behind these reforms, and demands their energetic prosecution.

The President's question as to with whom he and the Governments associated against Germany are dealing is therefore clearly and unequivocally answered, to the effect that the peace and armistice offer comes from a Government which, free from all arbitrary and irresponsible influence, is supported by the approval of the overwhelming majority of the German people.

SOLF,
Secretary of State of the Foreign Ministry.

Berlin, October 20.

IX.—President Wilson's Note to Germany of October 23, 1918.

Having received the solemn and explicit assurance of the German Government that it unreservedly accepts the terms of peace laid down in his address to the Congress of the United States on January 8, 1918, and the principles of settlement enunciated in his subsequent addresses, particularly the address of the 27th September, and that it desires to discuss the details of their application ;

And that this wish and purpose emanate, not from those who have hitherto dictated German policy and conducted the present war on Germany's behalf, but from Ministers who speak for the majority of the Reichstag and for an overwhelming majority of the German people ;

And having received also the explicit promise of the present German Government that the humane rules of civilized warfare will be observed both on land and sea by the German armed forces,

The President of the United States feels that he cannot decline to take up with the Governments with which the Government of the United States is associated the question of an armistice.

He deems it his duty to say again, however, that the only armistice he would feel justified in submitting for consideration would be one which should leave the United States and the Powers associated with her in a position to enforce any arrangements that may be entered into, and to make a renewal of hostilities on the part of Germany impossible. The President has, therefore, transmitted his correspondence with the present German Authorities to the Governments with which the Government of the United States is associated as a belligerent, with the suggestion that, if those Governments are disposed to effect peace upon the terms and principles indicated, their military advisers and the military advisers of the United States be asked to submit to the Governments associated against Germany the necessary terms of such an armistice as will fully protect the interests of the peoples involved and ensure to the Associated Governments the unrestricted power to safeguard and enforce the details of the peace to which the German Government has agreed, provided they deem such an armistice possible from the military point of view. Should such terms of armistice be suggested, their acceptance by Germany will afford the best concrete evidence of her unequivocal acceptance of the terms and principles of peace from which the whole action proceeds.

The President would deem himself lacking in candour did he not point out in the frankest possible terms the reason why extraordinary safeguards must be demanded. Significant and important as the constitutional changes seem to be which are spoken of by the German Foreign Secretary in his Note of the 20th October, it does not appear that the principle of a Government responsible to the German people has yet been fully worked out, or that any guarantees either exist or are in contemplation that the alterations of principle and of practice now partially agreed upon will be permanent.

Moreover, it does not appear that the heart of the present difficulty has been reached. It may be that future wars have been brought under the control of the German people: but the present war has not been; and it is with the present war that we are dealing. It is evident that the German people have no means of commanding the acquiescence of the military authorities of the Empire in the popular will: that the power of the King of Prussia to control the policy of the Empire is unimpaired: that the determining initiative still remains with those who have hitherto been the masters of Germany.

Feeling that the whole peace of the world depends now on plain speaking and straightforward action, the President deems it his duty to say, without any attempt to soften what may seem harsh words, that the nations of the world do not, and cannot trust the word of those who have hitherto been the masters of German policy, and to point out once more that in concluding peace and attempting to undo the infinite injuries and injustices of this war, the Government of the United States cannot deal with any but veritable representatives of the German people, who have been assured of a genuine constitutional standing as the real rulers of Germany. If it must deal with the military masters and the monarchical autocrats of Germany now, or if it is likely to have to deal with them later in regard to the international obligations of the German Empire, it must demand, not peace negotiations but surrender. Nothing can be gained by leaving this essential thing unsaid.

X.—Mr. Lansing's Note to Mr. Barclay of October 23, 1918.

Sir,

I have the honour to enclose herewith certain communications which have passed between the Government of the United States and the Government of Germany relative to an armistice and the terms of a Treaty of Peace between the belligerents in the present war, with the request that you transmit the same to your Government.

The President instructs me to make request that your Government take this correspondence under careful consideration and communicate, at its convenience, its views and conclusions concerning it.

The President desires especially an expression of the decision of your Government as to its willingness and readiness to acquiesce, and take part in, the course of action with regard to an armistice which is suggested in my Note of October 23, 1918, to the Chargé d'Affaires of Switzerland, in which is set forth the decision of the President with regard to the submission of the question of an armistice to the Governments with which the Government of the United States is associated in the prosecution of the war against Germany, and with regard to the manner in which the terms of an armistice are to be determined, provided that an armistice at this time is deemed possible from the military point of view.

I wish to point out to your Government that the President has endeavoured to safeguard with the utmost care the interests of the peoples at war with Germany in every statement made in the enclosed correspondence, and that it is his sincere hope that your Government will think that he has succeeded, and will be willing to co-operate in the steps which he has suggested.

Accept, Sir, the renewed assurances of my high consideration,

ROBERT LANSING.

[The communications enclosed in the Note are the three German Notes dated 4th October, 12th October, and 20th October, and the Replies of the Government of the United States dated 8th October, 14th October, and 23rd October.]

XI.—The German Note to President Wilson of October 27, 1918.

The German Government has taken cognizance of the answer of the President of the United States.

The President is aware of the far-reaching changes which have been carried out and are being carried out in the German Constitutional structure. The peace negotiations will be conducted by a people's Government, in whose hands rests both actually and constitutionally the power to make deciding conclusions. The military powers are also subject to it.

The German Government now awaits proposals for an armistice which shall be a first step towards a just peace, as the President has described it in his proclamations.

SOLF,
Secretary of State for Foreign Affairs.

XII.—The Austro-Hungarian Reply to President Wilson of October 27, 1918.

In answer to President Wilson's note of the 18th instant, addressed to the Austro-Hungarian Government, and in accordance with the President's decision to treat the question of armistice and peace separately with Austria-Hungary, the Austro-Hungarian Government has the honour to declare that it agrees, as with the President's former declarations, so also with the views expressed in his last note concerning the rights of the peoples of Austria-Hungary, especially those of Czecho-Slovaks and Jugo-Slavs. As, therefore, Austria-Hungary has accepted all the conditions on which the President has made the opening of negotiations for armistice and peace depend, the Austro-Hungarian Government considers that nothing stands in the way of such negotiations being opened. The Austro-Hungarian Government therefore declares itself ready, without awaiting the result of other negotiations, to commence negotiations for peace between Austria-

Hungary and the opposing States, and for immediate armistice on all Austro-Hungarian fronts, and requests the President to take introductory steps accordingly.—ANDRASSY.

XIII.—NOTE FROM THE VATICAN, DATED NOVEMBER 1, 1918, ON BEHALF OF AUSTRIA-HUNGARY.

The Holy Father, in his most earnest desire to see an end put as soon as possible to the war which for too long has devastated Europe, begs His Britannic Majesty's Government to give benevolent and immediate consideration to the request for a separate peace put forward by Austria-Hungary. After a request of this nature, the cessation of the sanguinary conflict appears to be imperiously called for by every principle of humanity.

Further, the August Pontiff, with a strong feeling for the sufferings of poor prisoners of war, especially on the approach of severe weather, trusts that, thanks especially to the noble and efficacious intervention of His Majesty's Government, these unfortunate people can by both parties be restored to their families.

APPENDIX II.

LORD CAVAN'S SECOND DISPATCH.

THE DEFEAT OF AUSTRIA.

WAR OFFICE,
4th December 1918.

THE Secretary of State for War has received the following Dispatch from General The Earl of Cavan, K.P., K.C.B., M.V.O., Commanding-in-Chief British Forces in Italy:—

GENERAL HEADQUARTERS,
BRITISH FORCES IN ITALY,
15th November 1918.

MY LORD,

I have the honour to submit the following report on the part played by the British troops in Italy from September 15, 1918, to the final defeat of the Austrian Army.

1. If reference only in general terms is made to the gallant troops of the XIth and XVIIIth Italian Corps which were under my command, it is not because their part was any less brilliant, but because this dispatch is written in my capacity of Commander-in-Chief of the British Forces in Italy and not in the capacity of Commander of the Tenth Italian Army.

2. Early in September, as it appeared unlikely that offensive operations would be undertaken in Italy in the near future, it was decided to assist France with some or all of the British troops in this country.

His Excellency General Diaz not only put no obstacle in the way, but further assured me that his one wish was to assist Marshal Foch in defeating the Germans with all the resources he had available.

In accordance with this idea the 7th, 23rd and 48th Divisions were reduced from 13 to 10 battalions, and the 9 battalions thus released were dispatched to France on September 13th and 14th.

The 7th Division was already at rest, and it was intended to dispatch this division as soon as a battle-worn division should arrive from France to replace it.

In order that it might be in a position to follow the 7th Division without delay the 23rd Division was relieved by troops of the 12th Italian Corps, the relief being completed on September 27th.

3. As a result of the tactical situation in France and the consequent demands on rolling stock the proposed exchange of divisions was postponed from day to day. The situation in Italy also changed, and finally all three divisions remained in this country.

4. On October 6th I went to Comando Supremo at General Diaz's request.

General Diaz at this interview offered me the Command of a mixed Italian-British Army with the view of undertaking offensive operations at an early date. I expressed my high appreciation of the honour conferred on me and the pleasure it would give me to accept this new command.

General Diaz impressed on me the vital importance of secrecy. In order to make as little apparent change as possible he suggested that the 48th Division should remain in position on the Asiago Plateau and pass temporarily under the command of General Pennella, Commanding the XIIth Italian Corps.

To this I agreed, with the stipulation that the 48th Division should rejoin my command at the earliest opportunity.

5. On October 13th General Diaz held a Conference of Army Commanders at Comando Supremo, at which he explained his plans for the forthcoming offensive.

The general plan for the main attack was to advance across the Piave with the Tenth, Eighth, and Twelfth Italian Armies—to drive a wedge between the Fifth and Sixth Austrian Armies—forcing the Fifth Army eastwards, and threatening the communications of the Sixth Army running through the Valmarino Valley.

The Fourth Army was simultaneously to take the offensive in the Grappa sector.

The task allotted to the Tenth Army was to reach the Livenza between Portobuffole and Sacile, and thus protect the flank of the Eighth and Twelfth Armies in their move northwards.

The co-ordination of the attacks of the Tenth, Eighth, and Twelfth Armies was entrusted to General Caviglia, the commander of the Eighth Italian Army.

6. On October 11th the Headquarters of the Tenth Army, the Army which had been placed under my command, were established near Treviso.

The Tenth Army in the first instance was to consist of the XIth Italian and XIVth British Corps.

The XIth Italian Corps was already holding a sector on the Piave extending from Ponte di Piave to Palazzon. The XIVth British Corps was concentrated in the Treviso area on the 16th of October.

7. The problem that faced the Tenth Army was not an easy one.

The breadth of the Piave on the front of attack was approximately one and a half miles, and consisted of numerous channels dotted with islands. The main island was the Grave di Papadopoli, which was some three miles long by one mile broad. The current varied according to the channels.

In the main channel it ran at a rate exceeding ten miles an hour in time of flood, and never dropped below three and a half miles an hour at summer level.

The enemy held the Grave di Papadopoli as an advanced post.

8. On October 21st the XIVth British Corps took over the northern portion of the XIth Italian Corps front from Salletuol to Palazzon.

Orders were issued that all troops visible to the enemy should wear Italian uniform, and that no British gun should fire a single shot previous to the general bombardment. By these means it was hoped to conceal the presence of British troops from the Austrians.

9. On the date of relief the Piave was in full flood, which not only made reconnaissances of the river bed impossible, but also raised the probability of changes in the main channels. This added considerably to my anxieties as regards bridging requirements.

10. Lieutenant-General Sir J. M. Babington, K.C.M.G., C.B., Commanding the XIVth British Corps, at once suggested the advisability of occupying the island of Grave di Papadopoli previous to the general advance.

With this opinion I concurred.

11. On the night of October 23rd-24th, the 2nd 1st Battalion of the Honourable Artillery Company and the 1st Battalion of the Royal Welsh Fusiliers, without any previous artillery preparation, crossed the main channel, surprised the Austrian garrison and occupied the northern half of the island.

The attacking troops were transported in small flat-bottomed boats, each holding six men, and rowed by two Italian pontiere. The movement owed its success to the careful arrangements made by the 7th Division, the untiring energy of Captain Odini, of the Italian Engineers, and of the Italian pontiere under his command and to the fine leading of Lieutenant-Colonel R. N. O'Connor, D.S.O., M.C., Commanding the 2nd/1st Honourable Artillery Company.

Both in the transport of the troops by boat and the subsequent bridging of the river, the pontiere gave us an assistance whose value it is impossible to over-estimate.

12. On the night of October 25th-26th the conquest of the island of Grave di Papadopoli was completed by a combined movement of the 7th British Division from the north and the 37th Italian Division from the south.

This very successful operation put the main channel of the Piave behind us and enabled us to begin our bridges and preparations for the main attack in comparative security, although the garrison of the island was subjected to a very heavy shelling all day on the 26th.

13. At 11.30 p.m. on the night of October 26th the bombardment of the hostile positions opened along the whole front. The fact that no single British gun had opened previous to this hour deserves special mention. Both heavy and field artillery were registered by the 6th Field Survey Company, R.E., and the fact that the bombardment and the subsequent barrage were excellent in every way reflects the greatest credit on all ranks of this company.

14. At 6.45 a.m. on October 27th the attack of the Tenth Army against the enemy defences east of the Piave opened.

On the right the XIth Italian Corps under General Paolini attacked with the 23rd Bersagliere Division under General Fara on its right, and the 37th Italian Division under General Castagnola on its left.

On the left the XIVth British Corps attacked with the 7th British Division under Major-General T. H. Shoubridge, C.B., C.M.G., D.S.O., on its right and the 23rd British Division under Major-General H. F. Thuillier, C.B., C.M.G., on its left.

15. The enemy offered considerable resistance in his front line, but the defenders were overwhelmed after a hard fight, and the advance was pushed forward by all units with the utmost determination. I would especially commend the action of the 22nd Battalion Manchester Regiment and the 11th Battalion Northumberland Fusiliers in this assault.

Unfortunately we lost a number of gallant men by drowning; the difficulty of keeping a footing in a strong current being very great when loaded with rifle and ammunition.

By the night of October 27th a large bridgehead had been gained and firmly held, and Stabiuzzo, S. Polo di Piave, Borgo Zanetti, Tezze, Borgo Malanotte, C. Tonon were all in our hands.

16. The bridging of the Piave was proceeding rapidly, though much interfered with by hostile airmen. The strength of the current was such that if a break occurred there was a great danger of the whole structure being washed away. Both bridges were frequently broken.

17. On the front of the Eighth Italian Army, but at an interval of ten kilometres to our left, a landing had also been effected, but difficulties in throwing bridges had been encountered, especially at the point of junction with my Army. Comando Supremo therefore allotted me the XVIIIth Corps, under the command of General Basso, with a view to passing it across by our bridges and attacking northwards and so clearing the front of the Eighth Army.

18. During the night of October 27th-28th portions of the 56th Italian Division, under the command of General Vigliani, and the 33rd Italian Division, under the command of General Sanna, both of the XVIIIth Corps, crossed the Piave by various bridges in the XIVth Corps Area and took over the front from Casa la Sega to Casa Tonon.

19. At 9 a.m. on 28th October the attack was renewed. During the night of 27th-28th October many of the bridges had been broken, and as a result the XVIIIth Italian Corps had been unable to deploy all the troops required. General Basso, with soldierly instinct, did not hesitate to continue the advance, which was resumed with splendid dash. By dark the Tenth Army had reached the line Roncadelle-Ormele-Tempio-Rai-C. Bonotto-C. Milanese-S. Lucia di Piave-Ponte-Priula. Patrols had been pushed in advance of this line towards and up to the River Monticano.

20. The success of these operations at once brought about the desired effect. The enemy's hold of the high ground about Susegana weakened, and the passage of the right of the Eighth Army about Nervesa was accomplished during the night 28th-29th October.

Having accomplished the rôle assigned to it, the XVIIIth Italian Corps reverted to the Eighth Army on the morning of 29th October.

21. On the morning of 29th October the attack was again renewed, and during the day the advance was carried up to the River Monticano from the neighbourhood of Fontanelle to Ramiera. The XIVth Corps Mounted Troops, under Lieutenant-Colonel Sir C. B. Lowther, D.S.O., Bart., acting vigorously in advance of the infantry, secured the bridge over the Monticano between Vazzola and Cimetta intact, although it had been prepared for demolition. This resolute action undoubtedly saved us many hours of delay in the pursuit.

By this date the enemy's defence showed manifest signs of weakening, and numerous fires in rear of his lines suggested that a far-reaching withdrawal was contemplated.

22. On 29th October the 23rd Bersagliere Division passed to the Third Army, with a view to clearing the front of that army by an attack southwards. Its place in the XIth Italian Corps was taken by the 10th Italian Division under General Gagliani. The 31st Italian Division, which included the 332nd American Regiment, under General de Angelis, had meanwhile joined the XIVth British Corps.

The enemy had rapidly occupied the line of the River Monticano, and on this line he offered his last serious resistance. During the evening of 29th October and the morning of 30th October passages were forced, and the enemy skilfully manœuvred out of the remainder of his defences, chiefly by very gallant work on the part of the 8th Battalion, Yorkshire Regiment.

From this moment the defeat became a rout.

23. By the evening of 30th October the Livenza was reached, at Francenigo and Sacile. On 31st October this river was reached, and crossed between Motta di Livenza and Sacile.

On this date the XVIIIth Italian Corps was again placed under the command of the Tenth Army.

The advance had, on the 30th, already caused the enemy to weaken on the front of the Third Army, and crossings of the Lower Piave were effected at a number of points on this date. On the 31st the Third Army was advancing rapidly to the Livenza.

24. 1st November was mainly devoted to bridging the Livenza, the pursuit of the enemy being entrusted to the Italian Cavalry Corps.

25. On 2nd November the advance was resumed, and on that date the Tenth Army reached the line Villotta-Praturlone-River Meduna (east of Pordenone)-S. Quirino-Aviano.

26. On 3rd November the Tagliamento was reached from S. Vito to the north of Spilimbergo, a little opposition being met with. On 4th November the 332nd American Regiment had their baptism of fire when forcing the passage of the Tagliamento. They took over 100 prisoners and suffered a few casualties when attacking the enemy rearguards, an operation which they carried out with the same dash as has always been shown by American troops.

27. At 3 p.m. on 4th November, when the armistice came into effect, the line of the Tenth Army was Basagliapenta-Meretto di Tomba-Coseano-S. Daniele-Pinzano.

28. It is difficult to say with certainty the number of prisoners captured by the Tenth Army, as, after 1st November, the cavalry passed back many prisoners through our cages, which had already proved inadequate to hold such vast numbers.

The share of the XIVth British Corps amounted to over 28,000 prisoners and 219 guns.

29. I should like to specially bring to your Lordship's

notice the work of the following officers in connection with these operations :—Brigadier-General W. W. Pitt-Taylor, C.M.G., D.S.O., Brigadier-General, General Staff, XIVth Corps, and Brigadier-General C. Ogston, C.M.G., D.S.O., D.A. and Q.M.G., XIVth Corps, to whose untiring efforts the regular supply of food and ammunition was largely due ; Brigadier-General R. C. Hudson, Commanding Heavy Artillery ; Brigadier-General J. McC. Steele, C.B., C.M.G., Commanding 22nd Infantry Brigade ; and Brigadier-General C. D. V. Cary-Barnard, D.S.O., Commanding 68th Infantry Brigade.

30. Meanwhile, as stated above, the 48th Division, under Major-General Sir H. B. Walker, K.C.B., D.S.O., has remained on the Asiago Plateau, forming part of the Sixth Italian Army.

Successful raids were carried out on 4th, 11th, and 23rd October, which resulted in the capture of 445 prisoners and twelve machine guns.

A further raid carried out on the night of 29th-30th October found the trenches facing Ave unoccupied.

This pointed to a withdrawal in the mountains, and on 30th October patrols pushed beyond Asiago found the enemy rearguards in position on the line M. Catz-Bosco-Camporovere.

At 5.45 a.m. on 1st November an attack was launched against this line. M. Catz was captured by the Royal Berkshire Regiment by 6.30 a.m., but no progress could be made on M. Interrotto.

On the morning of 2nd November the success gained on M. Catz by the 145th Infantry Brigade was wisely exploited. M. Mosciagh was in the hands of the 48th Division by 7.30 a.m., and the Interrotto position thus outflanked. The advance then became more rapid, and by dark the advanced guards had reached Vezzena, and thus set foot on Austrian soil. This division was therefore the first British division to enter enemy territory on the Western Front.

On the morning of 3rd November the advance was again

resumed, and by dark both Caldonazzo and Levico had been occupied.

At 3 p.m. on 4th November, when the armistice came into force, the leading troops were on the line Miola-eastern outskirts of Trent.

The captures in prisoners and guns made by the 48th Division cannot be accurately ascertained; they amounted to at least 20,000 prisoners and 500 guns. Included amongst the prisoners were the Commander of the 3rd Corps and three Divisional Commanders.

It must be remembered that this division was attacking very formidable mountain positions with only a fifth part of the artillery that would have been at its disposal had the initial attack started on the Altipiano. Its performance therefore in driving in the enemy's rearguards so resolutely, while climbing up to heights of 5,000 feet, is all the more praiseworthy.

During these operations the leadership of Brigadier-General G. C. Sladen, C.M.C., D.S.O., M.C., Commanding the 143rd Infantry Brigade, was particularly noticeable.

31. The infantry had been waiting for an opportunity to show that they could worthily emulate the performances of their comrades in France. When the opportunity came they fulfilled my highest anticipations.

32. The work of the Royal Artillery throughout was based on the valuable "Notes on Recent Fighting" sent to us from France, and the rapid advances in close support of the infantry were worthy of their great traditions.

33. The Royal Engineers were incessantly at work in bridging not only the Piave, but the Monticano, the Livenza, and later on the Meduna and the Tagliamento. Without their highly skilled and efficient work vigorous pursuit would have been impossible.

34. The Royal Air Force, under the command of Colonel P. B. Joubert de la Ferte, D.S.O., took a very prominent part in the battle, harassing the enemy's retreat so effectually that

many batteries and thousands of prisoners fell into our hands that would have otherwise escaped.

35. The Machine Gun Corps had frequent opportunities, which were fully taken advantage of, and their training and skill in moving warfare was well exemplified.

36. Under circumstances of the greatest difficulty the Signal Service kept me in communication with the various units under my command.

37. During the battle, I was in constant touch with His Excellency, General Caviglia, under whose general direction my Army was operating. He was always most kind and prompt in assistance and advice and I owe him very warm thanks for his generous encouragement.

The action of the XIth and XVIIIth Italian Corps has been only briefly referred to, but they bore a very noble and conspicuous part in the victory. My cordial thanks are due to their commanders for their most loyal co-operation.

My thanks are also due to His Royal Highness the Duke of Aosta and the Staff of the Third Army. The XIth Italian Corps had previously formed part of the Third Army. Careful and detailed arrangements for an attack had long been made, and owing to the advanced state of these preparations little in this direction remained for me to do.

38. The fresh influenza epidemic, which broke out shortly before the commencement of the operations, threw a heavy and additional strain on the medical services. Despite this the evacuation and care of both the sick and wounded was rapidly and satisfactorily carried out. All the arrangements were most ably organized by my Director of Medical Services, Major-General F. R. Newland, C.B., C.M.G.

39. The demands made upon the Transportation Services in consequence of the rapid move of troops and material from the Altipiano to the Piave were successfully met by my Deputy Director-General of Transportation, Brigadier-General G. L. Colvin, C.M.G., D.S.O.

40. The Chaplains of all Denominations with my Force

have invariably rendered the most devoted service, showing at all times the utmost solicitude for the welfare and comfort of the men.

41. Brigadier-General T. W. Hale, C.B., C.M.G., my Director of Ordnance Services, has promptly and efficiently met every demand that has been made on him.

42. The rapid advance during the operations entailed great strain on the Supply and Transport Services.

My thanks are due to Brigadier-General W. S. Swabey, C.B., C.M.G., and all ranks of these services who maintained the supply of both ammunition and rations in spite of bad roads, hastily constructed bridges and long distances from railheads.

43. Brigadier-General C. Delme-Radcliffe, C.B., C.M.G., C.V.O., and the Staff of the British Mission, as well as the Liaison Officers, both Italian and British, rendered much valuable service. The translation of orders and the carrying of important messages threw a heavy responsibility on these officers, and the task was carried out without a hitch or difficulty of any sort.

44. In their retreat the Austrians left many hospitals full of sick and wounded of all nationalities behind them. In many cases these hospitals were bereft of provisions and attendants. The British Red Cross, under the supervision of Colonel Sir Courtauld Thompson, K.B.E., C.B., spared no efforts to alleviate the sufferings of the inmates, and undoubtedly saved the lives of many Austrian as well as Italian patients.

45. I again desire to express my most grateful acknowledgment of the services rendered by my Major-General, General Staff, Major-General The Honourable J. F. Gathorne-Hardy, C.B., D.S.O., whose unerring judgment and readiness to help in any difficult situation did much to bring about the very decisive results of the battle of Vittorio.

I also desire to thank all subordinate members of my Staff for the smooth working of a difficult operation, and in particular my Chief Engineer, Major-General C. S. Wilson, C.B., C.M.G.; my G.O.C., R.A., Major-General W. H. Kay, D.S.O.; my D.A. and Q.M.G., Major-General H. L. Alexander, D.S.O., who met enormous demands for food for prisoners—which far exceeded the most sanguine estimate—as well as for a starving population and a never-ceasing flow of Italians, military and civil, returning to the liberated country; Lieutenant-Colonel C. H. Mitchell, C.B., C.M.G., D.S.O., head of the Intelligence Section; Colonel O. C. Mordaunt, D.S.O., Deputy-Director of Signals; Major The Honourable P. W. Legh, my Military Secretary; and Major-General J. A. Strick, D.S.O., Inspector-General of Communications.

46. Lastly, I have the very greatest pleasure in informing your Lordship that I have always been able to obtain the ready ear of Comando Supremo in all important matters. Their extreme courtesy and kindness to myself and to the British troops adds much to the happy memory of the campaign in Italy.

I have the honour to be, My Lord,
Your Lordship's obedient Servant,
CAVAN,
General, Commanding-in-Chief,
British Forces in Italy.

APPENDIX III.

THE ARMISTICE CONVENTION WITH AUSTRIA-HUNGARY, NOVEMBER 3, 1918.

I.—MILITARY CLAUSES.

1. The immediate cessation of hostilities by land, sea, and air.

2. Total demobilization of the Austro-Hungarian Army, and immediate withdrawal of all Austro-Hungarian forces operating on the front from the North Sea to Switzerland.

Within Austro-Hungarian territory, limited as in Clause 3 below, there shall only be maintained as an organized military force a maximum of 20 Divisions, reduced to pre-war peace effectives.

Half the Divisional, Corps, and Army artillery and equipment shall be collected at points to be indicated by the Allies and United States of America for delivery to them, beginning with all such material as exists in the territories to be evacuated by the Austro-Hungarian forces.

3. Evacuation of all territories invaded by Austria-Hungary since the beginning of war. Withdrawal within such periods as shall be determined by the Commander-in-Chief of the Allied forces on each front of the Austro-Hungarian Armies, behind a line fixed as follows :—

From Piz Umbrail to the north of the Stelvio it will follow the crest of the Rhætian Alps up to the sources of the Adige and the Eisach, passing thence by Mounts Reschen and Brenner and the heights of Oetz and Ziller; the line thence turns south, crossing Mount Toblach, and meeting the present frontier of the Carnic Alps. It follows this frontier up to Mount Tarvis, and after Mount Tarvis the watershed of the Julian Alps by the Col of Predil, Mount Mangart, the Tricorno (Terglou), and the watershed of the Cols di Podberdo, Podlaniscam, and Idria. From this point the line turns south-east towards the Schneeberg, excluding the whole basin of the Save and its tributaries; from the Schneeberg it goes down towards the coast in such a way as to include Castua, Mattuglia, and Volosca in the evacuated territories.

It will also follow the administrative limits of the present province of Dalmatia, including to the north Licarica and Trivania, and to the south territory limited by a line from the shore of Cape Planca to the summits of the watershed eastwards, so as to include in the evacuated area all the valleys and watercourses flowing towards Sebenico, such as the Cicola, Kerka, Butisnica, and their tributaries. It will also include all the islands in the north and west of Dalmatia, from Premuda, Selve, Ulbo, Scherda, Maon, Pago, and Puntadura in the north up to Meleda in the south, embracing Sant' Andrea, Busi, Lissa, Lesina, Tercola, Curzola, Cazza, and Lagosta, as well as the neighbouring rocks and islets and Pelagosa, only excepting the islands of Great and Small Zirona, Bua, Solta, and Brazza.

All territories thus evacuated will be occupied by the troops of the Allies and of the United States of America.

All military and railway equipment of all kinds (including coal), belonging to or within these territories, to be left *in situ*, and surrendered to the Allies according to special orders given by the Commanders-in-Chief of the forces of the Associated Powers on the different fronts. No new destruction, pillage, or requisition to be done by enemy troops in the territories to be evacuated by them and occupied by the forces of the Associated Powers.

4. The Allies shall have the right of free movement over all road and rail and waterways in Austro-Hungarian territory and of the use of the necessary Austrian and Hungarian means of transportation.

The Armies of the Associated Powers shall occupy such strategic points in Austria-Hungary at such times as they may deem necessary to enable them to conduct military operations or to maintain order.

They shall have the right of requisition on payment for the troops of the Associated Powers wherever they may be.

5. Complete evacuation of all German troops within 15 days, not only from the Italian and Balkan fronts, but from all Austro-Hungarian territory.

Internment of all German troops which have not left Austria-Hungary within that date.

6. The administration of the evacuated territories of Austria-Hungary will be entrusted to the local authorities under the control of the Allied and Associated Armies of Occupation.

7. The immediate repatriation without reciprocity of all Allied prisoners of war and interned subjects, and of civil populations evacuated from their homes, on conditions to be laid down by the Commanders-in-Chief of the forces of the Associated Powers on the various fronts.

8. Sick and wounded who cannot be removed from evacuated territory will be cared for by Austro-Hungarian *personnel*, who will be left on the spot with the medical material required.

II.—Naval Conditions.

1. Immediate cessation of all hostilities at sea, and definite information to be given as to the location and movements of all Austro-Hungarian ships.

Notification to be made to neutrals that freedom of navigation in all territorial waters is given to the naval and mercantile marines of the Allied and Associated Powers, all questions of neutrality being waived.

2. Surrender to the Allies and United States of America of 15 Austro-Hungarian submarines, completed between the years 1910 and 1918, and of all German submarines which are in or may hereafter enter Austro-Hungarian territorial waters. All other Austro-Hungarian submarines to be paid off and completely disarmed, and to remain under the supervision of the Allies and United States of America.

3. Surrender to the Allies and United States of America, with their complete armament and equipment, of:—

Three battleships,
Three light cruisers,
Nine destroyers,
Twelve torpedo-boats,
One minelayer,
Six Danube monitors,

to be designated by the Allies and the United States of America. All other surface warships (including river craft) are to be concentrated in Austro-Hungarian naval bases to be designated by the Allies and the United States of America, and are to be paid off and completely disarmed and placed under the supervision of the Allies and United States of America.

4. Freedom of navigation to all warships and merchant ships of the Allied and Associated Powers to be given in the Adriatic and up the River Danube and its tributaries in the territorial waters and territory of Austria-Hungary.

The Allies and Associated Powers shall have the right to sweep up all minefields and obstructions, and the positions of these are to be indicated.

In order to ensure the freedom of navigation on the Danube, the Allies and the United States of America shall be empowered to occupy or to dismantle all fortifications or defence works.

5. The existing blockade conditions set up by the Allied

and Associated Powers are to remain unchanged, and all Austro-Hungarian merchant ships found at sea are to remain liable to capture, save exceptions which may be made by a Commission nominated by the Allies and United States of America.

6. All naval aircraft are to be concentrated and immobilized in Austro-Hungarian bases to be designated by the Allies and United States of America.

7. Evacuation of all the Italian coasts and of all ports occupied by Austria-Hungary outside their national territory, and the abandonment of all floating craft, naval materials, equipment, and materials for inland navigation of all kinds.

8. Occupation by the Allies and the United States of America of the land and sea fortifications and the islands which form the defences and of the dockyards and arsenal at Pola.

9. All merchant vessels held by Austria-Hungary belonging to the Allies and Associated Powers to be returned.

10. No destruction of ships or of materials to be permitted before evacuation, surrender, or restoration.

11. All naval and mercantile marine prisoners of war of the Allied and Associated Powers in Austro-Hungarian hands to be returned without reciprocity.

APPENDIX IV.

Sir Douglas Haig's Seventh Dispatch.

THE LAST ADVANCE IN THE WEST.

War Office,
7th January 1919.

The Secretary of State for War has received the following dispatch from Field-Marshal Sir Douglas Haig, K.T., G.C.B., G.C.V.O., K.C.I.E., Commander-in-Chief of the British Armies in France :—

21st December 1918.

My Lord,

I have the honour to submit the following report on the operations of the forces under my command since the successful termination of the great defensive battles on the Somme and Lys Rivers, which were described in my last dispatch.

General Introduction.

(1) *State of the British Armies.*

At the end of April 1918, though the onrush of the German Armies had been stemmed for the time being, the situation on the Western Front, and particularly on the British portion of it, was still critical.

The immense weight of the enemy's first and heaviest onslaughts in March and April, and the unprecedented masses of men and material employed by him, had called for practically the whole strength of the British Armies to withstand them, and had left our forces greatly weakened. Although prompt steps had been taken by the home authorities to dispatch to France as rapidly as possible all reinforcements then available in England, as well as to recall considerable bodies of troops from other theatres of war, these reinforcements required time to arrive. A further period was needed to complete their training and equipment, to allow troops brought from abroad to become acclimatized, and to enable the new drafts to become assimilated within their various units.

Meanwhile it had become impossible to maintain at an effective strength the full number of our divisions. At the beginning of May no less than eight divisions had been reduced to cadres and were temporarily written off altogether as fighting units. Two other divisions were holding positions in line with reduced cadres which it was not yet possible to bring up to establishment.

Arrangements had been made at the end of April to hand over to the French for employment on a quiet part of their front a further five divisions, comprising the IX. Corps (see paragraph 10 below). These had only just been reconstituted, and, being badly in need of rest and training, were not yet considered fit to hold an active sector. In return for these five British divisions, and in accordance with Marshal Foch's views, presently explained, regarding the enemy's intentions, the French had dispatched a number of their divisions to be held in reserve in rear of the British right and to strengthen the Flanders front.

There remained available for operations on the British front forty-five British infantry divisions, most of which were below establishment. Fully three-fourths of them had been heavily engaged in one or other of the enemy's offensives, if not in both. All were urgently in need of rest; they contained a large number of young, partially trained and totally inexperienced recruits, and subordinate commanders had had little or no opportunity to become acquainted with their men.

(2) *The Position of our Allies.*

The French, though as yet they had been less heavily engaged than ourselves, had none the less been obliged to employ a substantial proportion of their reserves in the fighting south of the Somme and north of the Lys.

The American Army, though rapidly increasing in numbers and efficiency, was not yet ready to take the field in sufficient strength materially to affect the situation. In short, the German attacks, though they had failed to break the Allied line, had stretched the resources of the Allies to the uttermost; while before Amiens and Hazebrouck they had brought the enemy within a short distance of strategic points of great importance. In these circumstances, the possibility of an immediate renewal of the enemy's offensive could not but be viewed with grave anxiety.

(3) *The Enemy's Position.*

On the other hand, the enemy had undoubtedly paid heavily for his successes, and had used up a great number of divisions, among them his best and his most highly trained. The reserves which he was known to have had at his disposal at the beginning of the year would suffice, indeed, to make good his losses; but in his case, also, time would be required before the divisions which had suffered most would be fit to undertake a fresh attack against prepared positions.

At the commencement of the period under review the enemy was estimated to possess seventy-five divisions in reserve on the Western Front. It was evident that further German attacks could not long be postponed if the enemy was to achieve a decision before the weight of the American Army was thrown into the scale.

(4) *The Enemy's Intentions.*

At this period, early in May, the Allied High Command repeatedly expressed the opinion that the enemy would renew his attacks on a large scale on the front Arras-Amiens-Montdidier. The strategic results to be obtained by the capture of Amiens, the separation of the French and British Armies, and an advance towards the sea along the Valley of the Somme were very great, and might well have proved decisive. The enemy's opening offensive had already brought him within a measurable distance of success in this direction, and had carried his Armies through practically the whole of our organized lines of defence.

Since the conclusion of his attacks on this front in the first week of April, the enemy had had a considerable period of time in which to re-establish communications through the devastated area, and make his preparations for a fresh advance. This period of delay had also afforded us some opportunity, of which full use was being made with all the means and resources in our power, to lay out new trench lines and reconstruct such old systems as already existed. This work, however, was still far from complete, and our defences could not be compared with those which the enemy had already overrun.

(5) *The Policy of the British Armies.*

In short, the enemy still possessed a sufficient superiority of force to retain the initiative, and it was known that he would be compelled to act within a comparatively limited time if he were to turn his superiority to account before it passed from him. These were the two main factors which had to be taken into consideration when deciding the policy of the British Armies during the late spring and early summer. The common object of the French and ourselves was to tide over the period which must still elapse until the growth of the American Armies and the arrival of Allied reinforcements placed the opposing forces once more on a footing of equality.

The situation was an anxious one, but it was confidently expected that, if all measures open to us were undertaken promptly and executed with the energy and zeal demanded by the occasion, the enemy's future assaults would be met and overthrown as those had been which he had already made. If the Allies could preserve their front unbroken until August at the latest there was every hope that during the later portion of the year they would be able to regain the initiative, and pass to the offensive in their turn.

The period under review accordingly divides itself naturally into two main sections. During the first, the policy governing the action of the forces under my command was the maintenance of an active defence, whereby our line might be preserved unbroken, while every opportunity was taken to rest and train our sorely-tried Divisions. As the strength and efficiency of our Divisions were restored, minor operations of gradually increasing scope, but with limited objectives, could be carried out with greater frequency. These would serve to keep alive the fighting spirit of the troops, and could be used to effect local improvements in our line, where such improvement was considered necessary either for defence or for attack.

The second period arrived when the swelling list of German casualties and the steady influx of American and Allied reinforcements had produced an equilibrium of strength between the opposing forces. The complete success of the Allied counter-attack on the 18th July near Soissons marked this turning-point in the year's campaign, and commenced the second phase of the Allied operations. Thereafter the initiative lay with the Allies, and the growing superiority of their forces enabled them to roll back the tide of invasion with ever-increasing swiftness. At this point and in this connection I should like to pay my personal tribute to the foresight and determination of the French Marshal in whose hands the co-ordination of the action of the Allied Armies was placed.

PART I.

The Period of Active Defence.

(6) *Reorganization.*

During the period following the breakdown of the German attacks on the Lys the military centre of gravity moved to the south, and, as regards the British front, the months of May, June, and July, though full of incident of a minor character, in which the different troops concerned showed great gallantry and skill, can be dealt with comparatively shortly.

At the outset of this period, the most pressing need after that of filling up the gaps in our divisions, was to close the breaches which the German advances had made in our successive defensive systems. This work had been begun, indeed, in the early days of the Somme offensive, but much still remained to be accomplished before our positions could be regarded as reasonably secure.

Further, the depth to which the enemy had penetrated in the Somme and Lys valleys had disrupted important lateral lines of railway, and had created a situation of extreme gravity with regard to the maintenance of communications in Northern France. At Amiens, Béthune, and Hazebrouck much-used railway junctions had been brought under the effective fire of the enemy's guns, while the railway centre at St. Pol was threatened. To relieve the situation a comprehensive programme of railway construction was undertaken by us in conjunction with the French, so as to provide three separate routes for North and South traffic, which should be independent of Amiens. This involved extensive doublings and quadruplings of existing railways and the building of new lines for which some 200 miles of broad gauge track was laid during the period April-July.

All these various constructional needs threw an immense amount of work upon the staff of the departments concerned, and called for the employment of great quantities of skilled and unskilled labour. All available resources of men and material were concentrated upon satisfying them, and by the time that the great change in the general military situation had taken place, the essential part had been satisfactorily accomplished. In particular, a complete series of new defensive lines had been built, involving the digging of 5,000 miles of trench.

(7) *Minor Operations in May and June.*

While intense activity prevailed behind the lines, our fighting troops were not idle. Full use was made of harassing tactics by all arms, and in the Lys salient in particular the German troops crowded into this exposed area were continually subjected to a most effective system of artillery harassing fire.

The losses suffered by the enemy in the Lys sector and the destruction caused to his artillery and material were very great. Convincing evidence of this was obtained from prisoners' statements, and was furnished also by the extensive German graveyards afterwards found in this area, by the condition of the roads, and the litter of all kinds found near them and near battery positions and dumps. These tactics undoubtedly postponed the renewal of the German offensive on this front until the Allied counter-offensive made it impossible.

The chief centres of infantry activity during this period were on the fronts of the Fourth and Second Armies. Early in May small operations improved our line about Morlancourt.

These were followed on the 19th May by an admirably executed operation in which the 2nd Australian Division (Major-General N. M. Smyth) took Ville-sur-Ancre with 400 prisoners. Later, on the 10th June, the same division, in a highly successful night attack on a front of about two miles south of Morlancourt, effected a substantial advance, taking over 300 prisoners.

On the Second Army front, Locre Hospice and the small woods south-east of Dickebusch Lake, known as Scottish and Ridge Woods, were the scenes of very lively fighting, in which French forces took part. A successful minor operation by the French on the 20th May resulted in a valuable gain of ground in the neighbourhood of Locre Hospice and the capture of over 500 prisoners, though the Hospice itself was not secured by us till the first week in July. Ridge Wood changed hands several times prior to its final capture with 350 prisoners by the 6th Division (Major-General Sir T. O. Marden) and 33rd Division (Major-General Sir R. J. Pinney) on the 14th July.

A material improvement in our line was also effected by the capture on 3rd June of the small hill known as the Mont de Merris, west of Merris village, with nearly 300 prisoners, by the 1st Australian Division (Major-General Sir H. B. Walker) and troops of the 29th Division (Major-General D. E. Cayley). At other points there was much fighting of a minor character, notably about Aveluy Wood and in the neighbourhood of the Lawe River and Merville.

(8) *Operations in July; Hamel Captured.*

Two months of comparative quiet worked a great change in the condition of the British Armies. The drafts sent out from England had largely been absorbed, many of the reinforcements from abroad had already arrived, and the number of our effective infantry divisions had risen from forty-five to fifty-two. In artillery we were stronger than we had ever been.

Though the general situation did not warrant the adoption

of a definitely offensive policy, in view of the concentration of the bulk of the enemy's large reserves in Prince Rupprecht's Group of Armies opposite the British front, I now felt strong enough to undertake operations of a somewhat larger scope, which would at once strengthen our position for defence and fit in with future schemes.

The first of these, carried out at the end of June, east of Nieppe Forest, aimed at establishing our main line of resistance farther in advance of the wooded ground, which was constantly being shelled with gas. The assault, launched at 6 a.m. on the 28th June by the 5th Division (Major-General R. B. Stephens) and 31st Division (Major-General J. Campbell), without preliminary bombardment, took the enemy by surprise and was completely successful; the German defences west of the Plate Becque stream, on a front of 6,000 yards from Pont Tournant to La Becque, being captured, together with some 450 prisoners.

A necessary preliminary to any operation to disengage Amiens was the recapture of our old positions east of Hamel and Vaire Wood and the clearing of the Villers-Bretonneux Plateau. This was accomplished on the 4th July by the Australian Corps (Lieut.-General Sir J. Monash), with the aid of four companies of the 33rd American Division and sixty tanks.

The most striking characteristic of the attack was the close and effective co-operation between tanks and infantry. Moving up and down behind the barrage, the tanks either killed the enemy or forced him to take shelter in dug-outs, where he became an easy prey to the infantry. Hamel was taken by envelopment from the flanks and rear, the enemy was driven from Vaire Wood, and at the end of the day our troops had gained all their objectives and over 1,500 prisoners.

Our success at Hamel was followed by a series of admirably executed operations north of the Lys.

On the 11th July troops of the 1st Australian Division gave a striking example of their ascendancy over the German infantry opposite to them. At 11 a.m. on this day, four men went out on patrol near Merris and returned with between thirty and forty prisoners. Other patrols, pushed forward both by the 1st Australian and 31st Divisions, secured in two days no fewer than 223 prisoners and established a number of new posts well in advance of our former line.

Surprise played an important part in the successful attack by which the 9th Division (Major-General H. H. Tudor) took Meteren on 19th July, with some 350 prisoners. The village stood on high ground close to our line, and its capture provided greater depth to our defence.

For some time prior to this attack gas was discharged, in conjunction with a smoke and high-explosive shell bombardment. When at 7.55 a.m. on the 19th July our infantry advanced behind a barrage of smoke and high explosive the enemy was expecting only a gas discharge, and had in many cases put on gas masks.

The capture of Meteren was followed shortly after midnight on the 28th–29th July by a boldly conceived operation by the 1st Australian Division, which resulted in the capture of Merris, with 187 prisoners.

(9) *Operations on the French Front.*

By the end of July the reconstitution of the British Armies had been completed. The spirit of the men was as high as ever, and the success of their various local operations had had a good effect. I had once more at my command an effective striking force, capable of taking the offensive with every hope of success when the proper moment should arrive.

Meanwhile, events of the utmost and most critical importance had been taking place on the French front.

The British General Staff had always held the opinion that before the resumption of the enemy's main offensive on the Arras-Amiens-Montdidier front the attack on our northern flank in Flanders would be followed by a similar attack on the southern flank of the Allied Armies. This view had proved correct. Though probably delayed by his unexpectedly extensive commitments in the Lys battle, at the end of May the enemy had developed his plan of operations on the lines which we had foreseen, and had launched a violent surprise attack on the Aisne front. In this attack certain British divisions which had been sent there to rest became involved from the outset.

(10) *Operations of the IX. Corps in the Aisne Battle.*

At the end of April and early in May the 8th, 21st, 25th, and 50th Divisions, subsequently reinforced by the 19th Division, and constituting the IX. British Corps, under command of Lieut.-General Sir A. Hamilton-Gordon, had been placed at Marshal Foch's disposal as noted above. These divisions had been dispatched by him to the French Sixth Army, to take the place of certain French divisions concentrated behind Amiens.

Of these divisions, the 19th (Major-General G. D. Jeffreys), 21st (Major-General D. G. M. Campbell), 25th (Major-General Sir E. G. Bainbridge), and 50th Divisions (Major-General H. C. Jackson) had taken part in both the Somme battle and the battle of the Lys. The 8th Division (Major-General W. C. G. Heneker) had been involved south of the Somme in some of the heaviest fighting of the year, and had behaved with distinguished gallantry. All these divisions had but lately been filled up with young drafts, and, despite their high spirit and gallant record, were in no condition to take part in major operations until they had had several weeks' rest. During the first fortnight in May three of these divisions—the 21st, 8th, and 50th—were put into line on a front of about fifteen miles between Bermicourt and Bouconville, north-west of Reims.

About the 26th May prisoners taken by the French gave the first definite information regarding the great offensive launched by the enemy on the Aisne front on the morning of the 27th May. This attack, delivered by twenty-eight German divisions, supported by tanks, was directed against the Sixth French Army on a front of about thirty-five miles north-west of Reims. It involved the whole of the IX. British Corps, as well as the French Corps holding the Chemin des Dames on the left of the British sector.

Preceded by an artillery and trench mortar bombardment of great intensity, the German infantry broke into the battle positions of the Allied divisions. The enemy gained a footing on the Chemin des Dames at an early hour, and pressing on in the centre of his attack in overwhelming strength, forced the line of the Aisne on a wide front. By nightfall he had crossed the Vesle west of Fismes, and in the British sector, after very heavy and determined fighting, had compelled the left and centre of the IX. Corps, now reinforced by the 25th Division, to swing back to a position facing west and north-west between the Aisne and the Vesle.

On the 28th May and following days the enemy launched fresh attacks in great force on the whole battle front, pressing back our Allies to west of Soissons and south of Fère-en-Tardenois. The IX. British Corps, greatly reduced in numbers by severe and incessant fighting, was forced to withdraw across the Vesle, and thence gradually pressed back in a south-easterly direction between the Vesle and the Ardre. During the night of the 28th–29th May the 19th Division was brought up in 'buses, and put in to fill a gap in the French line across the Ardre Valley, deploying with great skill and steadiness. By the evening of the 30th May, at which date in the centre of his attack the enemy had reached the Marne, the rate of his advance in the British sector had begun to slacken.

During the next few days, however, fighting was still intense. On the southern and western portions of the battle front the enemy made deep progress, gaining the north bank of the Marne from Dormans to Château-Thierry and advancing astride the Aisne to the outskirts of the Villers-Cotterets Forest, and across the high ground north-east of Attichy. On the eastern flank of the salient created by the enemy's advance the British forces, at this date under the command of the French Fifth Army, withdrew gradually to the line Aubilly-Chambrecy-Boujacourt, where they were able to consolidate. Though the enemy's attacks continued persistently for some time longer, and on the 6th June culminated in two determined attempts upon the important position known as the Montagne de Bligny, which commands the valley of the Ardre, all these attacks were most gallantly repulsed, and the enemy's advance definitely stayed.

Throughout this long period of incessant fighting against greatly superior numbers the behaviour of all arms of the British forces engaged was magnificent. What they achieved is best described in the words of the French general under whose orders they came, who wrote of them: "They have enabled us to establish a barrier against which the hostile waves have beaten and shattered themselves. This none of the French who witnessed it will ever forget."

(II) *The Second Battle of the Marne.*

While our troops were still engaged in the fighting south-west of Reims a fresh battle had broken out on the 7th June on the French front between Noyon and Montdidier. In this case the enemy did not succeed in effecting a surprise, but the strain thrown upon the French Armies by these two attacks was considerable, and the situation was such that the German Command might reasonably be expected to endeavour to develop it with all the means at their disposal.

While, on the one hand, at the beginning of July it was known that Prince Rupprecht's reserve group of divisions about Douai and Valenciennes were still intact and opposite the British front, on the other hand, for a number of reasons, it was believed at French General Headquarters that the Germans were about to attack in strength east and west of Reims. It was apprehended, indeed, that the attack might spread even farther east into the Argonne and might endanger a wide sector of the French position. Marshal Foch accordingly withdrew the whole of the French forces, some eight divisions, from Flanders, and transferred them southwards to the French front. In addition he asked that four British divisions might be moved, two of them to areas south of the Somme and two to positions astride that river, so as to ensure the connection between the French and British Armies about Amiens and to enable him to move four French divisions farther east to his right flank. After carefully weighing the situation, I agreed to this proposal, and immediate orders were given for the movement.

On the 13th July a further request was received from Marshal Foch that these four British divisions might be placed unreservedly at his disposal, and that four other British divisions might be dispatched to take their places behind the junction of the Allied Armies. This request was also agreed to, and the 15th, 34th, 51st, and 62nd British Divisions, constituting the XXII. Corps, under command of Lieut.-General Sir A. Godley, were accordingly sent down to the French front.

Meanwhile, on the 15th July, the enemy had launched his expected attack east and south-west of Reims, and after making some progress at first and effecting the passage of the Marne, was held by the French, American, and Italian forces on those fronts. On the 18th July Marshal Foch launched the great counter-offensive which he had long been preparing on the front between Château-Thierry and Soissons, supporting this successful stroke by vigorous attacks also on other parts of the German salient. In this fighting the XXII. British Corps speedily became involved.

(12) *Operations by the XXII. Corps.*

On the 20th July the 51st and 62nd Divisions of the XXII. Corps, under command of Major-Generals G. T. C. Carter-Campbell and W. P. Braithwaite respectively, attacked in conjunction with the French on the eastern side of the salient south-west of Reims. The sector assigned to the British troops covered a front of 8,000 yards astride the Ardre River, and consisted of an open valley bottom, with steep wooded slopes on either side. Both valley and slopes were studded with villages and hamlets, which were for the most part intact and afforded excellent cover to the enemy.

On this front our troops were engaged for a period of ten days in continuous fighting of a most difficult and trying nature. Throughout this period steady progress was made, in the face of vigorous and determined resistance. Marfaux was taken on 23rd July, and on the 28th July British troops retook the Montagne de Bligny, which other British troops had defended with so much gallantry and success two months previously. In these operations, throughout which French artillery and tanks rendered invaluable assistance, the 51st and 62nd Divisions took 1,200 prisoners from seven different German divisions, and successfully completed an advance of over four miles.

Meanwhile, on the 23rd July, the 15th and 34th Divisions, under command of Major-Generals H. L. Reed and C. L. Nicholson respectively, attacked on the west side of the salient in the neighbourhood of Berzy-le-Sec and Parcy-Tigny, south-west of Soissons. These divisions also had many days of heavy and continuous fighting on different parts of this front until withdrawn during the first days of August, and acquitted themselves very gallantly side by side with their French comrades-in-arms. Many prisoners were taken by both divisions, and the 15th Division in particular earned distinction in the fierce struggle for Buzancy.

PART II.

The Period of Offensive Action.

(13) *The Situation at the End of July.*

The definite collapse of the ambitious offensive launched by the enemy on the 15th July, and the striking success of the Allied counter-offensive south of the Aisne, effected a complete change in the whole military situation. The German Army had made its effort and had failed. The period of its maximum strength had been passed, and the bulk of the reserves accumulated during the winter had been used up. On the other hand, the position of the Allies in regard to reserves had greatly improved. The fresh troops made available during the late spring and early summer had been incorporated and trained. The British Army was ready to take the offensive; while the American Army was growing rapidly, and had already given convincing proof of the high fighting quality of its soldiers.

At a conference held on the 23rd July, when the success of the attack of the 18th July was well assured, the methods by which the advantage already gained could be extended were discussed in detail. The Allied Commander-in-Chief asked that the British, French, and American Armies should each prepare plans for local offensives, to be taken in hand as soon as possible, with certain definite objectives of a limited nature. These objectives on the British front were the disengagement of Amiens and the freeing of the Paris-Amiens Railway by an attack on the Albert-Montdidier front. The *rôle* of the French and American Armies was to free other strategic railways by operations farther south and east.

In addition to the disengagement of Amiens, the situation on the British front presented strong arguments in favour of certain other schemes, such as the disengagement of Hazebrouck by the recapture of Kemmel Hill, combined with an operation in the direction of La Bassée. If successful, such an operation would have the effect of improving our position at Ypres and Calais. The Lys salient would be reduced, and the safety of the Bruay coal mines become less threatened.

These different operations had already been the subject of correspondence between Marshal Foch and myself, as well as of the earnest consideration of the British General Staff. Ultimately, I had come to the conclusion that of the tasks assigned to the British forces the operation east of Amiens should take precedence, as being the most important and the most likely to give large results.

It would depend upon the nature of the success which might be obtained in these different Allied operations whether they could be more fully exploited before winter set in. It was subsequently arranged that attacks would be pressed in a converging direction towards Mezières by the French and American Armies, while at the same time the British Armies, attacking towards the line St. Quentin-Cambrai, would strike directly at the vital lateral communications running through Maubeuge to Hirson and Mezières, by which alone the German forces on the Champagne front could be supplied and maintained.

As a secondary result of the advance of the British Armies towards the all-important railway centres about Maubeuge, the group of German Armies in Flanders would find their communications threatened from the south, and any operations which it might be possible for the Allies to undertake in that theatre at a later date would be powerfully assisted thereby. It was obviously of vital importance to the enemy to maintain intact his front opposite St. Quentin and Cambrai, and for this purpose he depended on the great fortified zone known as the Hindenburg Line.

(14) *General Scheme of British Operations.*

The brilliant success of the Amiens attack was the prelude to a great series of battles, in which, throughout three months of continuous fighting, the British Armies advanced without a check from one victory to another. The progress of this mighty conflict divides itself into certain stages, which themselves are grouped into two well-defined phases.

(*a*) During the first part of the struggle the enemy sought to defend himself in the deep belt of prepared positions and successive trench systems which extended from the spring-tide of the German advance, about Albert and Villers-Bretonneux, to the Hindenburg Line between St. Quentin and the Scarpe. From these positions, scene of the stubborn battles of the two preceding years, the German Armies were forced back step by step by a succession of methodical attacks which culminated in the breaking through of the Hindenburg Line defences.

(*b*) Thereafter, during the second period of the struggle our troops were operating in practically open country against an enemy who endeavoured to stand, on such semi-prepared or natural defensive positions as remained to him, for a period long enough to enable him to organize his retreat and avoid overwhelming disaster. The final stages of our operations, therefore, are concerned with the breaking of the enemy's resistance on these lines.

Throughout this latter period, the violence of our assaults and the rapidity of our advance towards the enemy's vital centres of communication about Maubeuge threatened to cut the main avenue of escape for the German forces opposite the French and American Armies. The position of the German Armies in Flanders, themselves unable to withstand the attacks of the Allied forces operating under the King of the Belgians, was equally endangered by our progress behind their left flank. To the south and north of the area in which our victorious Armies were driving forward through his weakening defence, the enemy was compelled to execute hasty withdrawals from wide tracts of territory.

The second phase had already reached its legitimate conclusion when the signing of the Armistice put an end to hostilities. Finally defeated in the great battles of the 1st and 4th November and utterly without reserves, the enemy at that date was falling back without coherent plan in widespread disorder and confusion.

FIRST PHASE: THE FIGHTING IN ENTRENCHED POSITIONS.

The Battle of Amiens (8th-12th August).

(15) *Plan of Operations.*

The plan of the Amiens operation was to strike in an easterly and south-easterly direction, using the Somme River to cover the left flank of our advance, with the object in the first place of gaining the line of the Amiens outer defences between Le Quesnel and Mericourt-sur-Somme, thereby freeing the main Paris-Amiens Railway. Having gained the Amiens defence line, the attack was to proceed without delay towards Roye, and to include the capture as soon as possible of the important railway junction of Chaulnes, thereby cutting the communications of the German forces in the Lassigny and Montdidier areas. If all went well, French troops would be in readiness to co-operate by pressing the enemy south-east of Montdidier.

Preliminary instructions to prepare to attack east of Amiens at an early date had been given to the Fourth Army Commander, General Rawlinson, on the 13th July, and on the 28th July the French First Army, under command of General Debeney, was placed by Marshal Foch under my orders for this operation. Further to strengthen my attack, I decided to reinforce the British Fourth Army with the Canadian Corps, and also with the two British divisions which were then held in readiness astride the Somme.

In order to deceive the enemy and to ensure the maximum effect of a surprise attack, elaborate precautions were taken to mislead him as to our intentions and to conceal our real purpose.

Instructions of a detailed character were issued to the formations concerned, calculated to make it appear that a British attack in Flanders was imminent. Canadian battalions were put into line on the Kemmel front, where they were identified by the enemy. Corps headquarters were prepared, and casualty clearing stations were erected in conspicuous positions in this area. Great activity was maintained also by our wireless stations on the First Army front, and arrangements were made to give the impression that a great concentration of tanks was taking place in the St. Pol area. Training operations, in which infantry and tanks co-operated, were carried out in this neighbourhood on days on which the enemy's long-distance reconnaissance and photographic machines were likely to be at work behind our lines.

The rumour that the British were about to undertake a large and important operation on the northern front quickly spread. In the course of our subsequent advances convincing evidence was obtained that these different measures had had the desired effect, and that the enemy was momentarily expecting to be attacked in strength in Flanders.

Meanwhile, the final details for the combined British and French attack had been arranged early in August, and the date for the assault fixed for the morning of the 8th. The front held by the Australian Corps on the right of the British line was extended southwards to include the Amiens-Roye road, and the Canadian Corps was moved into position by night behind this front. The assembly of tanks and of the Cavalry Corps was postponed until the last moment, and carried out as secretly as possible.

Partly as the result of successful minor operations of the Allies, and partly in consequence of the change in the general situation, the enemy during the first days of August withdrew from the positions still held by him west of the Avre and Ancre rivers. These movements did not affect our plans, but, on the other hand, a strong local attack launched by the enemy on the 6th August south of Morlancourt led to severe fighting, and undoubtedly rendered the task of the III. Corps more difficult.

(16) *The Troops Employed.*

The front of attack of General Rawlinson's Fourth Army extended for a distance of over eleven miles from just south of the Amiens-Roye road to Morlancourt exclusive. The troops employed were: On the right the Canadian Corps, under command of Lieut.-General Sir A. W. Currie, with the 3rd, 1st, and 2nd Canadian Divisions in line, and the 4th Canadian Division in close support; in the centre the Australian Corps, under command of Lieut.-General Sir J. Monash, with the 2nd and 3rd Australian Divisions in line and the 5th and 4th Australian Divisions in support; on the left, north of the Somme, the III. Corps, under the command of Lieut.-General Sir R. H. K. Butler, with the 58th and 18th Divisions in line and the 12th Division in support.

The attack of the French First Army, under General Debeney, was timed to take place about an hour later than the opening of the British assault, and was delivered on a front of between four and five miles between Moreuil inclusive and the British right. As the Allied troops made progress, the right of the French attack was to be gradually extended southwards until the southern flank of the Allied battle front rested on Braches.

Behind the British front the British Cavalry Corps, consisting of three Cavalry Divisions under command of Lieut.-General Sir C. T. McM. Kavanagh, was concentrated at zero hour east of Amiens. A special mobile force of two motor machine gun brigades and a Canadian cyclist battalion, under command of Brig.-General Brutinel, had orders to exploit success along the lines of the Amiens-Roye road.

(17) *The Battle Opened.*

At 4.20 a.m. on the 8th August our massed artillery opened intense fire on the whole front of attack, completely crushing the enemy's batteries, some of which never succeeded in coming into action. Simultaneously British infantry and tanks advanced to the assault. The enemy was taken completely by surprise, and under cover of a heavy ground mist our first objectives, on the line Demuin, Marcelcave, Cerisy, south of Morlancourt, were gained rapidly.

After a halt of two hours on this line by the leading troops, infantry, cavalry, and light tanks passed through and continued the advance, the different arms working in co-operation in a most admirable manner. At the close of the day's operations our troops had completed an advance of between six and seven miles. The Amiens outer defence line, including the villages of Caix, Harbonnières, and Morcourt, had been gained on the whole front of attack, except at Le Quesnel itself. Cavalry and armoured cars were in action well to the east of this line, and before dawn on the 9th August Le Quesnel also had been taken. North of the Somme the enemy was more alert as the result of the recent engagements in this sector, and succeeded by heavy fighting in maintaining himself for the time being in the village of Chipilly.

East of the line of our advance the enemy at nightfall was blowing up dumps in all directions, while his transport and limbers were streaming eastwards towards the Somme, affording excellent targets to our airmen, who made full use of their opportunities. Over 13,000 prisoners, between 300 and 400 guns, and vast quantities of ammunition and stores of all kinds remained in our possession.

The brilliant and predominating part taken by the Canadian and Australian Corps in this battle is worthy of the highest commendation. The skill and determination of these troops proved irresistible, and at all points met with rapid and complete success. The fine performance of the cavalry throughout all stages of the operation also deserves mention. Having completed their assembly behind the battle-front by a series of night marches, on the first day of the attack they advanced 23 miles from their points of concentration, and by the dash and vigour of their action, both on this and subsequent days, rendered most valuable and gallant service. The general success of all arms was made possible by the good staff work of my own staff at General Headquarters, and of the staffs of the Armies concerned. Under the able and experienced direction of the Fourth Army Commander, General Rawlinson, the preparations for the battle, including detailed artillery arrangements of an admirable nature, were carried out with a thoroughness and completeness which left nothing to chance. Without this excellent staff work neither the rapid concentration of troops, unknown to the enemy, nor the success of our initial assault and its subsequent development could have been accomplished.

Meanwhile, at 5.5 a.m., the attack of the French First Army had been launched successfully, and gained the line Pierrepont, Plessier, Fresnoy, all inclusive, in touch with Brutinel's Force on the Amiens-Roye Road west of Le Quesnoy. Three thousand three hundred and fifty prisoners and many guns were taken by the French forces on this day.

(18) *The Advance Continued.*

The sweeping character of this success, which in one day had gained our first objective and disengaged the Paris-Amiens

Railway, opened a clear field for the measures of exploitation determined upon to meet such an event.

The attack was continued on the 9th August. After meeting with considerable opposition on the line Beaufort-Vrely-Rosieres-Framerville, the enemy's resistance weakened under the pressure of our troops, and once more rapid progress was made. The 8th Hussars, 1st Cavalry Division (Major-General R. L. Mullens), took Meharicourt at a gallop; the 2nd and 3rd Cavalry Divisions (Major-Generals T. T. Pitman and A. E. W. Harman) also passed through our advancing infantry, capturing a number of prisoners and gaining much ground. That night we held Bouchoir, Rouvroy, Morcourt, and Framerville, and were on the western outskirts of Lihons and Proyart.

North of the Somme the III. Corps, including the 12th Division (Major-General H. W. Higginson) and a regiment of the 33rd American Division (Major-General G. Bell) attacked in the late afternoon and gained a line east of Chipilly, Morlancourt, and Dernancourt.

During the following days our operations continued successfully in close co-operation with the French. By the evening of the 12th August our infantry had reached the old German Somme defences of 1916, on the general line west of Damery, east of Lihons, east of Proyart, having repulsed with severe loss determined counter-attacks in the neighbourhood of Lihons. North of the Somme we were on the western outskirts of Bray-sur-Somme.

Montdidier had fallen to the French two days earlier, and on the whole front from the Oise River to the Roye road at Andechy our Allies had made deep and rapid progress.

On the night of the 12th August, as has been seen, our advance east of Amiens had reached the general line of the old Roye-Chaulnes defences. The derelict battle area which now lay before our troops, seared by old trench lines, pitted with shell holes, and crossed in all directions with tangled belts of wire, the whole covered by the wild vegetation of two years, presented unrivalled opportunities for stubborn machine-gun defence.

Attacks carried out on the 13th August proved the strength of these positions, and showed that the enemy, heavily reinforced, was ready to give battle for them. I therefore determined to break off the battle on this front, and transferred the front of attack from the Fourth Army to the sector north of the Somme, where an attack seemed unexpected by the enemy. My intention was for the Third Army to operate in the direction of Bapaume, so as to turn the line of the old Somme defences from the north. The French First Army now ceased to be under my command.

Meanwhile, south of the Somme, our pressure was to be maintained, so as to take advantage of any weakening on the part of the enemy and encourage in him the belief that we intended to persist in our operations on that front. During the succeeding days, local attacks gave us possession of Damery, Parvillers, and Fransart, and made progress also at other points.

(19) *The Results of the Battle of Amiens.*

The results of the battle of Amiens may be summarized as follows. Within the space of five days the town of Amiens and the railway centring upon it had been disengaged. Twenty German divisions had been heavily defeated by thirteen British infantry divisions and three cavalry divisions, assisted by a regiment of the 33rd American Division and supported by some four hundred tanks. Nearly 22,000 prisoners and over four hundred guns had been taken by us and our line had been pushed forward to a depth of some twelve miles in a vital sector. Further, our deep advance, combined with the attacks of the French Armies on our right, had compelled the enemy to evacuate hurriedly a wide extent of territory to the south of us.

The effect of this victory, following so closely after the Allied victory on the Marne, upon the *moral* both of the German and British troops was very great. Buoyed up by the hope of immediate and decisive victory, to be followed by an early and favourable peace, constantly assured that the Allied reserves were exhausted, the German soldiery suddenly found themselves attacked on two fronts and thrown back with heavy losses from large and important portions of their earlier gains. The reaction was inevitable and of a deep and lasting character.

On the other hand, our own troops felt that at last their opportunity had come, and that, supported by a superior artillery and numerous tanks, they could now press forward resolutely to reap the reward of their patient, dauntless, and successful defence in March and April. This they were eager to do, and as they moved forward during the ensuing months, from one success to another, suffering, danger, and losses were alike forgotten in their desire to beat the enemy and their confidence that they could do so.

Meanwhile, as a further and immediate result of our successes, the enemy was thrown back definitely upon a defensive policy, and began to straighten out the salients in his line. Between the 14th and 17th August he withdrew from his positions about Serre, and farther north indications multiplied of an intention shortly to abandon the salient in the Lys valley. Our patrols were already beginning to push forward on this front, and on the night of the 13th-14th August established posts south and east of Vieux Berquin. On the 18th and 19th August the capture of Outtersteene village and ridge with some 900 prisoners by the 31st, 29th, and 9th Divisions of the Second Army, hastened the enemy's movements on the Lys.

The Battle of Bapaume
(21st August—1st September).

(20) *Scheme of Operations.*

In deciding to extend the attack northwards to the area between the rivers Somme and Scarpe I was influenced by the following considerations.

The enemy did not seem prepared to meet an attack in this direction, and, owing to the success of the Fourth Army, he occupied a salient the left flank of which was already threatened from the south. A further reason for my decision was that the ground north of the Ancre River was not greatly damaged by shellfire, and was suitable for the use of tanks. A successful attack between Albert and Arras in a south-easterly direction would turn the line of the Somme south of Peronne, and gave every promise of producing far-reaching results. It would be a step forward towards the strategic objective St. Quentin-Cambrai.

This attack, moreover, would be rendered easier by the fact that we now held the commanding plateau south of Arras about Bucquoy and Ablainzevelle which in the days of the old Somme fighting had lain well behind the enemy's lines. In consequence we were here either astride or to the east of the intricate systems of trench lines which, in 1916, we had no choice but to attack frontally, and enjoyed advantages of observation which at that date had been denied us.

It was arranged that on the morning of the 21st August a limited attack should be launched north of the Ancre to gain the general line of the Arras-Albert Railway, on which it was correctly assumed that the enemy's main line of resistance was sited. The day of the 22nd August would then be used to get troops and guns into position on this front and to bring forward the left of the Fourth Army between the Somme and the Ancre. The principal attack would be delivered on the 23rd August by the Third Army and the divisions of the Fourth Army north of the Somme, the remainder of the Fourth Army assisting by pushing forward south of the river to cover the flank of the main operation. Thereafter, if success attended our efforts, the whole of both Armies were to press forward with the greatest vigour and exploit to the full any advantage we might have gained.

As soon as the progress of the Third Army had forced the enemy to fall back from the Mercatel spur, thereby giving us a secure southern flank for an assault upon the German positions on Orange Hill and about Monchy-le-Preux, the moment arrived for the First Army to extend the front of our attack to the north. Using the river Sensée to cover their left, in the same way as the river Somme had been used to cover the left of the Fourth Army in the battle of Amiens, the right of the First Army attacked east of Arras, and by turning from the north the western extremity of the Hindenburg Line compelled the enemy to undertake a further retreat. It was calculated correctly that this gradual extension of our front of attack would mislead the enemy as to where the main blow would fall, and would cause him to throw in his reserves piecemeal.

(21) *Opening Attacks: Albert.*

At 4.55 a.m. on the 21st August the IV. and VI. Corps of General Sir Julian Byng's Third Army, under command respectively of Lieut.-General Sir G. M. Harper and Lieut.-General Sir J. A. L. Haldane, attacked on a front of about nine miles north of the Ancre, from Miraumont to Moyenneville.

The opening assault was delivered by the divisions then in line—namely, the 42nd, New Zealand, and 37th Divisions of the IV. Corps, and the 2nd and Guards Divisions of the VI. Corps, supported by tanks, and carried the enemy's foremost defences rapidly and without difficulty. The 5th

Division and 63rd Division (Major-General C. E. Lawrie) of the IV. Corps, and the 3rd Division (Major-General C. J. Deverell) of the VI. Corps then passed through, and continued the advance. During this stage the thick fog, which at first had favoured us, led to some loss of direction. None the less, after much hard fighting, particularly about Achiet-le-Petit and Logeast Wood, where the enemy counter-attacked vigorously, our troops reached the general line of the railway on practically the whole front, capturing the above-named village and wood, together with Courcelles and Moyenneville, east of which places they crossed the railway.

The 21st Division of the V. Corps assisted by clearing the north bank of the Ancre about Beaucourt, and as a result of the whole operation the positions we required from which to launch our principal attack were gained successfully, with over 2,000 prisoners.

Early next morning the III. Corps of the Fourth Army, assisted by a small number of tanks, attacked with the 47th, 12th, and 18th Divisions, the 3rd Australian Division and the 38th Division co-operating on either flank. By this attack, in which the 18th Division (Major-General R. P. Lee) forced the passage of the river Ancre and captured Albert by a well-executed enveloping movement from the south-east, our line between the Somme and the Ancre was advanced well to the east of the Bray-Albert road. The left of the Fourth Army was brought forward in conformity with the remainder of our line, and over 2,400 prisoners and a few guns were taken by us.

(22) *The Main Attack Launched.*

These preliminary attacks cleared the way for the main operation. This was opened on the 23rd August by a series of strong assaults on practically the whole front of thirty-three miles from our junction with the French north of Lihons to Mercatel, in which neighbourhood the Hindenburg Line from Quéant and Bullecourt joined the old Arras-Vimy defence line of 1916. About 100 tanks were employed by us on different part of this front, and were of great assistance, particularly in overcoming the enemy's machine gunners. Many of these fought with great determination, continuing to fire until their guns were run over by the tanks.

On the eve of these operations I issued a note of instructions to the forces under my command, in which I drew attention to the favourable change which had taken place in the conditions under which operations were being conducted, and emphasized the necessity for all ranks to act with the utmost boldness and resolution. Wherever the enemy was found to be giving way, there the pressure was to be increased.

To this appeal all ranks and all Services responded during the strenuous fighting of the succeeding weeks with a whole-hearted and untiring devotion, for which no words of mine can adequately express my admiration and my gratitude. Divisions, which in the worst days of the March retreat had proved themselves superior to every hardship, difficulty and danger, once more rose to the occasion with the most magnificent spirit. Over the same ground that had witnessed their stubborn greatness in defence, they moved forward to the attack with a persistent vigour and relentless determination which neither the extreme difficulty of the ground, nor the obstinate resistance of the enemy, could diminish or withstand.

At 4.45 a.m. the Australian Corps attacked south of the Somme, employing the 32nd Division (Major-General T. S. Lambert), composed of men of Lancashire, Dorset, and Scotland, and the 1st Australian Division (Major-General T. W. Glasgow), and captured Herleville, Chuignolles, and Chuignes, with over 2,000 prisoners. The fighting about Chuignolles, on the Australian front, was very heavy, and great numbers of the enemy were killed.

At the same hour the 18th Division and the right brigade of the 38th Division of the III. and V. Corps recommenced their attacks about Albert, and by a well-executed operation, entailing hard fighting at different points, captured the high ground east of the town known as Tara and Usna Hills. At the same time two companies of the Welsh Regiment, part of the left brigade of the 38th Division, waded the Ancre in the neighbourhood of Hamel, and with great gallantry maintained themselves all day east of the river against constant counter-attacks.

Meanwhile, at different hours during the morning, the other divisions of the V. Corps and the IV. and VI. Corps (comprising respectively the 17th and 21st Divisions; the 42nd, New Zealand, 5th and 37th Divisions; and the 2nd, 3rd, Guards, 56th and 52nd Divisions) attacked along the whole front north of Albert, directing the chief weight of their assault upon the sector Miraumont-Boiry Becquerelle.

Our troops met with immediate success. On the right, progress was made by light forces of the 17th and 21st Divisions along the left bank of the Ancre north of Thiepval, but in this sector no deep advance was attempted during the day.

North of the Ancre, the attack of the VI. Corps was opened at 4 a.m., at which hour the 3rd Division took Gomiécourt with 500 prisoners. During the morning the attack spread along the front of the IV. Corps also. The enemy's main line of resistance was stormed and, penetrating deeply beyond it, our troops captured Bihucourt, Ervillers, Boyelles and Boiry Becquerelle, together with over 5,000 prisoners and a number of guns. Under the continued pressure of our attacks the enemy was becoming disorganized, and showed signs of confusion.

Our troops were now astride the Arras-Bapaume road, and closing down upon the latter town from the north and north-west. The position of the German divisions in the pronounced salient on the Thiepval Ridge was becoming perilous.

At 1 a.m. on the night of the 23rd–24th August the Third and Fourth Armies again attacked, and during the early morning the advance was resumed on the whole front from the Somme to Neuville Vitasse. On the right, the 3rd Australian Division took Bray-sur-Somme, and the 47th Division (Major-General Sir G. T. Gorringe), the 12th and 18th Divisions of the III. Corps carried our line forward across the high ground between Bray and La Boisselle. In the neighbourhood of the latter village and at certain other points heavy fighting took place, and a number of prisoners were taken.

On the front of the Third Army, the same divisions which had delivered the attacks on the previous day again moved forward against the beaten enemy and pressed him back rapidly. The German positions on the Thiepval Ridge were carried by a well-conceived and admirably executed concentric attack, directed upon the high ground about Pozières from the south-west and north-west. In this brilliant operation the brigade of the 38th Division, attacking on the right, crossed the Ancre at Albert during the early part of the night, and formed up close to the German lines on a narrow front between the Albert-Pozières road and the marshes of the Ancre. The left brigade of the same division waded breast deep through the flooded stream opposite Hamel, under heavy fire, and formed up in the actual process of a German counter-attack along the line held by the two companies who had crossed on the previous morning. At the given hour, the brigades of the 38th Division advanced in concert with the other divisions of the V. Corps on their left, and drove the enemy from the high ground about Ovillers and Thiepval. Continuing their advance, the divisions of the V. Corps gained Pozières, Courcelette and Martinpuich. Miraumont, which for three days had resisted our attacks, was taken by the 42nd Division (Major-General A. Solly-Flood) with many prisoners, and, pressing forward, the same division seized Pys. The 5th Division (Major-General J. Ponsonby) having captured Irles, cleared Loupart Wood in co-operation with the New Zealand Division (Major-General Sir A. H. Russell), tanks rendering valuable assistance to our infantry in both localities. New Zealand troops having taken Grevillers, reached Avesnes-les-Bapaume, and assisted also in the capture of Biefvillers by the 37th Division (Major-General H. B. Williams). Strong opposition was encountered on the high ground between Sapignies and Mory. Our troops pressed the enemy in these villages closely and farther north the Guards Division (Major-General G. P. T. Fielding) gained possession of St. Leger. On the left, troops of the 56th Division (Major-General Sir C. P. A. Hull) had heavy fighting about Croisilles and on the high ground north-west of that village known as Henin Hill. Important progress was made, and on their left the 52nd Division (Major-General J. Hill) took Henin-sur-Cojeul and gained a footing in St. Martin-sur-Cojeul.

Several thousand prisoners, many guns, and great quantities of material of every kind were captured by us on this day.

(23) *Bapaume Taken.*

During the next five days our troops followed up their advantage hotly, and in spite of increasing resistance from the German rearguards, realized a farther deep advance. The enemy clung to his positions in the later stages of this period with much tenacity. His infantry delivered many counter-attacks, and the progress of our troops was only won by hard and determined fighting.

During these days the 37th Division cleared Favreuil late in the evening of the 25th August, after much confused fighting. On the same day the 2nd Division captured Sapignies and Behagnies, taking a number of prisoners, and the 62nd Division drove the enemy from Mory.

On the 27th August the 18th Division secured possession of Trones Wood, after an all-day struggle, in the course of which troops of the 2nd Guards Division, fresh from reserve, made strong but unsuccessful counter-attacks. Next day the 12th Division and 58th Division (Major-General F. W. Ramsay) captured Hardecourt and the spur south of it, overcoming strong resistance. Both on the 27th and 28th August the 38th (Welsh) Division (Major-General T. A. Cubitt) was engaged in bitter fighting about Longueval and Delville Wood, and made progress in company with the 17th Division (Major-General P. R. Robertson) attacking towards Flers.

Yielding before the persistent pressure of our attacks, in the early morning of the 29th August the enemy evacuated Bapaume, which was occupied by the New Zealand Division. On the same day the 18th Division entered Combles, while to the north of Bapaume a gallant thrust by the 56th and 57th Divisions penetrated the enemy's positions as far as Riencourt-lez-Cagnicourt. Though our troops were unable at this time to maintain themselves in this village our line was established on the western and northern outskirts of Bullecourt and Hendecourt.

By the night of the 30th August the line of the Fourth and Third Armies north of the Somme ran from Clery-sur-Somme past the western edge of Marrières Wood to Combles, Lesbœufs, Bancourt, Fremicourt and Vraucourt, and thence to the western outskirts of Ecoust, Bullecourt and Hendecourt. Any farther advance would threaten the enemy's line south of Péronne along the east bank of the Somme, to which our progress north of the river had already forced him to retreat.

This latter movement had been commenced on the 26th August, on which date Roye was evacuated by the enemy, and next day had been followed by a general advance on the part of the French and British forces between the Oise and the Somme. By the night of the 29th August, Allied infantry had reached the left bank of the Somme on the whole front from the neighbourhood of Nesle, occupied by the French on the 28th August, northwards to Péronne. Farther south the French held Noyon.

(24) *The Fight for Mont St. Quentin and the Capture of Péronne.*

During these days an increase in hostile artillery fire, and the frequency and strength of the German counter-attacks indicated that our troops were approaching positions on which the enemy intended to stand, at any rate for a period. In the face of this increased resistance, by a brilliant operation commenced on the night of the 30th-31st August, the 2nd Australian Division (Major-General C. Rosenthal) stormed Mont St. Quentin, a most important tactical feature commanding Péronne and the crossings of the Somme at that town. Being prevented by floods and heavy machine-gun fire from crossing the river opposite Mont St. Quentin, the 5th Australian Infantry Brigade was passed across the Somme at Feuillières, two miles farther west, by means of hastily constructed bridges. By 10.15 p.m. on the 30th August, the brigade had captured the German trenches east of Clery, and was assembled in them ready for an assault which should turn the German positions from the north-west. At 5 a.m. on the 31st August the assault was launched, and, despite determined opposition, was completely successful. Both in the attack itself and in the course of repeated counter-attacks, delivered with great resolution by strong hostile forces throughout the remainder of the day and the greater part of the following night, fighting was exceptionally severe, and the taking of the position ranks as a most gallant achievement.

In this operation nearly 1,000 prisoners were taken, and great numbers of the enemy were killed. On the 1st September, as a direct consequence of it, Australian troops captured Péronne.

In support of the operation against Mont St. Quentin, on the morning of the 31st August the left of the Fourth Army (the 3rd Australian, 58th, 47th and 18th Divisions) attacked towards Bouchavesnes, Rancourt, and Fregicourt, and by successful fighting on this and the following day captured these villages with several hundred prisoners. On the Third Army front also there was hard fighting on both of these days. At the close of it we held Sailly Saillisel, Morval, Beaulencourt and Riencourt-lès-Bapaume, and were established on the ridges east of Bancourt, Fremicourt, Vaulx

Vraucourt and Longatte. Troops of the XVII. Corps, under command of Lieut.-General Sir C. Fergusson, completed the capture of Bullecourt and Hendecourt, and, following up their advantage, during the night took Riencourt-lez-Cagnicourt with 380 prisoners.

(25) *The Results of the Battle of Bapaume.*

The 1st September marks the close of the second stage in the British offensive. Having in the first stage freed Amiens by our brilliant success east of that town, in the second stage the troops of the Third and Fourth Armies, comprising 23 British divisions, by skilful leading, hard fighting, and relentless and unremitting pursuit, in ten days had driven 35 German divisions from one side of the old Somme battlefield to the other, thereby turning the line of the river Somme. In so doing they had inflicted upon the enemy the heaviest losses in killed and wounded, and had taken from him over 34,000 prisoners and 270 guns. For the remarkable success of the battle of Bapaume, the greatest credit is due to the excellence of the staff arrangements of all formations, and to the most able conduct of the operations of the Third Army by its Commander, General Byng.

In the obstinate fighting of the past few days the enemy had been pressed back to the line of the Somme River and the high ground about Rocquigny and Beugny, where he had shown an intention to stand for a time. Thereafter, his probable plan was to retire slowly, when forced to do so, from one intermediary position to another; until he could shelter his battered divisions behind the Hindenburg defences. The line of the Tortille River and the high Nurlu Plateau offered opportunities for an ordered withdrawal of this nature, which would allow him to secure his artillery as well as much of the material in his forward dumps.

On the other hand, the disorganization which had been

caused by our attacks on the 8th and 21st August had increased under the pressure of our advance, and had been accompanied by a steady deterioration in the *moral* of his troops. Garrisons left as rearguards to hold up our advance at important points had surrendered as soon as they found themselves threatened with isolation. The urgent needs of the moment, the wide extent of front attacked, and consequent uncertainty as to where the next blow would fall, and the extent of his losses had forced the enemy to throw in his reserve piecemeal as they arrived on the battle front. On many occasions in the course of the fighting elements of the same German division had been identified on widely separated parts of the battle front.

In such circumstances, a sudden and successful blow, of weight sufficient to break through the northern hinge of the defences to which it was his design to fall back, might produce results of great importance. At this date, as will be seen from the events described in paragraph 27, our troops were already in position to deliver such a stroke.

(26) *The Withdrawal from the Lys Salient.*

Meanwhile, during the process of the great events briefly recorded above and in immediate consequence of them, other events of different but scarcely less importance were taking place on the northern portion of our front.

The exhaustion of the enemy's reserves resulting from the Allied attacks made the shortening of the German line imperative. The obvious sector in which to effect such a shortening was the Lys front. The enemy had only maintained himself in the Lys salient under the constant fire of our guns at the expense of heavy casualties, not only to his infantry in line, but to his artillery and troops in back areas. With the abandonment of his projected offensive against the Channel Ports all reason had gone for remaining in so costly a salient, while the threat, carefully maintained by us, of a British attack provided an additional reason for withdrawing.

Accordingly, from about the 26th July the enemy had been actively employed in removing the ammunition and stores accumulated for his offensive, and as early as the 5th August he had begun to effect local withdrawals on the southern flank of the salient.

The development of our own and the French offensives hastened this movement, although immense quantities of ammunition still remained untouched. On the 18th August out patrols, whose activity had been constant, were able to make a considerable advance opposite Merville. Next day Merville itself was taken, and our line advanced on the whole front from the Lawe River to the Plate Becque.

During the following days, various other small gains of ground were made by us on the southern and western faces of the salient, but on the northern face the enemy as yet showed no signs of withdrawal, the various local operations carried out by us meeting with strong resistance. On the night of the 29th-30th August, however, impelled alike by the pressure exerted without remission by our troops on the spot and by the urgency of events elsewhere, the enemy commenced an extensive retirement on the whole of the Lys front.

In the early morning of the 30th August our troops found Bailleul unoccupied, and by the evening of that day our advanced detachments had reached the general line Lacouture, Lestrem, Noote Boom, east of Bailleul.

Thereafter, the enemy's withdrawal continued rapidly. At certain points, indeed, his rearguards offered vigorous resistance, notably about Neuve Eglise and Hill 63, captured with a number of prisoners by the 36th and 29th Divisions; but by the evening of the 6th September the Lys salient had disappeared. Kemmel Hill was once more in our hands, and our troops had reached the general line Givenchy, Neuve Chapelle, Nieppe, Ploegsteert, Voormezeele.

The Battle of the Scarpe
(26th August—3rd September).

(27) *The Retaking of Monchy-le-Preux.*

By the 25th August our advance had formed a salient of the German positions opposite Arras, and the proper moment had therefore come for the third stage of our operations, in which the First Army should extend the flank of our attack to the north. By driving eastwards from Arras, covered on the left by the rivers Scarpe and Sensée, the First Army would endeavour to turn the enemy's positions on the Somme battlefield, and cut his system of railway communications which ran south-westwards across their front.

At 3 a.m. on the 26th August, the Canadian Corps, Lieutenant-General Sir A. W. Currie commanding, on the right of General Horne's First Army, attacked the German positions astride the Scarpe River with the 2nd and 3rd Canadian Divisions (commanded by Major-Generals Sir H. E. Burstall and L. J. Lipsett) and the 51st Division. This attack, delivered on a front of about 5½ miles and closely supported by the left of the Third Army, was completely successful. By noon we had taken Wancourt and Guemappe, and had stormed the hill and village of Monchy-le-Preux. This latter position was one of great natural strength, well organized for defence, and commanded observation of much importance. Many prisoners were taken, and later in the day substantial progress was made to the east of these three villages, a strong counter-attack east of Monchy being successfully repulsed. North of the Scarpe the 51st Division pushed forward their line towards Roeux, so as to secure an easily defensible base of departure for this advance, and by a successful attack during the evening captured Greenland Hill.

Their opening success was followed up by the troops of the First Army with the greatest energy, and on the following day Cherisy, Vis-en-Artois, the Bois du Sart, Roeux and Gavrelle were taken. By the end of the month they had gained the high ground east of Cherisy and Haucourt, had captured Eterpigny, and cleared the area between the Sensée and Scarpe Rivers west of the Trinquis Brook. North of the Scarpe, Plouvain was held by us. Our progress brought our troops to within assaulting distance of the powerful trench system running from the Hindenburg Line at Quéant to the Lens defences about Drocourt, the breaking of which would turn the whole of the enemy's organized positions on a wide front southwards.

(28) *The Storming of the Drocourt-Quéant Line.*

On the 2nd September the Drocourt-Quéant Line was broken, the maze of trenches at the junction of that line and the Hindenburg system was stormed and the enemy was thrown into precipitate retreat on the whole front to the south of it. This gallant feat of arms was carried out by the Canadian Corps of the First Army, employing the 1st and 4th Canadian Divisions and the 4th English Division, and the XVII. Corps of the Third Army, employing the 52nd, 57th, and 63rd Divisions.

The assault of the Canadians was launched at 5 a.m. on a front of about 4½ miles south of the Trinquis Brook, our infantry being supported by 40 tanks of the 3rd Tank Brigade, and assisted by a mobile force of motor machine-gun units, Canadian cavalry, and armoured cars. The attack was a complete success, and by noon the whole of the elaborate system of wire, trenches, and strong points constituting the Drocourt-Quéant Line on the front of our advance was in our hands.

On the right the attack of the XVII. Corps, launched at the same hour by the 52nd and 57th Divisions, directed its main force on the triangle of fortifications marking the junction of the Hindenburg and Drocourt-Quéant lines north-west of the village of Quéant. Pressed with equal vigour it met with success equally complete. There was stern fighting in the network of trenches both north and south of Quéant, in which neighbourhood the 52nd (Lowland) Division performed distinguished service, and by the progress they made greatly assisted our advance farther north. Early in the afternoon our troops had cleared the triangle, and the 63rd Division (Major-General C. A. Blacklock) had passed through to exploit the success thus gained.

During the afternoon our farther progress met with considerable resistance from machine-gun nests sited in woods and villages and on the reverse slopes of the Dury Ridge. There was hard fighting until dusk, especially on the front of the 63rd Division and of the 4th Division (Major-General T. G. Matheson). By nightfall this opposition had been overcome, the 63rd Division had reached the railway east of Quéant, and the 57th Division, swinging to the right, was threatening that village and Pronville from the north. Our troops had pushed forward to a depth of over three miles along the Arras-Cambrai road, and had reached the outskirts of Buissy. Cagnicourt, Villers-les-Cagnicourt, and Dury were in our hands. During the day 8,000 prisoners had been taken and many guns.

Troops of the Third and Fourth Armies prolonged the line of attack as far south as Péronne. At all points important progress was made, though fighting was severe.

In the battle of the Scarpe, as in the battles of Amiens and Bapaume and the victories that followed them, staff work of a high order played an important part in our success. The greatest credit is due to the First Army Commander, General Horne, and his staff for the excellence of their arrangements.

(29) *The Enemy in Retreat.*

The result of the battles of Amiens, Bapaume, and the Scarpe now declared itself.

During the night of the 2nd-3rd September the enemy fell back rapidly on the whole front of the Third Army and the right of the First Army. By the end of the day he had taken up positions along the general line of the Canal du Nord from Péronne to Ytres and thence east of Hermies, Inchy-en-Artois, and Ecourt St. Quentin to the Sensée, east of Lecluse. On the following day he commenced to withdraw also from the east bank of the Somme south of Péronne, and by the night of the 8th September was holding the general line Vermand, Epehy, Havrincourt, and thence along the east bank of the Canal du Nord.

The withdrawal was continued on the front of the French forces on our right. On the 6th September French troops occupied Ham and Chauny, and by 8th September had reached the line of the Crozat Canal.

Throughout this hasty retreat our troops followed up the enemy closely. Many of his rearguards were cut off and taken prisoner; on numerous occasions our forward guns did great execution among his retiring columns, while our airmen took full advantage of the remarkable targets offered them. Great quantities of material and many guns fell into our hands.

In the battle of the Scarpe itself, in which ten British divisions attacked and overthrew thirteen German divisions, thereby giving the signal for this general retreat, our total captures amounted to over 16,000 prisoners and about 200 guns.

(30) *The Battle of Havrincourt and Epehy. 12th-18th September.*

North of Havrincourt, the Canal du Nord, behind which the enemy had taken shelter, with the open slopes leading down to it swept by the fire of the German positions on the east bank, could scarcely be taken except by a carefully organized attack.

From the neighbourhood of Havrincourt, southwards, the enemy's main line of resistance was the well-known Hindenburg Line, which, after passing through that village, ran south-east across the Beaucamp, La Vacquerie and Bonavis Ridges to the Scheldt Canal at Bantouzelle, whence it followed the line of the canal to St. Quentin. In front of this trench system strong German forces held formidable positions about Havrincourt and Epehy, which had to be taken before a final attack on the Hindenburg Line could be undertaken. By successful operations carried out during the second and third weeks of September these different defences were secured and our line advanced to within assaulting distance of the enemy's main line of resistance.

On the 12th September the IV. and VI. Corps of the Third Army attacked on a front of about five miles in the Havrincourt sector, employing troops of the New Zealand, 37th, 62nd and 2nd Divisions. The villages of Trescault and Havrincourt were taken by the 37th and 62nd Divisions respectively, and positions were secured which were of considerable importance in view of future operations.

On the right of the British front the IX. and Australian Corps continued to push forward with light forces. By the evening of the 17th September, as the result of skilful manœuvring and well-executed local attacks, they had captured Holnon village and wood and Maissemy, and were closely approaching Le Verguier and Templeux-le-Guerard.

Next day, at 7 a.m., on the 18th September, the Fourth and Third Armies attacked in heavy rain on a front of about seventeen miles from Holnon to Gouzeaucourt, the First French Army co-operating south of Holnon. A small number of tanks accompanied our infantry, and were of great assistance.

In this operation, our troops penetrated to a depth of

three miles through the deep, continuous, and well-organized defensive belt formed by the old British and German lines. On practically the whole front our objectives were gained successfully, the 1st, 17th, 21st, and 74th Divisions (Major-General E. S. Girdwood commanding the 74th Division), and the 1st and 4th Australian Divisions (the latter commanded by Major-General E. Sinclair-Maclagan) distinguishing themselves by the vigour and success of their attack. On the extreme right and in the left centre about Epehy the enemy's resistance was very determined, and in these sectors troops of the 6th, 12th, 18th, and 58th Divisions had severe fighting. Before nightfall, however, the last centres of resistance in Epehy were reduced, and both in this area and on our right about Gricourt local actions during the succeeding days secured for us the remainder of the positions required for an attack on the main Hindenburg defences.

At the close of these operations, in which fifteen British Divisions defeated twenty German Divisions and completed the fourth stage of our offensive, we had captured nearly 12,000 prisoners and 100 guns.

(31) *The Development of the Allied Plan.*

The details of the strategic plan outlined in paragraph 13 upon which future operations should be based, were the subject of careful discussion between Marshal Foch and myself. Preparations were already far advanced for the successful attack by which, on the 12th September, the First American Army, assisted by certain French divisions, drove the enemy from the St. Mihiel salient and inflicted heavy losses upon him in prisoners and guns. Ultimately, it was decided that as soon as possible after this attack four convergent and simultaneous offensives should be launched by the Allies as follows:—

By the Americans West of the Meuse in the direction of Mezières;

By the French west of Argonne in close co-operation with the American attack and with the same general objectives;

By the British on the St. Quentin-Cambrai front in the general direction of Maubeuge;

By Belgian and Allied forces in Flanders in the direction of Ghent.

By these attacks it was expected, as already indicated, that the important German forces opposite the French and Americans would be pressed back upon the difficult country of the Ardennes, while the British thrust struck at their principal lines of communication. In Flanders, it was intended to take advantage of the weakening of the German forces on this front to clear the Belgian coast by a surprise attack. Success in any one of these offensives might compel the enemy to withdraw to the line of the Meuse.

(32) *The Rôle of the British Armies.*

The results to be obtained from these different attacks depended in a peculiarly large degree upon the British attack in the centre. It was here that the enemy defences were most highly organized. If these were broken, the threat directed at his vital systems of lateral communication would of necessity react upon his defence elsewhere.

On the other hand, the long period of sustained offensive action through which the British armies had already passed had made large demands both upon the troops themselves and upon my available reserves. Throughout our attacks from the 8th August onwards, our losses, in proportion to the results achieved and the numbers of prisoners taken, had been consistently and remarkably small. In the aggregate, however, they were considerable, and in the face of them an attack upon so formidably organized a position as that which now confronted us could not be lightly undertaken. Moreover, the political effects of an unsuccessful attack upon a position so well known as the Hindenburg Line would be large, and would go far to revive the declining *moral* not only of the German Army but of the German people.

These different considerations were present to my mind. The probable results of a costly failure, or, indeed, of anything short of a decided success, in any attempt upon the main defences of the Hindenburg Line were obvious; but I was convinced that the British attack was the essential part of the general scheme, and that the moment was favourable.

Accordingly, I decided to proceed with the attack, and all preparatory measures, including the preliminary operations already recounted, were carried out as rapidly and as thoroughly as possible.

(33) *The Hindenburg Line.*

Between St. Quentin and the village of Bantouzelle the principal defences of the Hindenburg system lie sometimes to the west, but more generally to the east of the line of the Scheldt Canal.

The canal itself does not appear to have been organized as the enemy's main line of resistance, but rather as an integral part of a deep defensive system, the outstanding characteristic of which was the skill with which it was sited so as to deny us effective artillery positions from which to attack it. The chief *rôle* of the canal was that of affording cover to resting troops and to the garrisons of the main defensive trench lines during a bombardment. To this end the canal lent itself admirably, and the fullest use was made by the enemy of its possibilities.

The general configuration of the ground through which this sector of the canal runs produces deep cuttings of a depth in places of some sixty feet, while between Bellicourt and the neighbourhood of Vendhuille the canal passes through a tunnel for a distance of 6,000 yards. In the sides of the cuttings the enemy had constructed numerous tunnelled dugouts and concrete shelters. Along the top edge of them he had concealed well-sited concrete or armoured machine-gun emplacements. The tunnel itself was used to provide living accommodation for troops, and was connected by shafts with the trenches above. South of Bellicourt the canal cutting gradually becomes shallow, till at Bellenglise the canal lies almost at ground level. South of Bellenglise the canal is dry.

On the western side of the canal south of Bellicourt two thoroughly organized and extremely heavily wired lines of continuous trench run roughly parallel to the canal, at average distances from it of 2,000 and 1,000 yards respectively. Except in the tunnel sector, the double line of trenches known as the Hindenburg Line proper lies immediately east of the canal, and is linked up by numerous communication trenches with the trench lines west of it.

Besides these main features, numerous other trench lines, switch trenches and communication trenches, for the most part heavily wired, had been constructed at various points to meet local weaknesses or take advantage of local command of fire. At a distance of about 4,000 yards behind the most easterly of these trench lines lies a second double row of trenches known as the Beaurevoir-Fonsomme Line, very thoroughly wired and holding numerous concrete shelters and machine-gun emplacements. The whole series of defences, with the numerous defended villages contained in it, formed a belt of country varying from 7,000 to 10,000 yards in depth, organized by the employment of every available means into a most powerful system, well meriting the great reputation attached to it.

(34) *The Battle of Cambrai and the Hindenburg Line (27th September–5th October).*

The battle of Cambrai, which on the 5th October culminated in the capture of the last remaining sectors of the

Hindenburg Line, was commenced by the First and Third Armies.

Between the neighbourhood of St. Quentin and the Scheldt the Fourth, Third, and First Armies, in the order named, occupied on the evening of the 26th September a line running from the village of Selency (west of St. Quentin) to Gricourt and Pontruet and thence east of Villeret and Lempire to Villers Guislain and Gouzeaucourt, both exclusive. Thereafter the line continued northwards to Havrincourt and Mœuvres and thence along the west side of the Canal du Nord to the floods of the Sensee at Ecourt St. Quentin.

On the First and Third Army fronts strong positions covering the approaches to Cambrai between the Nord and Scheldt canals, including the section of the Hindenburg Line itself north of Gouzeaucourt, were still in the enemy's possession. His trenches in this sector faced south-west, and it was desirable that they should be taken in the early stages of the operation, so as to render it easier for the artillery of the Fourth Army to get into position. On the Fourth Army front, where the heaviest blow was to fall, the exceptional strength of the enemy's position made a prolonged bombardment necessary. I therefore decided that a very heavy bombardment, opened during the night of the 26th-27th September along the whole front of all three armies, should be followed on the morning of the 27th September by an attack delivered only by the First and Third Armies. In this way the enemy might be deceived as to the main point of attack, the First and Third Armies would be enabled to get nearer to their final objective, and the task of the Fourth Army artillery would be simplified.

(35) *The Battle opened.*

On the morning of the 26th September French and American forces attacked on both sides of the Argonne, between the Meuse and the Suippe river.

At 5.20 a.m. on the 27th September the Third and First British Armies attacked with the IV., VI., XVII., and Canadian Corps in the direction of Cambrai on a front of about 13 miles from Gouzeaucourt to the neighbourhood of Sauchy Lestrée. The success of the northern part of the attack depended upon the ability of our troops to debouch from the neighbourhood of Mœuvres, and to secure the crossings of the Canal du Nord in that locality. The northern portion of the Canal was too formidable an obstacle to be crossed in the face of the enemy. It was therefore necessary for the attacking divisions to force a passage on a comparatively narrow front about Mœuvres, and thereafter turn the line of the Canal farther north by a divergent attack developed fanwise from the point of crossing. This difficult manœuvre was carried out successfully, and on the whole front of attack our infantry, assisted by some sixty-five tanks, broke deeply into the enemy's position.

The attack proceeded according to plan from the commencement. On the right strong resistance was encountered at Beaucamp. Several strong counter-attacks were made during the day in this neighbourhood, but in spite of them troops of the 5th and 42nd Divisions successfully established the right flank of our attack between Beaucamp and Ribecourt. The 3rd Division moved forward with the Guards, forcing the crossings of the Canal in face of heavy fire from machine guns and forward field guns and captured Ribecourt and Flesquières. The Guards Division (Major-General T. G. Matheson) took Orival Wood and reached the neighbourhood of Premy Chapel, where the 2nd Division (Major-General C. E. Pereira) took up the advance.

In the centre the 52nd Division (Major-General F. J. Marshall), passing its troops across the Canal by bridgeheads previously established by the 57th Division, on the opening of the assault carried the German trench lines east of the Canal and gained the high ground overlooking Graincourt. On their left the 63rd Division and the 4th and 1st Canadian

Divisions (under command of Major-Generals Sir D. Watson and A. C. MacDonell) moved under cover of darkness down the west bank of the Canal between Mœuvres and Sains-lez-Marquion. In the half light of dawn these three divisions stormed the line of the Canal itself, and advanced on Graincourt, Anneux, Bourlon, and the slopes to the north of the latter village.

As soon as the line of the Canal had been secured our engineer troops commenced the construction of bridges, completing their task with remarkable speed and working with great gallantry under the fire of the German guns. Greatly assisted by their efforts our advance continued. Obstinate resistance was met with at Graincourt, and it was not until late in the day that the village was finally surrounded and captured by the 63rd Division. The 57th Division (Major-General R. W. R. Barnes) meanwhile had passed through and carried the line forward east of Anneux to Fontaine-Notre-Dame. Bourlon had been carried by the 4th Canadian Division, and the 3rd Canadian Division (Major-General F. O. W. Loomis) had passed through at Bourlon Wood, which was wholly in our possession.

On the left the 1st Canadian Division, having seized Sains-lez-Marquion early in the attack, advanced with the 11th Division (Major-General H. R. Davies) and took Haynecourt, while the latter division captured Epinoy and Oisy-le-Verger. On the extreme left the 56th Division of the XXII. Corps crossed the Canal, and having cleared Sauchy Lestrée and Sauchy Cauchy, moved northwards towards Palluel.

At the end of the day our troops had reached the general line Beaucamp–Ribecourt–Fontaine-Notre-Dame–east of Haynecourt–Epinoy–Oisy-le-Verger, and had taken over 10,000 prisoners and 200 guns.

Next day the advance on this front was continued, and Gouzeaucourt, Marcoing, Noyelles-sur-l'Escaut, Fontaine-Notre-Dame, Sailly, and Palluel were taken. At Marcoing our troops established themselves on the east bank of the

Scheldt Canal, and on the northern flank entered Aubencheul-au-Bac.

(36) *The Hindenburg Line broken.*

The heavy and continuous bombardment opened on the morning of the 27th September had been maintained by the Fourth Army along its whole front without intermission for two days. The intensity of our fire drove the enemy's garrisons to take refuge in their deep dugouts and tunnels, and made it impossible for his carrying parties to bring up food and ammunition.

At 5.50 a.m. on the 29th September, under an intense artillery barrage, General Rawlinson's Fourth Army attacked on a front of 12 miles, between Holnon and Vendhuille, with the IX., II. American (General G. W. Read commanding) and III. Corps, a strong force of tanks, manned by British and American crews, accompanying the infantry. On the right of the Fourth Army the French First Army continued the line of attack in the St. Quentin sector. On the left the V. and IV. Corps of the Third Army had attacked at an earlier hour between Vendhuille and Marcoing, and had heavy fighting about Villers Guislain, Gonnelieu, and Welsh Ridge.

On the Fourth Army front, the 46th Division (Major-General G. F. Boyd) greatly distinguished itself in the capture of Bellenglise. The village is situated in the angle of the Scheldt Canal, which, after running in a southerly direction from Bellicourt, here bends sharply to the east towards the Le Tronquoy Tunnel. Equipped with lifebelts, and carrying mats and rafts, the 46th Division stormed the western arm of the canal at Bellenglise and to the north of it, some crossing the canal on footbridges which the enemy was given no time to destroy, others dropping down the sheer sides of the canal wall, and, having swum or waded to the far side, climbing up the farther wall to the German trench lines on the eastern bank. Having captured these trenches, the attacking troops swung to the right and took from flank and rear the German defences along the eastern arm of the canal and on the high ground south of the canal, capturing many prisoners and German batteries in action before the enemy had had time to realize the new direction of the attack. So thorough and complete was the organization for this attack, and so gallantly, rapidly, and well was it executed by the troops, that this one division took on this day over 4,000 prisoners and 70 guns.

On the remainder of the front, also, our attack met with remarkable success. South of Bellenglise, the 1st Division (Major-General E. P. Strickland), with the 6th Division covering their flank, crossed the ridge north-west of Thorigny and reached the west end of the Le Tronquoy Tunnel. Here they gained touch with the 42nd Division, who had passed through the 46th Division and taken Lehaucourt and Magny la Fosse. North of Bellenglise, the 30th American Division (Major-General E. M. Lewis), having broken through the deep defences of the Hindenburg Line, stormed Bellicourt and seized Nauroy. On their left the 27th American Division (Major-General J. F. O'Ryan) met with very heavy enfilade machine-gun fire, but pressed on with great gallantry as far as Bony, where a bitter struggle took place for the possession of the village.

Fighting on the whole front of the II. American Corps was severe, and in Bellicourt, Nauroy, Gillemont Farm, and at a number of other points amid the intricate defences of the Hindenburg Line, strong bodies of the enemy held out with great obstinacy for many hours. These points of resistance were gradually overcome, either by the support troops of the American divisions or by the 5th and 3rd Australian Divisions (Major-Generals Sir J. J. T. Hobbs and J. Gellibrand), which, moving up close behind the American troops, were soon heavily engaged. On the left of the attack the 12th and 18th Divisions cleared the slopes above Vendhuille.

Meanwhile, the Third Army captured Masnières, and secured the crossings of the Scheldt Canal between that village and the outskirts of Cambrai, while the Canadian Corps made progress north-west of that town, taking St. Olle and Sancourt.

For the next two days our attacks continued on all fronts. On the 30th September the gap in the Hindenburg Line was enlarged by the capture of Thorigny and Le Tronquoy by the 1st and 32nd Divisions, thus securing possession of the Le Tronquoy Tunnel. On this day the enemy abandoned Villers Guislain and Gonnelieu, being threatened with envelopment, and withdrew behind the Scheldt Canal.

Next day, the IX. and Australian Corps attacked in conjunction with the French First Army, who occupied St. Quentin. Levergies was taken by the 32nd Division, and Australian troops captured Joncourt, Estrées, and Bony, establishing our line well to the north and east of the latter village.

In the Cambrai sector, the New Zealand and 3rd Divisions took Crevecœur and Rumilly, while north of Cambrai the Canadian Corps cleared the high ground west of Ramillies and entered Blécourt. The fighting on the Canadian front at this period was particularly severe, and our troops displayed great courage and determination. The enemy employed large forces, amounting to at least 11 divisions in the space of five days, in his attempt to check our advance, and counter-attacked frequently and in strength.

(37) *Montbrehain and Beaurevoir.*

During the first week of October the Cambrai battle was completed by a series of successful minor operations, in which the breach driven through the Hindenburg Line, and such prepared defences as lay behind it, was widened.

On the 3rd October the Fourth Army attacked between Sequehart and Le Catelet, and captured those villages and Ramicourt, together with the Beaurevoir-Fonsomme line on that front. In this operation the 50th Division took Gouy and Le Catelet after heavy and prolonged fighting, in which a number of counter-attacks were beaten off.

In the course of the next two days, other local improvements were effected in our line in this sector, and the villages of Montbrehain and Beaurevoir were captured after hard fighting, in which tanks did good service. Our advance compelled the enemy to evacuate the high ground about La Terrière, in the bend of the Scheldt Canal between La Catelet and Crevecoeur, with the result that on the 5th October the right of the Third Army was able to cross the Scheldt Canal and occupy the Hindenburg Line east of it, thereby greatly simplifying our arrangements for our next attack.

(38) *Results of breaking the Hindenburg Line.*

The great and critical assaults in which during these nine days of battle the First, Third, and Fourth Armies stormed the line of the Canal du Nord and broke through the Hindenburg Line mark the close of the first phase of the British offensive. The enemy's defence in the last and strongest of his prepared positions had been shattered. The whole of the main Hindenburg defences had passed into our possession, and a wide gap had been driven through such rear trench systems as had existed behind them. The effect of the victory upon the subsequent course of the campaign was decisive. The threat to the enemy's communications was now direct and instant, for nothing but the natural obstacles of a wooded and well-watered countryside lay between our armies and Maubeuge.

In the fighting of these days, in which thirty British and two American infantry divisions and one British cavalry division were engaged against thirty-nine German divisions, over 36,000 prisoners and 380 guns had been captured. Great as were the material losses the enemy had suffered, the effect of so overwhelming a defeat upon a *moral* already deteriorated was of even larger importance.

Combined with the events of Flanders presently narrated,

the advance we had made opened a new threat to the German positions on the Lys front.

(39) *The Battle in Flanders.*

As indicated above in paragraph 13, the general strategic plan of the Allies contemplated the development of operations on the Flanders front. The details of these operations were settled at a Conference held by the Commander-in-Chief of the Allied armies at Cassel on the 9th September. The force to be engaged was to be placed under the command of His Majesty the King of the Belgians, and was to consist of the Belgian Army, some French divisions, and all the artillery and a certain number of divisions of the Second British Army, commanded by General Sir H. Plumer. To the definite plan laid down I gladly gave my assent.

Accordingly at 5.30 a.m. on the 28th September the XIX. and II. Corps of the Second Army attacked without preliminary bombardment on a front of some 4½ miles south of the Ypres-Zonnebeke road. The 14th Division (Major-General P. C. B. Skinner), 35th Division (Major-General A. H. Marindin), 29th and 9th Divisions delivered the initial assault, being supported in the later stages of the battle by the 41st Division (Major-General Sir S. T. B. Lawford) and the 36th Division (Major-General C. Coffin). On the left of the II. Corps the Belgian Army continued the line of attack as far as Dixmude.

On both the British and Belgian fronts the attack was a brilliant success. The enemy, who was attempting to hold his positions with less than five divisions, was driven rapidly from the whole of the high ground east of Ypres, so fiercely contested during the battles of 1917. By the end of the day the British divisions had passed far beyond the farthest limits of the 1917 battles, and had reached and captured Kortewilde, Zandvoorde, Kruiseecke, and Becelaere. On their left Belgian troops had taken Zonnebeke, Poelcapelle, and Schaap Baillie, and cleared the enemy from Houthulst Forest.

South of the main attack, successful minor enterprises by the 31st, 30th (Major-General W. de L. Williams), and 34th British Divisions carried our line forward to St. Yves and the outskirts of Messines. Wytschaete was captured, and after sharp fighting our troops established themselves along the line of the ridge between Wytschaete and the canal north of Hollebeke.

During the succeeding days, despite continuous rain and great difficulties from the scarcity of practicable roads, the British and Belgian forces followed up the defeated enemy with the utmost vigour. On the 29th September our troops drove the German rearguards from Ploegsteert Wood and Messines and captured Terhand and Dadizeele. By the evening of the 1st October they had cleared the left bank of the Lys from Comines southwards, while north of that town they were close up to Wervicq, Gheluwe, and Ledeghem. On their left the Belgian Army had passed the general line Moorslede—Staden—Dixmude.

In these most successful operations and their subsequent developments the British forces alone captured at light cost over 5,000 prisoners and 100 guns.

(40) *The Withdrawal from Lens and Armentières.*

Once more the effect of our successes showed itself rapidly.

At the beginning of September the enemy had withdrawn from his outpost positions astride the La Bassée Canal, and the activity of our patrols led to sharp fighting, in which the 16th (Major-General A. B. Ritchie), 55th (Major-General Sir H. S. Jeudwine), and 19th Divisions advanced our line close up to the outskirts of La Bassée. Thenceforward the situation on the Lys front had remained practically unchanged until the 30th September, when the divisions of General Sir W. R. Birdwood's Fifth Army made certain small advances south of the Lys. On the 2nd October, however, the enemy once more began an extensive withdrawal, falling back on the whole front from south of Lens to Armentières. In the sector south of Lens, indeed, patrols of the 20th Division (Major-General G. G. S. Carey) met with considerable resistance on this day about Acheville and Mericourt, but progress was made. During the next two days the movement continued, under vigorous pressure from our troops. By the evening of the 4th October, north of Lens we had reached the general line Vendin le Vieil—Wavrin—Erquinghem—Houplines, where the increasing strength of the enemy's resistance indicated that he intended to stand at any rate for a time. South of Lens the withdrawal slackened about this date on the general line Fresnoy—Sallaumines—Vendin le Vieil, but shortly afterwards the development of our operations on the St. Quentin-Cambrai front forced upon the enemy a further retreat in this sector.

SECOND PHASE: THE FIGHTING IN OPEN COUNTRY.

THE SECOND BATTLE OF LE CATEAU (6th–12th October).

(41) The second and concluding phase of the British offensive now opened, in which the Fourth and Third Armies and the right of the First Army moved forward with their left flank on the canal line which runs from Cambrai to Mons and their right covered by the French First Army. This advance, by the capture of Maubeuge and the disruption of the German main lateral system of communications, forced the enemy to fall back upon the line of the Meuse and realized the strategic plan of the Allied operations.

The fighting which took place during this period, being in effect the development and exploitation of the Hindenburg Line victory, falls into three stages, the breaks between the different battles being due chiefly to the depth of our advances and the difficulties of re-establishing communications.

In the first of these stages, the Battle of Le Cateau, certain incomplete defences still held by the enemy were captured, and his troops compelled to evacuate Cambrai and fall back behind the line of the Selle River. In the second stage the Selle River was forced, and by a development of this operation our front pushed forward to the general line Sambre Canal—west edge of the Mormal Forest—Valenciennes, where we were in position for the final assault upon Maubeuge.

(42) Having completed their arrangements, at 4.30 a.m. and 5.10 a.m. respectively on the 8th October the Third and Fourth Armies attacked on a front of over seventeen miles from Sequehart to south of Cambrai. French troops continued the line of attack on our right as far south as St. Quentin. Farther south, French and American troops attacked on this day east of the Meuse and in Champagne, and made important progress.

On the British battle front our infantry and tanks penetrated the enemy's positions to a depth of between three and four miles, passing rapidly over the incomplete trench lines above referred to and gaining the open country beyond. Strong at the outset of our attack, during the later stages opposition weakened. Brancourt and Prémont were taken by the 30th American Division, while to the north of them the 66th Division (Major-General H. K. Bethell), attacking beside the 25th Division (Major-General J. R. E. Charles), captured Serain. Villers Outreaux was cleared by the 38th Division, with the assistance of tanks, after heavy fighting, and late in the afternoon Malincourt was captured. The New Zealand Division passed through Lesdain and took Esnes, while on the left of the attack the 3rd, 2nd, and 63rd Divisions captured Seranvillers, Forenville, and Niergnies after very heavy fighting, in the course of which the enemy counter-attacked with tanks. On the extreme left the 57th Division made progress in the southern outskirts of Cambrai.

As the result of this attack the enemy's resistance temporarily gave way. His infantry became disorganized and retired steadily eastwards, while our airmen reported that the roads converging on Le Cateau were blocked with troops and transport. Several thousand prisoners and many guns fell into our hands. During the following night the Canadian Corps captured Ramillies and crossed the Scheldt Canal at Pont d'Aire. Canadian patrols entered Cambrai from the north and joined hands with patrols of the 57th Division working through the southern portion of the town. Next morning at 5.20 a.m. the Fourth and Third Armies resumed the attack on the whole front, cavalry assisting in the advance. By nightfall our troops were within two miles of Le Cateau, had captured Bohain, and were attacking Caudry from the south. Cambrai was in our hands, and our troops were three miles to the east of the town.

In this day's fighting cavalry again did valuable and gallant work, hurrying the enemy in his retreat and preventing him from completing the destruction of the railway which runs from St. Quentin to Busigny and Cambrai. When our infantry were held up by heavy machine-gun fire from Cattigny Wood and Clary, a dashing charge by the Fort Garry Horse gained a footing in Cattigny Wood and assisted our infantry to press forward. Farther east, Dragoon Guards and Canadian Cavalry were instrumental in the capture of Honnechy, Reumont and Troisvilles.

On the 10th October our progress continued, though the enemy's resistance gradually stiffened as our troops approached the line of the river Selle, and attempts made by the cavalry to cross that stream had to be abandoned. That night we had reached the outskirts of Riquerval Wood, and held the west bank of the Selle River thence as far as Viesly, whence our line ran past St. Hilaire and Avesnes, taken by the Guards and 24th Divisions, to the Scheldt at Thun St. Martin.

During these days the French First Army on our right advanced its line east of St. Quentin, clearing the west bank of the Oise-Sambre Canal as far north as Bernot.

(43) *The Withdrawal from Laon.*

By this advance, in which twenty British infantry, two British cavalry, and one American infantry division routed twenty-four German divisions and took from them 12,000 prisoners and 250 guns, we gained full possession of the important lateral double line of railway running from St. Quentin through Busigny to Cambrai. During the repair of such portions of it as had been destroyed and the removal of delay action mines left by the enemy, our line was carried forward by local operations. By the 13th October we had reached the Selle River at all points south of Haspres, and had established bridgeheads at a number of places.

Meanwhile, on the 7th October, under close pressure from our troops, the enemy had extended the flank of his withdrawal south of Lens, and on that day the 8th Division had captured Biache St. Vaast and Oppy, with some hundreds of prisoners. After the launching of our attack on the 8th October, this movement continued with increased rapidity. By the evening of the 13th October, our troops had reached the western suburbs of Douai, and were close up to the west banks of the Sensée Deviation and Haute Deule Canals on the whole front from Arleux (south of Douai) to Vendin le Vieil.

During this period also our Allies had been pushing forward steadily on both sides of the Argonne. Held by their attacks on his southern flank, while to the north the British offensive was driving forward rapidly behind his right, the enemy was forced to evacuate his positions in the Laon salient. Signs of a widespread German withdrawal were reported on the 11th October, and by the evening of the 13th October Laon was in French hands.

(44) *The Advance in Flanders Resumed.*

While these great events were taking place to the south of them, the Allied Forces in Flanders were busily engaged in re-establishing adequate communications in the area of the old Ypres battles. By dint of great exertions, and the most careful organization of traffic routes, by the end of the second week in October the restoration of the Allied systems of communications was sufficiently far advanced to permit of a resumption of the offensive.

Accordingly, at 5.35 a.m. on the 14th October, the British, Belgian, and French forces, under command of His Majesty the King of the Belgians, attacked on the whole front between the Lys River at Comines and Dixmude.

The British sector extended for a distance of between 9 and 10 miles from Comines to the hamlet of St. Pieter, on the Menin-Roulers road. The assault was launched by the X., XIX., and II. Corps of General Plumer's Second Army, under command respectively of Lieut-General R. B. Stephens, Lieut-General Sir E. E. Watts, and Lieut-General Sir C. W. Jacob, employing respectively the 30th and 34th Divisions, the 41st and 35th Divisions, and the 36th, 29th and 9th Divisions.

The Allied attack was again attended by complete success. The two southern British Corps advanced their line according to programme to the southern edge of the rising ground overlooking Wervicq, Menin, and Wevelghem, in spite of very considerable resistance. Meanwhile, the II. Corps, after heavy fighting, penetrated to a depth of between three and four miles eastwards, capturing Moorseele and making progress beyond it to within a short distance of Gulleghem and Steenbeek. On our left Belgian troops reached Iseghem, French troops surrounded Roulers, while farther north other Belgian divisions took Cortemarck.

During the ensuing days our success was vigorously exploited. By the afternoon of the 16th October we held the north bank of the Lys from Frelinghien to opposite Harlebeke, and had crossed the river at a number of points. To the north of us our Allies also had made striking progress. Before nightfall on the 15th October Thourout was surrounded, and next day the enemy retired rapidly. Ostend fell on the 17th October, and three days later the northern flank of the Allied line rested on the Dutch frontier.

In these operations and others of a lesser nature, carried out on the last day of the month after the withdrawal next mentioned, the British forces operating on this battle front captured over 6,000 prisoners and 210 guns.

(45) *The Evacuation of Lille.*

Our advance north of the Lys had brought our troops far to the east of the Lille defences on the northern side, while our progress on the Le Cateau front had turned the Lille defences from the south. The German forces between the Sensée and the Lys were once more compelled to withdraw, closely followed by our troops, who constantly drove in their rearguards and took a number of prisoners. The enemy was given no opportunity to complete the removal of his stores and the destruction of roads and bridges, or to evacuate the civil population.

The movement began on the 15th October, when, in spite of considerable opposition, our troops crossed the Haute Deule Canal on a wide front north of Pont-a-Vendin. By the evening of the 17th October the 8th Division of General Sir A. Hunter Weston's VIII. Corps had entered Douai and the 57th and 59th Divisions (Major-General N. M. Smyth) of Lieut.-General Sir R. C. B. Haking's XI. Corps were on the outskirts of Lille. At 5.50 a.m. on the 18th October our troops had encircled Lille, which was clear of the enemy. During the day our line was carried far to the east of these towns and east of Roubaix and Tourcoing, occupied by the

40th and 31st Divisions (Major-General Sir W. E. Feyton commanding 40th Division) of Lieut-General Sir H. B. de Lisle's XV. Corps. Thereafter our troops pressed forward steadily, until by the evening of the 22nd October they had reached the general line of the Scheldt on the whole front from Valenciennes to the neighbourhood of Avelghem.

The Battle of the Selle River (17th-25th October).

(46) *The Forcing of the River Crossings.*

Meanwhile, communications on the Le Cateau front were improving, and it was possible to recommence operations of a more than local character for the forcing of the Selle positions and the attainment of the general line Sambre et Oise Canal—west edge of the Forêt de Mormal—Valenciennes. This advance would bring the important railway junction at Aulnoye within effective range of our guns.

Our operations were opened on the 17th October by an attack by the Fourth Army on a front of about ten miles from Le Cateau southwards, in conjunction with the French First Army operating west of the Sambre et Oise Canal. The assault launched at 5.20 a.m. was delivered by the IX., II. American, and XIII. Corps, employing respectively the 46th, 1st, and 6th Divisions, the 30th and 27th American Divisions, and the 50th and 66th Divisions.

The enemy was holding the difficult wooded country east of Bohain and the line of the Selle north of it in great strength, his infantry being well supported by artillery. During the first two days his resistance was obstinate; but the attacking British and American troops made good progress. By the evening of the 19th October, after much severe fighting, the enemy had been driven across the Sambre et Oise Canal at practically all points south of Catillon, whence our line followed the valley of the Richemont east and north of Le Cateau.

This success was followed at 2 a.m. on the 20th October by an attack upon the line of the Selle River north of Le Cateau. The troops employed were the 38th, 17th, 5th, 42nd, 62nd, Guards, and 19th Divisions of the Third Army, and the 4th Division on the right of the First Army in that order from right to left.

On this occasion also the enemy's resistance was serious, and he had been able to erect wire entanglements along the greater part of the line. Our advance was strongly contested at every point, frequent counter-attacks being made. Supported by a number of tanks which had successfully crossed the river, our infantry, after severe fighting about Neuvilly, Amerval, Solesmes and Haspres, gained their objectives on the high ground east of the Selle, pushing out patrols as far as the river Harpies. North of Haspres other troops of the First Army continued to make progress on both sides of the Scheldt Canal, reaching the slopes overlooking the left bank of the Ecaillon River and occupying Denain.

(47) The capture of the Selle positions was followed almost immediately by the larger operation for the attainment of the required general line above mentioned running from the Sambre Canal along the edge of the Mormal Forest to the neighbourhood of Valenciennes.

The original front of attack stretched from east of Mazinghien to Maison Bleue, north-east of Haussy, a distance of some fifteen miles. The assault was opened by the Fourth Army at 1.20 a.m. on the 23rd October, and was delivered by the IX. and XIII. Corps, employing respectively the 1st and 6th Divisions and the 25th and 18th Divisions. The Third Army again attacked with the V., IV., VI., and XVII. Corps, employing respectively the 33rd and 21st Divisions, the 5th, 42nd, 37th, and New Zealand Divisions, the 3rd and 2nd Divisions, and the 19th Division. On the second day the 61st Division of the XVII. Corps and the 4th Division and 51st Division of the XXII. Corps, First Army, extended the line of attack for a further five miles northwards to the Scheldt.

The unfavourable weather of the preceding days had made it difficult to locate the enemy's batteries, and during the earlier stages of the battle hostile artillery fire was heavy. Despite this, and in spite of determined opposition at many points from the German machine-gunners, in two days our infantry and tanks realized an advance of six miles over difficult country. About many of the woods and villages which lay in the way of our attack there was severe fighting, particularly in the large wood known as the Bois l'Eveque and at Pommereuil, Bousies, Forest, and Vendegies-sur-Ecaillon. This latter village held out till the afternoon of the 24th October, when it was taken by an enveloping attack by troops of the 19th Division and 61st Division.

At the end of that day the western outskirts of the Forêt de Mormal had been reached, our troops were within a mile of Le Quesnoy and to the north-west of that town had captured the villages of Ruesnes and Maing. Local operations during the following three days gave us Englefontaine and established our line well to the north and east of the Le Quesnoy—Valenciennes railway, from the outskirts of Le Quesnoy, past Sepmeries and Artres to Famars.

(48) *The Enemy's Position at the End of October.*

By this time the rapid succession of heavy blows dealt by the British forces had had a cumulative effect, both moral and material, upon the German Armies. The difficulty of replacing the enemy's enormous losses in guns, machine guns and ammunition had increased with every fresh attack, and his reserves of men were exhausted. In the Selle battle the twenty-four British and two American Divisions engaged had captured a further 20,000 prisoners and 475 guns from the thirty-one German divisions opposed to them, and had advanced to a great depth with certainty and precision. Though troops could still be found to offer resistance to our initial assault, the German infantry and machine-gunners were no longer reliable, and cases were being reported of their retiring without fighting in front of our artillery barrage.

The capitulation of Turkey and Bulgaria and the imminent collapse of Austria—consequent upon Allied successes which the desperate position of her own armies on the Western front had rendered her powerless to prevent—had made Germany's military situation ultimately impossible. If her armies were allowed to withdraw undisturbed to shorter lines the struggle might still be protracted over the winter. The British Armies, however, were now in a position to prevent this by a direct attack upon a vital centre, which should anticipate the enemy's withdrawal and force an immediate conclusion.

The Battle of the Sambre (1st-11th November).

(49) The principal British attack was to take place at the beginning of November, as soon as possible after the capture of Valenciennes, which I regarded as a necessary preliminary. In view of the likelihood of fresh withdrawals, time was of importance. Accordingly, at 5.15 a.m. on the 1st November, the XVII. Corps of the Third Army and the XXII. and Canadian Corps of the First Army attacked on a front of about six miles south of Valenciennes, and in the course of two days of heavy fighting inflicted a severe defeat on the enemy. During these two days the 61st Division (Major-General F. J. Duncan), 49th Division (Major-General H. J. G. Cameron) and 4th Division (Major-General C. H. T. Lucas) crossed the Rhonelle River, capturing Maresches and Preseau after a stubborn struggle, and established themselves on the high ground two miles to the east of it. On their left the 4th Canadian Division captured Valenciennes and made progress beyond the town.

As a consequence of this defeat the enemy on the 3rd November withdrew on the Le Quesnoy—Valenciennes front and our line was advanced. There were indications that a further withdrawal was contemplated both in the Tournai salient, where the line of the Scheldt was turned by our progress on the battle front, and also in the area to the south of us, where the enemy's positions were equally threatened by our advance. Our principal attack was ready.

(50) The front of the decisive attack delivered by the Fourth, Third and First Armies on the 4th November extended for a distance of about thirty miles from the Sambre, north of Oisy, to Valenciennes.

The nature of the country across which our advance was to be made was most difficult. In the south the river had to be crossed almost at the outset. In the centre the great Forest of Mormal, though much depleted by German woodcutting, still presented a formidable obstacle. In the north the fortified town of Le Quesnoy, and several streams which ran parallel to the line of our advance offered frequent opportunities for successful defence. On the other hand, our troops had never been so confident of victory or so assured of their own superiority.

After an intense bombardment our troops moved forward to the assault at about dawn, under a most effective artillery barrage, and very soon had penetrated the enemy's positions on the whole battle front. Throughout the day their pressure was never relaxed, and by the evening they had advanced to a depth of five miles, reaching the general line Fesmy—Landrecies—centre of Forêt de Mormal—Wargnies-le-Grand—five miles east of Valenciennes—Onnaing—Scheldt Canal opposite Thiers.

On the right of the attack the 1st Division of the IX. Corps, under the command of Lieut.-General Sir W. P. Braithwaite, starting at 5.45 a.m., captured Catillon, and proceeded to pass troops across the Sambre at this place and at the lock some two miles to the south of it. This difficult operation was accomplished with remarkable rapidity and skill, and by 7.45 a.m., the 1st Battalion Cameron Highlanders and the

1st Battalion Northampton Regiment were east of the river. Bois l'Abbaye, Hautreve, and La Groise were captured in turn, and though held up for a time at Fesmy, our troops took this place also in a renewed attack at 4 p.m., subsequently advancing well to the east of it.

The 32nd Division on the left of the IX. Corps met strong resistance all along the river line. By hard fighting they forced a crossing at Ors, and, pushing forward, took Mezières and Heurtebise, reaching the outskirts of La Folie. Later in the day other troops of this division, having crossed the river south of Landrecies, moved against La Folie from the north, and the village was captured.

Meanwhile the XIII. Corps, under command of Lieut.-General Sir T. L. N. Morland, had attacked at 6.15 a.m., with the 25th, 50th, and 18th Divisions, and quickly overran the enemy's positions, despite strong opposition, which at Preux-au-Bois was maintained until the village was completely surrounded by our infantry and tanks. Severe fighting took place also about Landrecies, where a battalion of the 1st Guard Reserve Division had been specially detailed to hold the bridgehead. Troops of the 25th Division, having overcome this resistance, crossed the Sambre north and south of Landrecies by means of rafts, and captured the town.

The divisions of the Third Army in the centre of the attack also encountered stiff resistance at first, but when this was overcome made rapid progress. The 38th and 17th Divisions of the V. Corps, under command of Lieut.-General C. D. Shute, pushed far into the Forest of Mormal. Before dawn on the 5th November, the 38th Division had reached the eastern edge of the forest, while the 17th Division, after sharp fighting about Locquignol, had penetrated a mile to the east of that village.

On the IV. Corps front the 37th and New Zealand Divisions repulsed a counter-attack north of Ghissignies early in the battle with great loss to the enemy. Thereafter the 37th Division took Louvignies and Jolimetz, with over 1,000 prisoners, and during the late afternoon and evening pushed on to the centre of the forest. By 8 a.m. the New Zealand Division had already surrounded Le Quesnoy. Without attempting to take the town by direct assault, the New Zealand troops swept past, and far to the east of it, capturing Herbignies by the evening. Meanwhile we had gained a footing on the ramparts surrounding Le Quesnoy, and at 4 p.m. the German garrison over 1,000 strong surrendered.

Opposite Orsinval the 62nd Division of the VI. Corps attacked at 5.20 a.m., and as soon as that village had been taken the Guards Division of the same corps attacked on the left of them. Both divisions had hard fighting, but made good progress, capturing Frasnoy and Preux-au-Sart, and reaching the western outskirts of Gommegnies. On the front of the XVII. Corps on the left of the Third Army the enemy's resistance was less vigorous, though sharp fighting took place about Wargnies-le-Petit. This village and Wargnies-le-Grand were taken by the 24th Division (Major-General A. C. Daly) during the afternoon, while the 19th Division captured Bry and Eth.

On the front of th First Army the XXII. Corps and the Canadian Corps advanced against little opposition, except on their right. Here the 11th and 56th Divisions, having crossed the Aunelle River and captured the villages of Le Triez, Sebourg, and Sebourquiaux, were counter-attacked on the high ground east of the Aunelle and pressed back slightly. The 4th and 3rd Canadian Divisions on their left reached the outskirts of Rombies, and the eastern side of the marshes north of Valenciennes.

In these operations and their developments twenty British divisions utterly defeated thirty-two German divisions, and captured 19,000 prisoners and more than 450 guns. On our right the French First Army, which had continued the line of attack southwards to the neighbourhood of Guise, kept pace with our advance, taking 5,000 prisoners and a number of guns.

(51) *The Return to Mons.*

By this great victory the enemy's resistance was definitely broken. On the night 4th-5th November his troops began to fall back on practically the whole battle front. Throughout the following days, despite continuous rain, which imposed great hardships on our troops, infantry and cavalry pressed forward with scarcely a check, maintaining close touch with the rapidly retreating Germans.

On the 5th November the troops of the Fourth Army realized a further advance of some four miles, penetrating beyond Prisches and Maroilles. On the Third Army front the 5th, 21st, and 33rd Divisions pushed forward well to the east of Mormal Forest, while farther north by the evening we were approaching Bavai. Only on the First Army front was the resistance encountered at all serious. Here, after regaining during the morning the ridge east of the Aunelle, and capturing Roisin, Meaurain, and Angreau, the divisions of the XXII. Corps were held up for a time in front of Angre and along the line of the Honnelle River.

Throughout the day, the roads packed with the enemy's troops and transport afforded excellent targets to our airmen, who took full advantage of their opportunities despite the unfavourable weather. Over thirty guns, which bombs and machine-gun fire from the air had forced the enemy to abandon, were captured by a battalion of the 25th Division in the fields near Le Preseau.

On the 6th November considerable opposition was again encountered on the front of the First Army, as well as on the left of the Third Army. Angre, however, was captured, and the Honnelle River crossed, while Canadian troops took Baisieux and Quievrechain. During the night of the 6th-7th November the enemy's resistance again weakened, and early on the morning of the 7th November the Guards Division entered Bavai. Next day Avesnes fell into our hands, Hautmont was captured, and our troops reached the outskirts of Maubeuge.

Meanwhile to the north of the Mons-Condé Canal our success was bearing fruit. During the night of the 7th-8th November numerous explosions were observed behind the German lines, and on the following morning the VIII. Corps and I. Corps (Lieut.-General Sir Arthur Holland) of the First and Fifth Armies were able to move forward, occupying Condé and crossing the Scheldt on a considerable front south of Antoing. Farther north the enemy abandoned his bridgehead at Tournai, and the western portion of the town was occupied by our troops.

On the 9th November the enemy was in general retreat on the whole front of the British Armies. The fortress of Maubeuge was entered by the Guards Division and the 62nd Division (Major-General Sir R. D. Whigham), while the Canadians were approaching Mons. The progress of the Fifth Army was accentuated, and Peruwelz, Antoing, and Tournai captured. The Second Army crossed the Scheldt on its whole front and reached the outskirts of Renaix.

Next day, the advance of the five British Armies continued, cavalry and cyclists operating in advance of the infantry. Only in the neighbourhood of Mons was any substantial opposition met with. Here the Canadians advancing towards the town from south and west, and working round it on the north, encountered an organized and tenacious machine-gun defence. Farther north our cavalry were on the outskirts of Ath, and our line was far to the east of Tournai. Renaix had been captured, and our troops were approaching Grammont.

In the early morning of the 11th November the 3rd Canadian Division captured Mons, the whole of the German defending force being killed or taken prisoners.

(52) *The Armistice.*

At 11 a.m. on the 11th November, in accordance with instructions received from the Commander-in-Chief of the Allied Armies, hostilities were suspended. At that hour the right of the Fourth Army was east of the Franco-Belgian frontier and thence northwards our troops had reached the general line Sivry—Erquelinnes—Boussu—Jurbise—Herghies—Ghislenghien—Lessines—Grammont.

The military situation on the British front on the morning of the 11th November can be stated very shortly. In the fighting since 1st November our troops had broken the enemy's resistance beyond possibility of recovery, and had forced on him a disorderly retreat along the whole front of the British Armies. Thereafter, the enemy was capable neither of accepting nor refusing battle. The utter confusion of his troops, the state of his railways, congested with abandoned trains, the capture of huge quantities of rolling stock and material, all showed that our attack had been decisive. It had been followed on the north by the evacuation of the Tournai salient, and to the south, where the French forces had pushed forward in conjunction with us, by a rapid and costly withdrawal to the line of the Meuse.

The strategic plan of the Allies had been realized with a completeness rarely seen in war. When the armistice was signed by the enemy his defensive powers had already been definitely destroyed. A continuance of hostilities could only have meant disaster to the German Armies and the armed invasion of Germany.

(53) *The Work of the Troops.*

In three months of epic fighting the British Armies in France have brought to a sudden and dramatic end the great wearing-out battle of the past four years.

In our admiration for this outstanding achievement, the long years of patient and heroic struggle by which the strength and spirit of the enemy were gradually broken down cannot be forgotten. The strain of those years was never ceasing, the demands they made upon the best of the Empire's manhood are now known. Yet throughout all those years, and amid the hopes and disappointments they brought with them the confidence of our troops in final victory never wavered. Their courage and resolution rose superior to every test, their cheerfulness never failing however terrible the conditions in which they lived and fought. By the long road they trod with so much faith and with such devoted and self-sacrificing bravery we have arrived at victory, and to-day they have their reward.

The work begun and persevered in so steadfastly by those brave men has been completed during the present year with a thoroughness to which the event bears witness, and with a gallantry which will live for all time in the history of our country. The annals of war hold record of no more wonderful recovery than that which, three months after the tremendous blows showered upon them on the Somme and on the Lys, saw the undefeated British Armies advancing from victory to victory, driving their erstwhile triumphant enemy back to and far beyond the line from which he started, and finally forcing him to acknowledge unconditional defeat.

The great series of victories won by the British forces between the 8th August and the 11th November is the outstanding feature of the events described in this Dispatch. At Amiens and Bapaume, in the breaking of the Drocourt-Quéant and Hindenburg systems, before Le Cateau and on the Selle, in Flanders and on the Sambre, the enemy was again and again brought to battle and defeated.

In the decisive contests of this period, the strongest and most vital parts of the enemy's front were attacked by the British, his lateral communications were cut and his best divisions fought to a standstill. On the different battle fronts

187,000 prisoners and 2,850 guns were captured by us, bringing the total of our prisoners for the present year to over 201,000. Immense numbers of machine guns and trench mortars were taken also, the figures of those actually counted exceeding 29,000 machine guns and some 3,000 trench mortars. These results were achieved by 59 fighting British divisions, which in the course of three months of battle engaged and defeated 99 separate German divisions.

This record furnishes the proof of the skill of our commanders and their staffs, as well as of the fine fighting qualities of the British regimental officer and soldier. It is a proof also of the overwhelmingly decisive part played by the British Armies on the Western front in bringing the enemy to his final defeat.

It is an accepted military doctrine that in good defensive positions any given force can hold up an attacking force of considerably greater numbers. This doctrine was proved in the fighting of March and April of this year, when, despite the enormous superiority of force which the enemy was able to concentrate against the right of the British Armies, all his efforts to effect a definite break-through were frustrated by our defence. Yet, as has been seen, when the tide of battle turned and the British Armies advanced to the attack, throughout practically the whole of the long succession of battles which ended in the complete destruction of the German powers of resistance, the attacking British troops were numerically inferior to the German forces they defeated.

It would be impossible to devise a more eloquent testimony to the unequalled spirit and determination of the British soldier of all ranks and services. We have been accustomed to be proud of the great and noble traditions handed down to us by the soldiers of bygone days. The men who form the Armies of the Empire to-day have created new traditions which are a challenge to the highest records of the past and will be an inspiration to the generations who come after us.

Infantry.

Despite the enormous development of mechanical invention in every phase of warfare, the place which the infantryman has always held as the main substance and foundation of an army is as secure to-day as in any period of history. The infantryman remains the backbone of defence and the spearhead of the attack. At no time has the reputation of the British infantryman been higher, or his achievement more worthy of his renown. During the past three months, the same infantry divisions have advanced to the attack day after day and week after week with an untiring, irresistible ardour which refused to be denied. No praise can be too high for the valour they have shown, no gratitude too deep for the work they have accomplished.

Artillery.

Four years of scientific warfare have seen a consistent and progressive development in the power and influence of artillery, both in the actual infantry battle and in all the stages which lead up to it. Despite the handicap under which we started the war, British artillery has played a large part in that development and of late has dominated the enemy's artillery to an ever-increasing degree. The influence of this fact upon the *moral* both of our own and the enemy's troops could scarcely be exaggerated.

During the present year the greater number of guns available for our use and the amount and regularity of our ammunition supply, combined with the enemy's weakened powers of resistance, due to the bitter fighting of the past two years, have for the most part led to the substitution of sudden and intense outburst of fire for the prolonged destructive bombardments which preceded our attacks in 1917. All ranks of the artillery have adapted themselves to these new conditions with complete success, and in the rapid movements of the latter stages of our advance have shown the highest technical skill and most indefatigable energy. The accuracy and intensity of our barrages, frequently arranged at short notice and with little opportunity being given for ranging or previous reconnoitring of the ground, have contributed largely to the success of our infantry attacks. The intimate co-operation between artillery and infantry, which is the first requisite in modern war, has been a marked feature of our operations.

Cavalry.

The more open character of the recent fighting at once brought prominently to notice the fact that cavalry is still a necessary arm in modern war. On a number of occasions, to some of which short reference has been made in this Report, important results have been obtained by the use of cavalry, particularly in combination with light tanks and mobile machine-gun units. Such increased opportunities as have been offered them have been seized and utilized by the cavalry with promptness and effect. Both in the development of the successes of our infantry attacks and in following up the various withdrawals thereby forced upon the enemy, the different cavalry units have performed work of the highest value.

Royal Air Force.

During the past year the work of our airmen, in close co-operation with all fighting branches of the Army, has continued to show the same brilliant qualities which have come to be commonly associated with that Service; while the ever-increasing size of the Royal Air Force and the constant improvement in the power and performance of machines, combined with the unfailing keenness of pilots and observers, have enabled intense activity to be maintained at all times.

Some idea of the magnitude of the operations carried out can be gathered from the fact that, from the beginning of January 1918 to the end of November, nearly 5,500 tons of bombs were dropped by us, 2,953 hostile aeroplanes were destroyed, in addition to 1,178 others driven down out of control, 241 German observation balloons were shot down in flames, and an area of over 4,000 square miles of country has been photographed, not once but many times.

The assistance given to the infantry by our low-flying aeroplanes during the battles of March and April was repeated during the German offensives on the Aisne and Marne, on both of which occasions British squadrons were dispatched to the French battle front and did very gallant service. During our own attacks, hostile troops and transport have been constantly and heavily attacked with most excellent results.

Both by day and night our bombing squadrons have continually attacked the enemy's railway junctions and centres of activity, reconnaissance machines have supplied valuable information from both far and near, while artillery machines have been indefatigable in their watch over German batteries and in accurate observation for our own guns. In these latter tasks our balloons have done most valuable work and have kept pace with admirable energy and promptness with the ever-changing battle line.

Tanks.

Since the opening of our offensive on 8th August, tanks have been employed in every battle, and the importance of the part played by them in breaking the resistance of the German infantry can scarcely be exaggerated. The whole scheme of the attack of the 8th August was dependent upon tanks, and ever since that date on numberless occasions the success of our infantry has been powerfully assisted or confirmed by their timely arrival. So great has been the effect produced upon the German infantry by the appearance of

British tanks that in more than one instance, when for various reasons real tanks were not available in sufficient numbers, valuable results have been obtained by the use of dummy tanks painted on frames of wood and canvas.

It is no disparagement of the courage of our infantry, or of the skill and devotion of our artillery, to say that the achievements of those essential arms would have fallen short of the full measure of success achieved by our Armies had it not been for the very gallant and devoted work of the Tank Corps, under the command of Major-General H. J. Elles.

Trench Mortars.

Throughout the period under review the personnel of the trench mortar batteries, both heavy, medium, and light, have continued to discharge their duties with skill and efficiency whenever opportunity offered for the effective use of their arms. During the period of trench warfare the heavier types of trench mortars well maintained their superiority over the enemy, while during the war of movement later in the campaign numerous instances were reported when the lighter types have been used with effect well forward in the attack in overcoming the resistance of hostile strong points.

Machine Gun Corps.

The high reputation earned by the different units of the Machine Gun Corps during the defensive battles of the spring has been well maintained under the changed conditions of the latter part of the year. The great value of the machine gun in the attack, when handled with energy and decision, has been proved again and again. The consistent failure of the enemy's frequent counter-attacks has been due in no small degree to the skilful use of these weapons.

Royal Engineers.

Reference has already been made to the vast amount of work carried out on new defences during the earlier part of the period under review. In the construction of the 5,000 miles of new trench 20 million cubic yards of earth were shifted, while the wire entanglements erected in front of the trench lines consumed 23,500 tons of barbed wire and 15 million wooden or steel pickets.

During the period of our offensive all branches of the Royal Engineers and the Engineer units of the Dominions have shown the greatest energy and skill in the discharge of their different tasks. On many occasions, particularly in the construction of bridges under fire and in the removal of mines, they have shown courage of the highest order.

In the course of our advance some 700 road bridges, exclusive of pontoon bridges, were constructed. Many of these, and in addition a large number of footbridges for infantry assault, were constructed under heavy shell and machine-gun fire. Notable instances of the cool pluck and determination displayed in this work were furnished by a field company of the 38th Division, which in a crossing of the Selle River lost 50 per cent. of its effectives, yet completed its bridge, and by the fine performance of Engineer troops of the 1st Division at the crossing of the Sambre on the 4th November.

The work of the tunnelling companies has demanded equally with that of the field companies great courage and skill. In the period from the 8th August to the termination of hostilities nearly 14,000 German mines and traps of various descriptions, totalling over 540 tons of explosives, had been discovered and rendered harmless by the different tunnelling companies, while a further amount of nearly 300 tons of explosives had been withdrawn from our own demolition charges and minefields.

The provision of water for the troops presented a problem of great difficulty, which was met with equal energy and success. Many miles of new water mains were laid, and over 400 mechanical pumping plants, giving a daily yield of some 20 million gallons of water, were installed as our troops advanced. In addition to work of the kind performed by the transportation services, Engineer troops were responsible also for the repair of some 3,500 miles of roads, including the filling in of some 500 road craters.

Gas Services.

Prior to the commencement of the advance several important gas operations, in which large quantities of gas were discharged, were carried out successfully by the Special Brigade. After our advance had begun, immediate advantage was taken of any temporary stabilization of the line to carry out a large number of useful operations of a lesser character, wherever it was possible to do so without danger to the lives of French civilians.

Some idea of the magnitude of the work performed and of the energy and zeal displayed by all ranks can be gained from the fact that the 21 Special Companies, with the assistance of two American companies attached for instruction, discharged during the period March–November a total of over 2,250 tons of gas. Between the 11th March and the 7th October gas was discharged on 119 nights out of 210, and no less than 301 separate operations were successfully carried out, in addition to a large number of others, which, when all preparations had been completed, had to be abandoned in consequence of changes in the tactical situation. In all these different operations all ranks of the Gas Services have shown their accustomed courage and devotion to duty.

Signal Services.

The constant movement of the line and the shifting of headquarters has again imposed an enormous strain upon all ranks of the Signal Service. The depth of our advance, and the fact that during the latter part of it the whole of the British Armies were simultaneously involved, made the maintenance of signal communications most difficult. The fact that in such circumstances the needs of the Army were met reflects the highest credit upon the zeal and efficiency of all ranks.

Transportation Services.

Attention has already been drawn to the work thrown upon the Transportation Services as the result of the German advances during the early part of the year. From the commencement of the British offensive in August the situation became reversed. Defensive measures were abandoned, and the energies of all concerned were centred upon the reconstruction of the railway system recaptured from the enemy. In spite of the fact that the enemy, as he withdrew, used every modern artifice for the destruction of railways, roads, bridges, and water supplies, the Railway Construction troops were able to meet all demands and accomplished successfully an unparalleled programme of railway reconstruction. By the end of October no less than 1,050 miles of line, much of which had been destroyed, had been brought into service for our Armies. This included 485 miles of new track and some 4,000 feet of bridging.

The following is an instance of the speed with which the work of reconstruction was carried out. On the 17th October, Lille was evacuated by the enemy. On the 25th October the first train of supplies for the civil population entered the city, the railway having been carried across the Lys River at Armentières by a bridge constructed in the short space of four days. Some idea of the extent of the traffic dealt with can be gathered from the fact that in a period of six months nearly seven million officers and other ranks were carried by the broad and metre gauge railways. The number of ton miles worked by the light railway systems during a similar period amounted to over 21 millions.

The troops engaged upon this work have been drawn from the British Railway Companies and from Canada. They have worked continuously for months under great pressure. The energy and efficiency displayed in administration and execution are beyond all praise. I desire to acknowledge the great assistance rendered by the British railways and local authorities at home in supplying personnel, locomotives, wagons, and plant, the valuable service of Canadian railway troops, and the loyal co-operation and assistance of the French railways.

A similar expansion is to be noticed in the work of the Roads Directorate. In June 1917, the mileage of roads maintained was 1,640; in October of 1918 it was 4,412. During a period of six months of the present year 1,500,000 tons of road stone and 685,000 sleepers and pit props were used upon the roads. The enormous demand for material is reflected in a greatly increased output from the quarries and forests worked by us.

The work at the Base Ports has been discharged during the past year with an efficiency and dispatch undiminished by the fact that the ports have been persistently and heavily attacked by hostile aircraft. During the period under review the Channel Train Ferry Service, opened in February last, has proved of inestimable value.

As the result of the enemy's advance in the spring, the length of Inland Waterways operated by the British fell to less than 250 miles. By October, however, the mileage operated had risen to 464 miles, and, throughout our advance, every effort has been made to open up for navigation the waterways uncovered by the enemy's retreat. Very satisfactory results have been obtained and very valuable and important service has been rendered by the personnel concerned.

Supply Services.

The demands made by our Armies upon the Supply Services throughout the period under review were great and increasing. Every advance made supply more difficult, and during the later stages of our offensive the work was complicated by the necessity of feeding many thousands of liberated civilians in the reconquered territories. Despite the magnitude of their task, these services rose magnificently to the demands made upon them. It is in no small degree due to their excellent organization and administration that our Armies in the Field have never lacked food, clothing, equipment, guns, or munitions. The greatest testimony to the efficiency of these services is the rapidity of our advances, which otherwise would have been impossible. Their work was unostentatious, but its effect was far reaching.

Forestry.

During the twelve months ended on the 31st October 1918, over two and a half million tons of timber have been cut for the use of the British and French Armies by the different units under the control of the Forestry Directorate. The work has been carried out with admirable thoroughness and efficiency in close co-operation with the Forestry Authorities of other Allied Armies, and has resulted in a very material saving of transport.

The Omnibus Park.

In my last Dispatch I referred to the invaluable work performed by the Auxiliary Omnibus Park throughout the German offensive. During the period under review further heavy calls have been made upon it in connection with our advance. In all, a total of nearly 800,000 troops have been carried and over 2,500,000 miles have been run by the Omnibus

Park. In accomplishing this task all ranks concerned have once more shown the same zeal and devotion to duty which distinguished their previous conduct.

The Labour Corps.

Throughout the period under review the demands upon the Labour Corps were incessant. The British labour companies were composed entirely of men medically unfit for active operations, and more than half their number owed their incapacity to wounds or sickness incurred while serving with fighting units. The men of the Corps, however, made light of their disabilities. Many companies worked for months on end under shell fire, long marches were willingly undertaken, and the essential work entrusted to them was cheerfully performed often under conditions entailing all the hardship and strain without the excitement of actual fighting. The successive British advances imposed upon all ranks daily increasing work and responsibilities. It is to the credit of the Corps and of the excellent system of command and administration developed in it during the earlier part of the year that the Labour Companies have invariably answered all demands made upon them.

Medical Services.

During the period under review the Medical Services, under the direction of Lieut.-General C. H. Burtchaell, deserve special commendation for the initiative, energy, and success which have characterized all branches of their work. The rapid advance of the troops and the extended front on which operations were carried out during the final stages of the offensive created problems in connection with the collection, evacuation, and treatment of wounded which had not been met with in the earlier phases of the war. These difficulties were met with the most admirable promptness and efficiency.

My thanks are due to the consulting surgeons and physicians

for the invaluable assistance given by them in the application of new methods to the treatment of wounds and disease; to the R.A.M.C. Officers and Permanent Staffs of the Convalescent Depôts for work which enabled many thousands of men to be restored to the fighting ranks; to the untiring and devoted work of the British Red Cross Society, the Order of St. John, and all members of the Nursing Services, whose unremitting kindness and constancy have done much to alleviate the sufferings of the sick and wounded; and finally for the very valuable services rendered by the Base Hospital Units and by individual officers of the Medical Corps of the United States of America, attached to the British Army.

The Chaplain's Department.

Under the direction of the Principal Chaplain, the Rev. J. M. Simms, and the Deputy Chaplain-General, The Right Rev. Bishop Gwynne, the clergy of all denominations ministering to the Army have earned the admiration and affection of all ranks. I desire once more to express on behalf of all officers and men my profound appreciation of their unfailing devotion and self-sacrifice.

Administrative Services and Departments.

To all other Administrative Services and Departments I desire to express the thanks of the fighting forces for the loyal and efficient manner in which they have carried out their essential tasks. During a period of great strain and incessant work they have contributed in their various spheres to the smooth working of the Army machine, and are entitled to a full share in the victory of our arms.

The Navy and Home Authorities.

The thanks of all ranks of the British Armies in France and Flanders are once more due to the Royal Navy and Mercantile Marine for their magnificent work, which throughout the heavy demands of the past year has at all times enabled our needs to be supplied.

We thank also the different Home Authorities and the workers in the great munition factories, both men and women, for the magnificent support they have given us through all stages of the war. We understand and appreciate the value of the work they have done.

Our Allies.

At the moment when the final triumph of the Allied cause is assured, we and all others of the Allied and Associated Armies can look back on the years that have gone with a satisfaction undimmed by any hint of discord or conflict of interest and ideals. Few alliances of the past can boast such a record. Few can show a purpose more tenaciously and faithfully pursued, or so fully and gloriously realized. If the complete unity and harmony of our action is to be ascribed in part to the justice of our cause, it is due also to the absolute loyalty with which that cause has been pursued by all those entrusted with the control of the different Allied Armies that have fought side by side with ours.

I propose to submit at a later date a further and final dispatch dealing with the advance of the British Armies to the Rhine and the occupation of the Cologne bridgehead.

I have the honour to be, my Lord,

Your Lordship's obedient servant,

D. HAIG, Field-Marshal,

Commanding-in-Chief, British Armies in France.

APPENDIX V.

TERMS OF ARMISTICE WITH GERMANY.

(Signed at 5 a.m. on November 11th.)

A.—Clauses relating to Western Front.

I.—Cessation of operations by land and in the air six hours after the signature of the Armistice [viz., at 11 a.m.].

II.—Immediate evacuation of invaded countries—Belgium, France, Alsace-Lorraine, Luxemburg—so ordered as to be completed within fourteen days from the signature of the Armistice.

German troops which have not left the above-mentioned territories within the period fixed will become prisoners of war.

Occupation by the Allied and United States Forces jointly will keep pace with evacuation in these areas.

All movements of evacuation and occupation will be regulated in accordance with a Note (Annexure 1).

III.—Repatriation, beginning at once, to be completed within fourteen days, of all inhabitants of the countries above enumerated (including hostages, persons under trial, or convicted).

IV.—Surrender in good condition by the German Armies of the following equipment :—

5,000 guns (2,500 heavy, 2,500 field).
30,000 machine-guns.
3,000 *Minenwerfer*.
2,000 aeroplanes (fighters, bombers—firstly D. 7's —and night bombing machines).

The above to be delivered *in situ* to the Allied and United States troops in accordance with the detailed conditions laid down in the Note (Annexure 1).

V.—Evacuation by the German Armies of the countries on the left bank of the Rhine. These countries on the left bank of the Rhine shall be administered by the local authorities under the control of the Allied and United States Armies of occupation.

The occupation of these territories will be carried out by Allied and United States garrisons holding the principal crossings of the Rhine (Mayence, Coblenz, Cologne), together with bridgeheads at these points of a 30 kilometre [about 19 miles] radius on the right bank, and by garrisons similarly holding the strategic points of the regions.

A neutral zone shall be set up on the right bank of the Rhine between the river and a line drawn 10 kilometres [6¼ miles] distant, starting from the Dutch frontier to the Swiss frontier. In the case of inhabitants, no person shall be prosecuted for having taken part in any military measures previous to the signing of the Armistice.

No measure of a general or official character shall be taken which would have, as a consequence, the depreciation of industrial establishments or a reduction of their *personnel*.

Evacuation by the enemy of the Rhinelands shall be so ordered as to be completed within a further period of sixteen days—in all thirty-one days after the signature of the Armistice.

All movements of evacuation and occupation will be regulated according to the Note (Annexure 1).

VI.—In all territory evacuated by the enemy there shall be no evacuation of inhabitants; no damage or harm shall be done to the persons or property of the inhabitants.

No destruction of any kind to be committed.

Military establishments of all kinds shall be delivered intact, as well as military stores of food, munitions, equipment not removed during the periods fixed for evacuation.

Stores of food of all kinds for the civil population, cattle, etc., shall be left *in situ*.

Industrial establishments shall not be impaired in any way, and their *personnel* shall not be moved.

VII.—Roads and means of communication of every kind, railroads, waterways, main roads, bridges, telegraphs, telephones shall be in no manner impaired.

All civil and military *personnel* at present employed on them shall remain.

5,000 locomotives, 150,000 wagons, and 5,000 motor lorries in good working order, with all necessary spare parts and fittings, shall be delivered to the Associated Powers within the period fixed for the evacuation of Belgium and Luxemburg.

The railways of Alsace-Lorraine shall be handed over within the same period, together with all pre-war *personnel* and material.

Further, material necessary for the working of railways in the country on the left bank of the Rhine shall be left *in situ*.

All stores of coal and material for upkeep of permanent way, signals, and repair shops shall be left *in situ* and kept in an efficient state by Germany, as far as the means of communication are concerned, during the whole period of the Armistice.

All barges taken from the Allies shall be restored to them. The Note appended as Annexure 2 regulates the detail of these measures.

VIII.—The German Command shall be responsible for revealing all mines or delay-action fuses disposed on territory evacuated by the German troops, and shall assist in their discovery and destruction.

The German Command shall also reveal all destructive

measures that may have been taken (such as poisoning or pollution of springs, wells, etc.), under penalty of reprisals.

IX.—The right of requisition shall be exercised by the Allied and United States Armies in all occupied territory, save for settlement of accounts with authorized persons.

The upkeep of the troops of occupation in the Rhineland (excluding Alsace-Lorraine) shall be charged to the German Government.

X.—The immediate repatriation, without reciprocity, according to detailed conditions which shall be fixed, of all Allied and United States prisoners of war; the Allied Powers and the United States of America shall be able to dispose of these prisoners as they wish. However, the return of German prisoners of war interned in Holland and Switzerland shall continue as heretofore. The return of German prisoners of war shall be settled at peace preliminaries.

XI.—Sick and wounded who cannot be removed from evacuated territory will be cared for by German *personnel*, who will be left on the spot, with the medical material required.

B.—Clauses relating to the Eastern Frontiers of Germany.

XII.—All German troops at present in any territory which before the war belonged to Russia, Rumania, or Turkey, shall withdraw within the frontiers of Germany as they existed on August 1st, 1914; and all German troops at present in territories which before the war formed part of Russia must likewise return to within the frontiers of Germany as above defined as soon as the Allies shall think the moment suitable, having regard to the internal situation of these territories.

XIII.—Evacuation by German troops to begin at once; and all German instructors, prisoners, and civilian as well as military agents now on the territory of Russia (as defined on August 1st, 1914) to be recalled.

XIV.—German troops to cease at once all requisitions and

seizures, and any other undertaking with a view to obtaining supplies intended for Germany in Rumania and Russia, as defined on August 1st, 1914.

XV.—Abandonment of the Treaties of Bukarest and Brest-Litovsk and of the Supplementary Treaties.

XVI.—The Allies shall have free access to the territories evacuated by the Germans on their Eastern frontier, either through Danzig or by the Vistula, in order to convey supplies to the populations of these territories or for the purpose of maintaining order.

C.—Clause relating to East Africa.

XVII.—Unconditional evacuation of all German forces operating in East Africa within one month.

D.—General Clauses.

XVIII.—Repatriation, without reciprocity, within a maximum period of one month, in accordance with detailed conditions hereafter to be fixed, of all civilians interned or deported who may be citizens of other Allied or Associated States than those mentioned in Clause III.

XIX.—With the reservation that any future claims and demands of the Allies and United States of America remain unaffected, the following financial conditions are required:—

Reparation for damage done.

While the Armistice lasts no public securities shall be removed by the enemy which can serve as a pledge to the Allies for the recovery or reparation for war losses.

Immediate restitution of the cash deposit in the National Bank of Belgium, and, in general, immediate return of all documents, specie, stocks, shares, paper money, together with plant for the issue thereof, touching public or private interests in the invaded countries.

Restitution of the Russian and Rumanian gold yielded to Germany or taken by that Power.

This gold to be delivered in trust to the Allies until the signature of peace.

E.—Naval Conditions.

XX.—Immediate cessation of all hostilities at sea, and definite information to be given as to the location and movements of all German ships.

Notification to be given to neutrals that freedom of navigation in all territorial waters is given to the Naval and Mercantile Marines of the Allied and Associated Powers, all questions of neutrality being waived.

XXI.—All Naval and Mercantile Marine prisoners of war of the Allied and Associated Powers in German hands to be returned, without reciprocity.

XXII.—Handing over to the Allies and the United States of all submarines (including all submarine cruisers and minelayers) which are present at the moment with full complement in the ports specified by the Allies and the United States. Those that cannot put to sea to be deprived of crews and supplies, and shall remain under the supervision of the Allies and the United States. Submarines ready to put to sea shall be prepared to leave German ports immediately on receipt of wireless order to sail to the port of surrender, the remainder to follow as early as possible. The conditions of this Article shall be carried [out] within fourteen days after the signing of the Armistice.

XXIII.—The following German surface warships, which shall be designated by the Allies and the United States of America, shall forthwith be disarmed and thereafter interned in neutral ports, or, failing them, Allied ports, to be designated by the Allies and the United States of America, and placed under the surveillance of the Allies and the United States of America, only caretakers being left on board, namely :—

6 Battle Cruisers.
10 Battleships.
8 Light Cruisers, including two minelayers.
50 Destroyers of the most modern types.

All other surface warships (including river craft) are to be concentrated in German Naval bases to be designated by the Allies and the United States of America, and are to be paid off and completely disarmed and placed under the supervision of the Allies and the United States of America. All vessels of the auxiliary fleet (trawlers, motor-vessels, etc.) are to be disarmed. All vessels specified for internment shall be ready to leave German ports seven days after the signing of the Armistice. Directions of the voyage will be given by wireless.

NOTE.—A declaration has been signed by the Allied Delegates and handed to the German Delegates, to the effect that, in the event of ships not being handed over owing to the mutinous state of the Fleet, the Allies reserve the right to occupy Heligoland as an advanced base to enable them to enforce the terms of the Armistice. The German Delegates have on their part signed a Declaration that they will recommend the Chancellor to accept this.

XXIV.—The Allies and the United States of America shall have the right to sweep up all minefields and obstructions laid by Germany outside German territorial waters, and the positions of these are to be indicated.

XXV.—Freedom of access to and from the Baltic to be given to the Naval and Mercantile Marines of the Allied and Associated Powers. To secure this, the Allies and the United States of America shall be empowered to occupy all German forts, fortifications, batteries, and defence works of all kinds in all the entrances from the Kattegat into the Baltic, and to sweep up all mines and obstructions within and without German territorial waters without any questions of neutrality being raised, and the positions of all such mines and obstructions are to be indicated.

XXVI.—The existing blockade conditions set up by the Allied and Associated Powers are to remain unchanged, and all German merchant ships found at sea are to remain liable to capture. The Allies and United States contemplate the provisioning of Germany during the Armistice as shall be found necessary.

XXVII.—All Naval aircraft are to be concentrated and immobilized in German bases to be specified by the Allies and the United States of America.

XXVIII.—In evacuating the Belgian coasts and forts Germany shall abandon all merchant ships, tugs, lighters, cranes, and all other harbour materials, all materials for inland navigation, all aircraft and air materials and stores, all arms and armaments, and all stores and apparatus of all kinds.

XXIX.—All Black Sea ports are to be evacuated by Germany; all Russian warships of all descriptions seized by Germany in the Black Sea are to be handed over to the Allies and the United States of America; all neutral merchant ships seized are to be released; all warlike and other materials of all kinds seized in those ports are to be returned, and German materials as specified in Clause XXVIII. are to be abandoned.

XXX.—All merchant ships in German hands belonging to the Allied and Associated Powers are to be restored in ports to be specified by the Allies and the United States of America without reciprocity.

XXXI.—No destruction of ships or of materials to be permitted before evacuation, surrender, or restoration.

XXXII.—The German Government shall formally notify the neutral Governments of the world, and particularly the Governments of Norway, Sweden, Denmark, and Holland, that all restrictions placed on the trading of their vessels with the Allied and Associated countries, whether by the German Government or by private German interests, and whether in return for specific concessions, such as the export of shipbuilding materials or not, are immediately cancelled.

XXXIII.—No transfers of German merchant shipping of any description to any neutral flag are to take place after signature of the Armistice.

F.—Duration of Armistice.

XXXIV.—The duration of the Armistice is to be 36 days, with option to extend, During this period, on failure of execution of any of the above clauses, the Armistice may be denounced by one of the contracting parties on 48 hours' previous notice.

G.—Time Limit for Reply.

XXXV.—This Armistice to be accepted or refused by Germany within 72 hours of notification.

APPENDIX VI.

Sir Douglas Haig's Final Dispatch.

THE ADVANCE INTO GERMANY.

General Headquarters,
British Armies in France,
21st March 1919.

Sir,

I have the honour to submit the following final Dispatch in which is described the advance of the British Forces into Germany and the occupation of the bridgehead east of the Rhine at Cologne. I include in this Dispatch a brief review of the chief features of military interest which stand out among the operations of the British Armies on the Western front during the time I have been in command of them. I take this last opportunity also to refer by name to some few of the many able and gallant officers who have assisted me in my task, and to thank them personally.

PART I.

The Advance into Germany

(11th Nov. 1918—31st Dec. 1918).

Arrangements for the Advance.

(1) At 11.00 on the 11th November 1918, at which hour and date the armistice granted to Germany by the Allies took

effect, the British front extended over a distance of about 60 miles from the neighbourhood of Montbliart, East of Avesnes, to just North of Grammont (*vide* attached map).* This front from South to North was held by troops of the Fourth, Third, First, Fifth, and Second British Armies, all of whom were in hot pursuit of the enemy at the moment when the armistice came into operation.

The provisions of the armistice had settled in general terms the course to be followed subsequently by the belligerent groups of Armies. To co-ordinate the action of the Allied Armies, instructions of a more detailed character were issued by Marshal Foch to all concerned, and these formed the basis of the orders given by me during the period covered by this Dispatch.

Troops were at once directed not to advance East of the line reached by them at the time when hostilities ceased, and certain parties of Germans taken prisoner after that hour were returned to the enemy. Outposts were established along this line both for the sake of military security and in order to prevent all possibility of fraternization. Behind these outposts the remainder of our forces were grouped and concentrated.

It was arranged that the forward movement of the different Allied Armies should be carried out by certain definite stages, through separate zones of action. The zone allotted to the British Armies extended from the front then held by us in an easterly direction as far as the German frontier, whence it continued in a North-easterly direction to the Cologne Bridgehead. The boundaries of this zone and the stages of the advance are shown on the attached map. †

In order to permit the enemy to withdraw his troops from the area immediately in front of us, our positions were maintained unchanged until the morning of the 17th November. Thereafter, to avoid all possibility of collision between the opposing forces, the movement of troops towards the frontier

* Not reproduced. † Not reproduced.

was regulated so as to preserve a safety zone of 10 kilometres in depth between our advanced detachments and the enemy's rearguards.

The general advance into Germany was directed to begin on the 1st December. On the 12th December, French, American, and British forces would cross the Rhine at Mayence, Coblentz, and Cologne, and commence the occupation of bridgeheads having a radius of 30 kilometres from the crossings at those towns. By that date, the enemy was bound by the terms of the armistice to have withdrawn his military forces a distance of 10 kilometres from the right bank of the Rhine and from the perimeter of the Rhine bridgeheads.

Readjustment of the British Forces.

(2) As we progressed eastwards, the front held by the British Armies, already short, would automatically be decreased. On the other hand, the maintenance of supply across and beyond the battle areas presented difficulties which would grow rapidly as our communications lengthened. These two considerations made it both feasible and necessary to effect a redistribution of troops, so that the extent of the forces advancing into Germany should be no more than was absolutely necessary to meet military requirements.

I decided that the opening stages of our advance should be carried out by the Second and Fourth Armies, under command of the two senior Army Commanders—General Plumer and General Rawlinson—and that each Army should consist of four Corps, each of four divisions. To ensure rapidity of movement and to facilitate supply, the artillery and auxiliary arms and services accompanying these Armies were cut down to a minimum, and all surplus units then attached to them were transferred to the First, Third, and Fifth Armies. Arrangements were made for reorganizing these last-mentioned Armies and for withdrawing them to areas farther West.

The Advance to the German Frontier.

(3) At 05.00 on the morning of the 17th November the 2nd Cavalry Division covering the front of the Fourth Army, and the 1st and 3rd Cavalry Divisions covering the front of the Second Army crossed the line reached on the 11th November and commenced the march to the German Frontier. The leading infantry divisions moved forward on the following day.

The advance was carried out under active service conditions, cavalry leading, and all military precautions being taken. Among all arms, the general bearing, smartness, and march discipline of the troops were of a high order, reflecting credit on the Army and the nation. All traces of the desperate fighting and forced marches of the previous months had been removed, and men, horses, guns, and vehicles appeared as though turned out for parade. Throughout the advance, despite long distances covered under difficult conditions, indifferent billets, and the absence of the usual opportunities for bathing or renewing clothes, the same general standard of excellence was maintained in a remarkable degree.

The first troops to complete the portion of our advance which lay through Belgium were patrols of the 2nd Cavalry Division, who arrived on the German frontier in the neighbourhood of Beho on the night of the 28-29th November. Next day the frontier was reached by the 1st Cavalry Division along the whole front of our advance. The infantry, who had been marching steadily in rear of the cavalry, closed up behind them in readiness for the advance into Germany.

During this part of our march the various stages above referred to were strictly observed, except that in front of our general advance detachments of cavalry had been sent forward to keep order in Charleroi and Namur in response to requests received from the local authorities. Everywhere our troops were received with the utmost enthusiasm by the population of the liberated districts.

In every town and village streets were festooned with flags

and spanned by triumphal arches bearing messages of welcome. Men, women, and children thronged to meet our troops and exchange greetings in French and English. Nor was their gratitude confined to demonstrations such as these. Wherever our men were billeted during their advance everything possible was done for their comfort. In many cases refreshment was pressed upon them without payment, and on all sides, despite the shortage of food from which the occupied districts of Belgium had long suffered, the generosity of the civil population found means to supplement the rations of our troops.

During this period large numbers of released prisoners of war, French and British, came through our lines and were passed back to collecting stations. The enemy seems to have liberated the majority of the Allied prisoners west of the Rhine without making any provision for their feeding and conveyance. The result was that much unnecessary suffering was caused to these unfortunate individuals, while a not inconsiderable additional burden was placed upon our own transport and supplies.

Supply Difficulties.

(4) Throughout the whole of the advance, and especially in the stage which followed the crossing of the German frontier, very great, but unavoidable, difficulties were encountered in connection with supply.

At the time of the armistice railheads were on the general line Le Cateau, Valenciennes, Lille, Courtrai, and for many miles in front of them bridges had been broken and track torn up or destroyed by mines. Even after the cessation of hostilities delay-action mines, which the enemy had laid in the course of his retreat without preserving exact record of their location, went up from time to time, causing serious interruption to traffic. The clearing of these mines was a work of considerable risk, and the fact that comparatively so few mines exploded after trains had begun to run is entirely due to the great courage and skill with which officers, non-commissioned officers and men of the Tunnelling Companies performed the difficult and dangerous task of detecting them and rendering them harmless. The work of reconstruction, therefore, was most arduous, continuing day and night. The speed with which it was completed reflects great credit upon all ranks of the British Railway Companies and the Canadian Railway Troops Corps, as well as on the Railway Construction Engineers who controlled their work. Credit is due also to the personnel of the Railway Operating Division, who were called upon to keep traffic open with scarcely any of the ordinary traffic facilities.

Though roads had been pushed farther ahead the same general conditions applied to them, while the extraordinary amount of traffic which it was necessary to direct along them made maintenance very difficult. Up to the night of the 25-26th November, on which date the railway was carried across the gap between Valenciennes and Mons, the Corps of the Second Army were still based on the railheads west of the river Scheldt, and supplies had to be brought forward by double and treble echelons of lorries. At the close of this period divisions were being fed by means of narrow one-way roads at distances of from 80 to 100 miles from their railheads. This imposed a great strain on the personnel of the Motor Transport Units and Mobile Repair Shops, who were compelled to work long hours under very trying and anxious conditions. I am glad to express my deep appreciation of the devoted service rendered by all ranks.

Until roads and railways could be got through to the areas which the enemy had not damaged the progress of our troops was necessarily limited by our ability to supply them. Only by the greatest effort on the part of the departments concerned with reconstruction and supply, and at the expense of considerable hardship to the leading troops of the Fourth and Second Armies, and in particular the cavalry, could the programme of our advance be maintained. Troops were denied frequently and for long periods comforts which they had been accustomed to obtain even under battle conditions. Nothing beyond bare necessities could be got forward to them. Even these were at times short in some units, and on more than one occasion the only available supplies of food were the current day's issue carried on the man.

Many other causes conspired to render the problem of supply one of serious difficulty throughout our advance. At the date of the armistice the amount of available rolling stock had been no more than sufficient to meet the requirements of our Armies. The advance to the Rhine added over 200 miles to the distances to be covered, and greatly reduced the amount of rolling stock available by largely increasing the time required for each train to complete its journey. The necessity for supplying the civil population of the territories through which the Allied Armies were advancing and the resumption of French civilian traffic put an additional strain upon our pooled resources. This strain was not met by rolling stock taken over from the enemy, which came in very slowly, and was much of it unfit for immediate service.

In this connection it is not out of place to refer to the work done by the British Army in providing food and medical attendance for the civil population of the liberated districts through which we passed, a population which in France alone amounted to nearly 800,000 persons. This duty, though very willingly accepted by us, none the less made no small demands upon both rail and road transport. In France it entailed the supply and distribution of more than 5,000,000 rations during a period exceeding six weeks, until the French were able to complete their arrangements for relieving us of the task. The service we were able to render in the name of humanity has been most generously acknowledged by the French authorities.

The fulfilment of our programme under such conditions would have been impossible without the exercise of great patience and whole-hearted co-operation on the part of the troops. Nor was it less dependent upon the untiring energy and efficiency displayed by commanders and staffs in the methodical arrangement of the details of our advance and the concentration of our resources. I desire to place on record my appreciation of the careful forethought of the Staff and of the excellent conduct of all ranks under very trying conditions.

It will readily be understood from the foregoing that had our advance been conducted against active opposition, even from a beaten and demoralized enemy, our progress must have been greatly delayed. The difficulties of supply would have been enormously increased in many ways, among which would have been the necessity of bringing forward large quantities of ammunition. Bridges, railways, and roads would have been destroyed in front of us or blown up after we had passed, by delay-action mines. Immense loss would have been caused to property of all descriptions and incalculable suffering inflicted upon the inhabitants of the invaded districts of Belgium, France, and Luxembourg.

Further Readjustment of Troops.

(5) Towards the close of the advance to the German frontier, a further readjustment was effected in the disposition of my troops.

The sector allotted to the British Forces in the general scheme for the occupation of the Rhine Provinces was too narrow to admit of the employment of more than a single Army Command. I therefore directed that the German territory to be occupied by us should be held by General Plumer's Second Army, which for this purpose should be composed as follows :—The II. Corps (9th, 29th, and New Zealand Divisions), the VI. Corps (Guards, 2nd, and 3rd Divisions), the IX. Corps (1st, 6th, and 62nd Divisions), the Canadian Corps (1st and 2nd Canadian Divisions), and the 1st Cavalry Division. The various changes and transfers necessary to give effect to this arrangement involved the taking over by the Second Army of the whole of the British front of advance, and the gradual withdrawal of the troops of the Fourth Army to the area west of the frontier and about Namur.

The Advance into Germany.

(6) On the morning of the 1st December, a date for ever memorable as witnessing the consummation of the hopes and efforts of 4½ years of heroic fighting, the 1st Cavalry Division crossed the frontier between Belgium and Germany. On the same day the 2nd and 1st Canadian Divisions of the Canadian Corps and the 29th and 9th Divisions of the II. Corps resumed their march towards the frontier.

On this date, however, the supply situation became critical, trains due on the 30th November failing to arrive until the night of the 1st-2nd December. In consequence for two days the Army remained practically stationary, and it was not until the 4th December that progress was resumed.

In this stage of our march the line of our advance traversed the northern portion of the Ardennes, and, particularly on the right in the Canadian Corps area, the country through which our troops were passing was of a most difficult character. Practicable roads were few, villages were far apart, and facilities for billeting very limited. Our way lay across a country of great hills rising to over 2,000 feet, covered by wide stretches of forest, and cut by deep and narrow valleys, along the steep sides of which the roads wound in countless sudden curves. Marches were long, while the surface of the roads, which had already borne the traffic of the retreating German Armies, suffered anew under the passage of our columns. Even under conditions approximating to those of peace, severe demands were made upon the spirit and endurance of the troops.

British Troops in Cologne.

(7) On the 6th December, in response to a request previously made by the German authorities, and in order that the town might not be left without troops after the withdrawal of the

enemy's military forces, the 2nd Brigade of the 1st Cavalry Division was sent forward to Cologne. A detachment of armoured cars of the 17th (A.C.) Battalion, Tank Corps, escorted the General Officer Commanding 1st Cavalry Division into Cologne, and thereafter picketed the bridges, being the first British troops to cross the Rhine. A great concourse of people thronged the streets of the city to watch the arrival of our troops. Next day, the 28th Infantry Brigade of the 9th Division arrived at Cologne by rail, and on the 8th December the 1st Cavalry Division reached the Rhine on the whole British front, securing the crossings of the river.

While during the following days our infantry continued their movement, on the 11th December the Military Governor, Lieut.-General Sir Charles Fergusson, arrived by train at Cologne. Accompanied by an escort of the 9th Lancers, he proceeded through crowded streets to the Hotel Monopol, where he took up the duties of his office. As the Military Governor reached the entrance to the hotel, the Union Jack was hoisted above the building and floated out for the first time over the roof-tops of the city.

The Occupation of the Cologne Bridgehead.

(8) On the 12th December, the day fixed for that event by the general scheme of advance, the 1st Cavalry Division crossed the Rhine and commenced the occupation of the Cologne Bridgehead, the perimeter of which they reached on the following day.

On the 13th December the 2nd and 1st Canadian Divisions and the 29th and 9th Divisions of the Canadian and II. Corps passed across the Rhine at Cologne and Bonn respectively in four columns, each of the strength of a division. During the following three days they pushed forward to the bridgehead perimeter, gradually relieving the cavalry, and by the evening of the 16th December had completed the occupation of the bridgehead.

Before Christmas Day the troops of the Second Army had

reached their final areas in the occupied territories of Germany. The military organization of the bridgehead, so as to secure the crossing of the Rhine and render possible the rapid deployment of troops for action east of it, had been commenced, and was proceeded with steadily during the remainder of the year. In the course of this work, on the 28th December the perimeter of the bridgehead was slightly amended (*vide* attached map),* so as to accord with the boundaries of the German Communal Districts, and thus simplify the work of administration.

Conduct of the Troops.

(9) In concluding this part of my Dispatch, I desire to acknowledge with gratitude and pride the exemplary conduct of the troops, both throughout the different stages of their arduous advance and since its successful completion.

Among all services and in all Armies, both those which took part in the advance and those which remained behind, the period following the armistice has indeed been one of no little difficulty. For those that went forward, the real hardships of the long marches, poor billets, and indifferent food constituted a strange contrast to ideas which had been formed of victory. For all, the sudden relaxation of the enduring tension of battle, and the natural desire of the great majority for an early return to civil life, could not but lead at times to a certain impatience with delays, and with the continuance, under conditions of apparent peace, of restrictions and routine duties gladly borne while the future of their country was at stake. Despite these disturbing factors, and the novelty of finding themselves masters in a conquered country, instances of misbehaviour have been remarkably few, and chiefly of a minor character. The inborn courtesy and good temper of the British soldier have guided them in their attitude towards the inhabitants of the occupied districts. The spreading of a better understanding of the causes of the temporary shortage of supplies, of the difficulties of demobilization and of the

* Not reproduced.

continued necessity for keeping a strong Army in the field, has generally dispelled any incipient feelings of discontent.

The discipline, self-respect, and strong sense of responsibility which carried our men through to victory, have in general been fully maintained amid changed conditions and new surroundings.

PART II.

Features of the War.

A Single Great Battle.

(10) In this, my final Dispatch, I think it desirable to comment briefly upon certain general features which concern the whole series of operations carried out under my command. I am urged thereto by the conviction that neither the course of the war itself nor the military lessons to be drawn therefrom can properly be comprehended, unless the long succession of battles commenced on the Somme in 1916 and ended in November of last year on the Sambre are viewed as forming part of one great and continuous engagement.

To direct attention to any single phase of that stupendous and incessant struggle and seek in it the explanation of our success, to the exclusion or neglect of other phases possibly less striking in their immediate or obvious consequences is, in my opinion, to risk the formation of unsound doctrines regarding the character and requirements of modern war.

If the operations of the past 4½ years are regarded as a single continuous campaign, there can be recognized in them the same general features and the same necessary stages which between forces of approximately equal strength have marked all the conclusive battles of history. There is in the first instance the preliminary stage of the campaign in which the opposing forces seek to deploy and manœuvre for position, endeavouring while doing so to gain some early advantage which might be pushed home to quick decision. This phase came to an end in the present war with the creation of continuous trench lines from the Swiss frontier to the sea.

Battle having been joined, there follows the period of real struggle in which the main forces of the two belligerent Armies are pitted against each other in close and costly combat. Each commander seeks to wear down the power of resistance of his opponent and to pin him to his position, while preserving or accumulating in his own hands a powerful reserve force with which he can manœuvre, and, when signs of the enemy becoming morally and physically weakened are observed, deliver the decisive attack. The greatest possible pressure against the enemy's whole front must be maintained, especially when the crisis of the battle approaches. Then every man, horse, and gun is required to co-operate, so as to complete the enemy's overthrow and exploit success.

In the stage of the wearing out struggle losses will necessarily be heavy on both sides, for in it the price of victory is paid. If the opposing forces are approximately equal in numbers, in courage, in *moral*, and in equipment, there is no way of avoiding payment of the price or of eliminating this phase of the struggle.

In former battles this stage of the conflict has rarely lasted more than a few days, and has often been completed in a few hours. When armies of millions are engaged, with the resources of great empires behind them, it will inevitably be long. It will include violent crises of fighting which, when viewed separately and apart from the general perspective, will appear individually as great indecisive battles. To this stage belong the great engagements of 1916 and 1917 which wore down the strength of the German Armies.

Finally, whether from the superior fighting ability and leadership of one of the belligerents, as the result of greater resources or tenacity, or by reason of higher *moral*, or from a combination of all these causes, the time will come when the other side will begin to weaken and the climax of the battle is reached. Then the commander of the weaker side must choose whether he will break off the engagement, if he can, while there is yet time, or stake on a supreme effort what reserves remain to him. The launching and destruction of Napoleon's last reserves at Waterloo was a matter of minutes. In this World War the great sortie of the beleaguered German Armies, commenced on the 21st March 1918, lasted for four months, yet it represents a corresponding stage in a single colossal battle.

The breaking down of such a supreme effort will be the signal for the commander of the successful side to develop his greatest strength, and seek to turn to immediate account the loss in material and *moral* which their failure must inevitably produce among his opponent's troops. In a battle joined and decided in the course of a few days or hours, there is no risk that the lay observer will seek to distinguish the culminating operations by which victory is seized and exploited from the preceding stages by which it has been made possible and determined. If the whole operations of the present war are regarded in correct perspective, the victories of the summer and autumn of 1918 will be seen to be as directly dependent upon the two years of stubborn fighting that preceded them.

The Length of the War.

(11) If the causes which determined the length of the recent contest are examined in the light of the accepted principles of war, it will be seen that the duration of the struggle was governed by, and bore a direct relation to, certain definite factors which are enumerated below.

In the first place, we were unprepared for war, or at any rate for a war of such magnitude. We were deficient in both trained men and military material, and, what was more important, had no machinery ready by which either men or material could be produced in anything approaching the requisite quantities. The consequences were twofold. Firstly, the necessary machinery had to be improvised hurriedly, and improvisation is never economical and seldom satisfactory. In this case the high-water mark of our fighting strength in infantry was only reached after $2\frac{1}{2}$ years of conflict, by which time heavy casualties had already been incurred. In consequence, the full man power of the Empire was never developed in the field at any period of the war.

As regards material, it was not until midsummer 1916 that the artillery situation became even approximately adequate to the conduct of major operations. Throughout the Somme battle the expenditure of artillery ammunition had to be watched with the greatest care. During the battles of 1917 ammunition was plentiful, but the gun situation was a source of constant anxiety. Only in 1918 was it possible to conduct artillery operations independently of any limiting consideration other than that of transport.

The second consequence of our unpreparedness was that our Armies were unable to intervene, either at the outset of the war or until nearly two years had elapsed, in sufficient strength adequately to assist our Allies. The enemy was able to gain a notable initial advantage by establishing himself in Belgium and northern France, and throughout the early stages of the war was free to concentrate an undue proportion of his effectives against France and Russia. The excessive burden thrown upon the gallant Army of France during this period caused them losses the effect of which has been felt all through the war and directly influenced its length. Just as at no time were we as an Empire able to put our own full strength into the field, so at no time were the Allies as a whole able completely to develop and obtain the full effect from their greatly superior man power. What might have been the effect of British intervention on a larger scale in the earlier stages of the war is shown by what was actually achieved by our original Expeditionary Force.

It is interesting to note that in previous campaigns the side which has been fully prepared for war has almost invariably gained a rapid and complete success over its less well-prepared opponent. In 1866 and 1870, Austria and then France were overwhelmed at the outset by means of superior preparation. The initial advantages derived therefrom were followed up by such vigorous and ruthless action, regardless of loss, that there was no time to recover from the first stunning blows. The German plan of campaign in the present war was undoubtedly based on similar principles. The margin by which the German onrush in 1914 was stemmed was so narrow and the subsequent struggle so severe that the word "miraculous" is hardly too strong a term to describe the recovery and ultimate victory of the Allies.

A further cause adversely influencing the duration of the war on the Western front during its later stages, and one following indirectly from that just stated, was the situation in other theatres. The military strength of Russia broke down in 1917 at a critical period when, had she been able to carry out her military engagements, the war might have been shortened by a year. At a later date, the military situation in Italy in the autumn of 1917 necessitated the transfer of five British divisions from France to Italy at a time when their presence in France might have had far-reaching effects.

Thirdly, the Allies were handicapped in their task and the war thereby lengthened by the inherent difficulties always associated with the combined action of armies of separate nationalities, differing in speech and temperament, and, not least important, in military organization, equipment, and supply.

Finally, as indicated in the opening paragraph of this part of my Dispatch, the huge numbers of men engaged on either side, whereby a continuous battle front was rapidly established from Switzerland to the sea, outflanking was made impossible and manœuvre very difficult, necessitated the delivery of frontal attacks. This factor, combined with the strength of the defensive under modern conditions, rendered a protracted wearing-out battle unavoidable before the enemy's power of resistance could be overcome. So long as the opposing forces are at the outset approximately equal in numbers and *moral* and there are no flanks to turn, a long struggle for supremacy is inevitable.

The Extent of our Casualties.

(12) Obviously the greater the length of a war the higher is likely to be the number of casualties incurred in it on either side. The same causes, therefore, which served to protract the recent struggle are largely responsible for the extent of our casualties. There can be no question that to our general unpreparedness must be attributed the loss of many thousands of brave men whose sacrifice we deeply deplore, while we regard their splendid gallantry and self-devotion with unstinted admiration and gratitude.

Given, however, the military situation existing in August 1914, our total losses in the war have been no larger than were to be expected. Neither do they compare unfavourably with those of any other of the belligerent nations, so far as figures are available from which comparison can be made. The total British casualties in all theatres of war—killed, wounded, missing, and prisoners, including native troops—are approximately three millions (3,076,388). Of this total, some two and a half millions (2,568,834) were incurred on the Western front. The total French losses—killed, missing, and prisoners, but exclusive of wounded—have been given officially as approximately 1,831,000. If an estimate for wounded is added, the total can scarcely be less than 4,800,000, and of this total it is fair to assume that over four millions were incurred on the Western front. The published figures for Italy—killed and wounded only, exclusive of prisoners—amount to 1,400,000, of which practically the whole were incurred in the Western theatre of war.

Figures have also been published for Germany and Austria. The total German casualties—killed, wounded, missing, and prisoners—are given at approximately six and a half millions (6,485,000), of which the vastly greater proportion must have been incurred on the Western front, where the bulk of the German forces were concentrated and the hardest fighting took place. In view of the fact, however, that the number of

German prisoners is definitely known to be considerably understated, these figures must be accepted with reserve. The losses of Austria-Hungary in killed, missing, and prisoners are given as approximately two and three-quarter millions (2,772,000). An estimate of wounded would give a total of over four and a half millions.

The extent of our casualties, like the duration of the war, was dependent on certain definite factors which can be stated shortly.

In the first place, the military situation compelled us, particularly during the first portion of the war, to make great efforts before we had developed our full strength in the field or properly equipped and trained our Armies. These efforts were wasteful of men, but in the circumstances they could not be avoided. The only alternative was to do nothing and see our French Allies overwhelmed by the enemy's superior numbers.

During the second half of the war, and that part embracing the critical and costly period of the wearing-out battle, the losses previously suffered by our Allies laid upon the British Armies in France an increasing share in the burden of attack. From the opening of the Somme Battle in 1916 to the termination of hostilities the British Armies were subjected to a strain of the utmost severity which never ceased, and consequently had little or no opportunity for the rest and training they so greatly needed.

In addition to these particular considerations, certain general factors peculiar to modern war made for the inflation of losses. The great strength of modern field defences and the power and precision of modern weapons, the multiplication of machine guns, trench mortars, and artillery of all natures, the employment of gas and the rapid development of the aeroplane as a formidable agent of destruction against both men and material, all combined to increase the price to be paid for victory.

If only for these reasons, no comparisons can usefully be

made between the relative losses incurred in this war and any previous war. There is, however, the further consideration that the issues involved in this stupendous struggle were far greater than those concerned in any other war in recent history. Our existence as an Empire, and civilization itself as it is understood by the free Western nations, were at stake. Men fought as they have never fought before in masses.

Despite our own particular handicaps and the foregoing general considerations, it is satisfactory to note that, as the result of the courage and determination of our troops, and the high level of leadership generally maintained, our losses even in attack over the whole period of the battle compare favourably with those inflicted on our opponents. The approximate total of our battle casualties in all arms, and including Overseas troops, from the commencement of the Somme Battle in 1916 to the conclusion of the Armistice, is 2,140,000. The calculation of German losses is obviously a matter of great difficulty. It is estimated, however, that the number of casualties inflicted on the enemy by British troops during the above period exceeds two and a half millions. It is of interest, moreover, in the light of the paragraph next following, that more than half the total casualties incurred by us in the fighting of 1918 were occasioned during the five months, March–July, when our Armies were on the defensive.

Why we Attacked whenever Possible.

(13) Closely connected with the question of casualties is that of the relative values of attack and defence. It is a view often expressed that the attack is more expensive than defence. This is only a half statement of the truth. Unquestionably, unsuccessful attack is generally more expensive than defence, particularly if the attack is pressed home with courage and resolution. On the other hand, attack so pressed home, if skilfully conducted, is rarely unsuccessful; whereas, in its later stages especially, unsuccessful defence is far more costly than attack.

Moreover, the object of all war is victory, and a purely defensive attitude can never bring about a successful decision, either in a battle or in a campaign. The idea that a war can be won by standing on the defensive and waiting for the enemy to attack is a dangerous fallacy, which owes its inception to the desire to evade the price of victory. It is an axiom that decisive success in battle can be gained only by a vigorous offensive. The principle here stated has long been recognized as being fundamental, and is based on the universal teaching of military history in all ages. The course of the present war has proved it to be correct.

To pass for a moment from the general to the particular, and consider in the light of the present war the facts upon which this axiom is based.

A defensive *rôle* sooner or later brings about a distinct lowering of the *moral* of the troops, who imagine that the enemy must be the better man, or at least more numerous, better equipped with and better served by artillery or other mechanical aids to victory. Once the mass of the defending infantry become possessed of such ideas, the battle is as good as lost. An army fighting on enemy soil, especially if its standard of discipline is high, may maintain a successful defence for a protracted period, in the hope that victory may be gained elsewhere, or that the enemy may tire or weaken in his resolution and accept a compromise. The resistance of the German armies was undoubtedly prolonged in this fashion, but in the end the persistence of our troops had its natural effect.

Further, a defensive policy involves the loss of the initiative, with all the consequent disadvantages to the defender. The enemy is able to choose at his own convenience the time and place of his attacks. Not being influenced himself by the threat of attack from his opponent, he can afford to take risks, and by greatly weakening his front in some places can concentrate an overwhelming force elsewhere with which to attack. The defender, on the other hand, becomes almost entirely ignorant of the dispositions and plans of his opponent, who is thus in a position to effect a surprise. This was clearly exemplified during the fighting of 1918. As long as the enemy was attacking, he obtained fairly full information regarding our dispositions. Captured documents show that, as soon as he was thrown once more on the defensive and the initiative returned to the Allies, he was kept in comparative ignorance of our plans and dispositions. The consequence was that the Allies were able to effect many surprises, both strategic and tactical.

As a further effect of the loss of the initiative and ignorance of his opponent's intentions, the defender finds it difficult to avoid a certain dispersal of his forces. Though for a variety of reasons, including the fact that we had lately been on the offensive, we were by no means entirely ignorant of the enemy's intentions in the spring of 1918, the unavoidable uncertainty resulting from a temporary loss of the initiative did have the effect of preventing a complete concentration of our reserves behind the point of the enemy's attack.

An additional reason, peculiar to the circumstances of the present war, which in itself compelled me to refuse to adopt a purely defensive attitude so long as any other was open to me, is to be found in the geographical position of our Armies. For reasons stated by me in my Dispatch of the 20th July 1918, we could not afford to give much ground on any part of our front. The experience of the war has shown that if the defence is to be maintained successfully, even for a limited time, it must be flexible.

The End of the War.

(14) If the views set out by me in the preceding paragraphs are accepted, it will be recognized that the war did not follow any unprecedented course, and that its end was neither sudden nor should it have been unexpected. The rapid collapse of Germany's military power in the latter half of 1918 was the logical outcome of the fighting of the previous

two years. It would not have taken place but for that period of ceaseless attrition which used up the reserves of the German Armies, while the constant and growing pressure of the blockade sapped with more deadly insistence from year to year at the strength and resolution of the German people. It is in the great battles of 1916 and 1917 that we have to seek for the secret of our victory in 1918.

Doubtless, the end might have come sooner had we been able to develop the military resources of our Empire more rapidly and with a higher degree of concentration, or had not the defection of Russia in 1917 given our enemies a new lease of life.

So far as the military situation is concerned, in spite of the great accession of strength which Germany received as the result of the defection of Russia, the battles of 1916 and 1917 had so far weakened her Armies that the effort they made in 1918 was insufficient to secure victory. Moreover, the effect of the battles of 1916 and 1917 was not confined to loss of German man power. The moral effects of those battles were enormous, both in the German Army and in Germany. By their means our soldiers established over the German soldiers a moral superiority which they held in an ever-increasing degree until the end of the war, even in the difficult days of March and April 1918.

The Value of Cavalry in Modern War.

(15) From time to time as the war of position dragged on and the enemy's trench systems remained unbroken, while questions of man power and the shortage of shipping became acute, the wisdom or necessity of maintaining any large force of mounted men was freely discussed. In the light of the full experience of the war the decision to preserve the Cavalry Corps has been completely justified. It has been proved that cavalry, whether used for shock effect under suitable conditions or as mobile infantry, have still an indispensable part to play in modern war. Moreover, it cannot safely be assumed

that in all future wars the flanks of the opposing forces will rest on neutral States or impassable obstacles. Whenever such a condition does not obtain opportunities for the use of cavalry must arise frequently.

Throughout the great retirement in 1914, our cavalry covered the retirement and protected the flanks of our columns against the onrush of the enemy, and on frequent occasions prevented our infantry from being overrun by the enemy's cavalry. Later in the same year, at Ypres, their mobility multiplied their value as a reserve, enabling them rapidly to reinforce threatened portions of our line.

During the critical period of position warfare, when the trial of strength between the opposing forces took place, the absence of room to manœuvre made the importance of cavalry less apparent. Even under such conditions, however, valuable results may be expected from the employment of a strong force of cavalry when, after there has been severe fighting on one or more fronts, a surprise attack is made on another front. Such an occasion arose in the operations before Cambrai at the close of 1917, when the cavalry were of the greatest service; while throughout the whole period of trench fighting they constituted an important mobile reserve.

At a later date, when circumstances found us operating once more in comparatively open country, cavalry proved themselves of value in their true *rôle*. During the German offensive in March 1918, the superior mobility of cavalry fully justified their existence. At the commencement of the battle, cavalry were used under the Fifth Army over wide fronts. So great, indeed, became the need for mounted men that certain units which had but recently been dismounted were hurriedly provided with horses and did splendid service. Frequently, when it was impossible to move forward other troops in time, our mounted troops were able to fill gaps in our line and restore the situation. The absence of hostile cavalry at this period was a marked feature of the battle. Had the German command had at their disposal even two or three well-trained cavalry divisions, a wedge might have been driven between the French and British Armies. Their presence could not have failed to add greatly to the difficulties of our task.

In the actions already referred to east of Amiens, the cavalry were again able to demonstrate the great advantage which their power of rapid concentration gives them in a surprise attack. Operating in close concert with both armoured cars and infantry, they pushed ahead of the latter, and by anticipating the arrival of German reserves assisted materially in our success. In the battle of the 8th October, they were responsible for saving the Cambrai—Le Cateau—St. Quentin Railway from complete destruction. Finally, during the culminating operations of the war when the German Armies were falling back in disorganized masses, a new situation arose which demanded the use of mounted troops. Then our cavalry, pressing hard upon the enemy's heels, hastened his retreat and threw him into worse confusion. At such a time the moral effect of cavalry is overwhelming, and is in itself a sufficient reason for the retention of that arm.

On the morning of the Armistice, two British Cavalry Divisions were on the march east of the Scheldt, and before the orders to stop reached them they had already gained a line ten miles in front of our infantry outposts. There is no doubt that, had the advance of the cavalry been allowed to continue, the enemy's disorganized retreat would have been turned into a rout.

The Value of Mechanical Contrivances.

(16) A remarkable feature of the present war has been the number and variety of mechanical contrivances to which it has given birth, or has brought to a higher state of perfection.

Besides the great increase in mobility made possible by the development of motor transport, heavy artillery, trench mortars, machine guns, aeroplanes, tanks, gas, and barbed wire have in their several spheres of action played very prominent parts in operations, and as a whole have given a greater driving power to war. The belligerent possessing a preponderance of such mechanical contrivances has found himself in a very favourable position as compared with his less well provided opponent. The general superiority of the Allies in this direction during the concluding stages of the recent struggle undoubtedly contributed powerfully to their success. In this respect the Army owes a great debt to science and to the distinguished scientific men who placed their learning and skill at the disposal of their country.

It should never be forgotten, however, that weapons of this character are incapable of effective independent action. They do not in themselves possess the power to obtain a decision, their real function being to assist the infantry to get to grips with their opponents. To place in them a reliance out of proportion to their real utility—to imagine, for example, that tanks and aeroplanes can take the place of infantry and artillery—would be to do a disservice to those who have the future of these new weapons most at heart by robbing them of the power to use them to their best effect.

Every mechanical device so far produced is dependent for its most effective use upon the closest possible association with other arms, and in particular with infantry and artillery. Aeroplanes must rely upon infantry to prevent the enemy from overrunning their aerodromes, and, despite their increasing range and versatility of action, are clearly incapable in themselves of bringing about a decision. Tanks require the closest artillery support to enable them to reach their objectives without falling victims to the enemy's artillery, and are dependent upon the infantry to hold the position they have won.

As an instance of the interdependence of artillery and tanks, we may take the actions fought east of Amiens on the 8th August 1918 and following days. A very large number of tanks were employed in these operations, and they carried out their tasks in the most brilliant manner. Yet a scrutiny of the artillery ammunition returns for this period discloses the fact that in no action of similar dimensions had the expenditure of ammunition been so great.

Immense as the influence of mechanical devices may be, they cannot by themselves decide a campaign. Their true *rôle* is that of assisting the infantryman, which they have done in a most admirable manner. They cannot replace him. Only by the rifle and bayonet of the infantryman can the decisive victory be won.

Close and Complete Co-operation between all Arms and Services.

(17) This war has given no new principles; but the different mechanical appliances above mentioned—and in particular the rapid improvement and multiplication of aeroplanes, the use of immense numbers of machine guns and Lewis guns, the employment of vast quantities of barbed wire as effective obstacles, the enormous expansion of artillery and the provision of great masses of motor transport—have introduced new problems of considerable complexity concerning the effective co-operation of the different arms and services. Much thought has had to be bestowed upon determining how new devices could be combined in the best manner with the machinery already working.

The development of the Air Service is a matter of general knowledge, and figures showing something of the work done by our airmen were included in my last Dispatch. The combining of their operations with those of the other arms, and particularly of the artillery, has been the subject of constant study and experiment, giving results of the very highest value. As regards machine guns, from a proportion of one gun to approximately 500 infantrymen in 1914, our establishment of machine guns and Lewis guns had risen at the end of 1918 to one machine gun or Lewis gun to approximately 20 infantrymen. This great expansion was necessarily accompanied by a modification of training and methods both for attack and defence, and resulted ultimately in the establishment of the Machine Gun Corps under an Inspector-General.

During the same period, the growth of our artillery was even more remarkable, its numbers and power increasing out of all proportion to the experience of previous wars. The 486 pieces of light and medium artillery with which we took the field in August 1914 were represented at the date of the Armistice by 6,437 guns and howitzers of all natures, including pieces of the heaviest calibre.

This vast increase so profoundly influenced the employment of artillery, and was accompanied by so intimate an association with other arms and services, that it merits special comment.

In the first place, big changes were required in artillery organization, as well as important decisions concerning the proportions in which the different natures of artillery and artillery ammunition should be manufactured. These changes and decisions were made during 1916, and resulted in the existing artillery organization of the British Armies in France.

In order to gain the elasticity essential to the quick concentration of guns at the decisive point, to enable the best use to be made of them, and to facilitate ammunition supply and fire control, Artillery Commanders, acting under Army and Corps Commanders, were introduced and Staffs provided for them. This enabled the large concentrations of guns required for our offensives to be quickly absorbed and efficiently directed. The proportions required of guns to howitzers, and of the lighter to the heavier natures, were determined by certain factors—namely, the problem of siting in the comparatively limited areas available the great numbers of pieces required for an offensive; the "lives" of the different types of guns and howitzers—that is, the number of rounds which can be fired from them before they become unserviceable from wear, and questions of relative accuracy and fire effect upon particular kinds of targets.

The results attained by the organization established in

1916 is in itself strong evidence of the soundness of the principles upon which it was based. It made possible a high degree of elasticity, and by the full and successful exploitation of all the means placed at its disposal by science and experience, ensured that the continuous artillery battle which began on the Somme should culminate, as it did, in the defeat of the enemy's guns.

The great development of air photography, sound ranging, flash spotting, air-burst ranging, and aerial observation brought counter-battery work and harassing fire both by day and night to a high state of perfection. Special progress was made in the art of engaging moving targets with fire controlled by observation from aeroplanes and balloons. The work of the Field Survey Sections in the location of hostile battery positions by re-section and the employment of accurate maps was brought into extended use. In combination with the work of the Calibration Sections in the accurate calibration of guns and by careful calculation of corrections of range required to compensate for weather conditions, it became possible to a large extent to dispense with registration, whereby the chance of effecting surprise was greatly increased. In the operations east of Amiens on the 8th August 1918, in which over 2,000 guns were employed, practically the whole of the batteries concentrated for the purpose of the attack opened fire for the first time on the actual morning of the assault.

The use of smoke shell for covering the advance of our infantry and masking the enemy's positions was introduced and employed with increasing frequency and effect. New forms of gas shell were made available, and their combination with the infantry attack carefully studied. The invention of a new fuze known as "106," which was first used in the battle of Arras 1917, enabled wire entanglements to be easily and quickly destroyed, and so modified our methods of attacking organized positions. By bursting the shell the instant it touched the ground and before it had become buried, the destructive effect of the explosion was greatly increased. It became possible to cut wire with a far less expenditure of time and ammunition, and the factor of surprise was given a larger part in operations.

Great attention was paid to the training of personnel, and in particular the Chapperton Down Artillery School, Salisbury Plain, was formed for training artillery, brigade commanders, and battery commanders; while Artillery Schools in France were organized for the training of subalterns and non-commissioned officers.

A short examination of our principal attacks will give a good idea of the increasing importance of artillery. On the first day of the Somme Battle of 1916 the number of artillery personnel engaged was equal to about half the infantry strength of the attacking divisions. On this one day a total of nearly 13,000 tons of artillery ammunition was fired by us on the Western front. Our attacks at Arras and Messines on the 9th April and 7th June 1917 saw the total expenditure of artillery ammunition nearly doubled on the first days of those battles, while the proportion of artillery personnel to infantry steadily grew.

During the period following the opening of the Somme Battle, the predominance of our artillery over that of the enemy gradually increased, till at the time of the Arras Battle it had reached a maximum. In the course of the summer and autumn of 1917, however, the enemy constantly reinforced his artillery on our front, being enabled to do so owing to the relaxation of pressure elsewhere.

The Battle of Ypres in the autumn of 1917 was one of intense struggle for artillery supremacy. By dint of reducing his artillery strength on other parts of the Western front, and by bringing guns from the East, the enemy definitely challenged the predominance of our artillery. In this battle, therefore, the proportion of our artillery to infantry strength was particularly large. In the opening attack on the 31st July our artillery personnel amounted to over 80 per cent. of the infantry engaged in the principal attack on our front, and our total expenditure of artillery ammunition on this day exceeded 23,000 tons. During the succeeding weeks the battle of the rival artilleries became ever more violent. On the two days 20th and 21st September, about 42,000 tons of artillery ammunition were expended by us, and in the successful attack of the 4th October, which gave us the main ridge about Broodseinde, our artillery personnel amounted to 85 per cent. of the infantry engaged in the assault.

During the winter of 1917–1918 the enemy so greatly added to his artillery strength by batteries brought from the Russian front that in his spring offensive he was able temporarily to effect a definite local artillery superiority. This state of affairs was short lived. Even before the breakdown of the German offensive, our guns had regained the upper hand. In the battles later in the year the superiority of our batteries once more grew rapidly, until the defeat of the German artillery became an accomplished fact. From the commencement of our offensive in August 1918 to the conclusion of the Armistice, some 700,000 tons of artillery ammunition were expended by the British Armies on the Western front. For the fortnight from the 21st August to 3rd September our average daily expenditure exceeded 11,000 tons, while for the three days of crucial battle on the 27th, 28th, and 29th September nearly 65,000 tons of ammunition were fired by our artillery.

The tremendous growth of our artillery strength above described followed inevitably from the character of the wearing-out battle upon which we were engaged. The restricted opportunities for manœuvre and the necessity for frontal attacks made the employment of great masses of artillery essential.

The massing of guns alone, however, could not have secured success without the closest possible combination between our batteries and the infantry they were called upon to support, as well as with the other arms. The expansion was accompanied, therefore, by a constant endeavour to improve the knowledge of all ranks of both artillery and infantry and the air service concerning the work and possibilities of the other arms.

An intelligent understanding of " the other man's job " is the first essential of successful co-operation. To obtain the best results from the vast and complex machine composing a modern army, deep study of work other than one's own is necessary for all arms. For this study much time is needed, as well as much practical application of the principles evolved; and for reasons already explained, opportunity sufficient for adequate training could not be found. None the less, the best possible use was made of such opportunities as offered, and much was in fact accomplished.

The Signal Service.

(18) As a natural corollary to the general increase of our Forces, the Signal Service, required alike for the proper co-ordination of supply and for the direction and control of the battle, has grown almost out of recognition. From an original establishment of under 2,400 officers and men, trained and equipped chiefly for mobile warfare, at the end of 1918 the personnel of the Signal Service had risen to 42,000, fully equipped with all the latest devices of modern science to act efficiently under all conditions as the nervous system to the whole vast organism of our Army.

The commencement of trench warfare and the greater use of artillery led to a rapid development of the signal system, which as fresh units were introduced became more and more elaborate. At the same time, the increase in the power and range of artillery made the maintenance of communications constantly more difficult. Many miles of deep trenches were dug in which cables containing 50 to 100 circuits were buried to gain protection from shell fire. The use of wireless communication gradually became more widely spread, and finally constituted part of the Signal establishment of all formations down to divisions. To provide an alternative method of communication with front line troops, in 1915 carrier pigeons were introduced, and a special branch of the Signal Service was formed controlling ultimately some 20,000 birds. In 1917 a Messenger Dog Service was started for similar purposes, and did good work on a number of occasions.

The expansion of the work of the Signal Service in the more forward areas was accompanied by a similar development on the Lines of Communication, at General Headquarters, Armies and Corps. Construction and Railway Companies were formed and about 1,500 miles of main telegraph and telephone routes constructed in the Lines of Communication area alone, in addition to many miles in Army areas. Provision had to be made for communicating with London, Paris, and Marseilles, as well as between the different Allied Headquarters. On the advance of our forces to the Rhine telephone communication was established between General Headquarters at Montreuil and Cologne. Signal communication entailing the putting up of many thousands of miles of wire was provided also for the control of railway traffic, while to supplement electric communication generally a Dispatch Rider Letter Service was maintained by motor cyclists.

The amount of Signal Traffic dealt with became very great, and on the Lines of Communication alone more than 23,000 telegrams have been transmitted in twenty-four hours. Similarly, at General Headquarters as many as 9,000 telegrams have been dealt with in twenty-four hours, besides 3,400 letters carried by Dispatch Rider; an Army Headquarters has handled 10,000 telegrams and 5,000 letters in the same space of time, and a Corps 4,500 telegrams and 3,000 letters. In addition to telegrams and letters, there has been at all times a great volume of telephone traffic.

Something of the extent of the constructional work required, in particular to meet the constant changes of the battle line and the movement of Headquarters, can be gathered from the fact that as many as 6,500 miles of field cable have been issued in a single week. The average weekly issue of such cable for the whole of 1918 was approximately 3,300 miles.

Rearward Services and Personnel; Transportation.

(19) The immense expansion of the Army from 6 to over 60 infantry divisions, combined with the constant multiplication of auxiliary arms, called inevitably for a large increase in the size and scope of the services concerned in the supply and maintenance of our fighting forces.

As the Army grew and became more complicated, the total feeding strength of our forces in France rose until it approached a total of 2,700,000 men. The vastness of the figures involved in providing for their needs will be realized from the following examples. For the maintenance of a single division for one day, nearly 200 tons dead weight of supplies and stores are needed, representing a shipping tonnage of nearly 450 tons. In an army of 2,700,000 men, the addition of one ounce to each man's daily rations involves the carrying of an extra 75 tons of goods.

To cope with so great a growth, the number of existing directorates had gradually to be added to or their duties extended, with a corresponding increase in demands for personnel. The supervision of ports was entrusted to the Directorate of Docks, which controlled special companies for the transhipping of stores. By the end of November 1918 the number of individual landings in France at the various ports managed by us exceeded 10½ million persons. During the 11 months, January to November 1918, the tonnage landed at these ports averaged some 175,000 tons per week.

To the Directorate of Transport, originally concerned with the administration of horse vehicles and pack animals, fell the further duty of exploiting mechanical road traction. Despite the employment of over 46,700 motor vehicles, including over 30,000 lorries, the number of horses and mules rose greatly, reaching a figure exceeding 400,000. The replacement, training, and distribution of these animals was the duty of the Directorate of Remounts. The Directorate of Veterinary

Services reduced losses and prevented the spread of disease, while the Inspector of Horse Feeding and Economies ensured that the utmost value was obtained from the forage and grain consumed.

To meet the requirements of mechanical and horse traffic, the upkeep or construction of a maximum of some 4,500 miles of roadway was entrusted to the Directorate of Roads. Some idea of the work involved may be obtained from the fact that for ordinary upkeep alone 100 tons of road material are required per fortnight for the maintenance of one mile of road. Under this Directorate were organized a number of Road Construction Companies, together with Quarry Companies to supply the necessary metal. In the month of October 1918 over 85,000 tons of road material were conveyed weekly by motor transport alone, involving a petrol mileage of over 14,000,000 weekly. The total output of stone from the commencement of 1918 to the date of the armistice amounted to some 3,500,000 tons.

For the working of the existing railways and for the construction or repair of many miles of track, both normal and narrow gauge, railway troops of every description, Operating Companies, Construction Companies, Survey and Reconnaissance Companies, Engine Crew Companies, Workshop Companies, Wagon Erecting Companies, and Light Railway Forward Companies had to be provided. Under the Directorate of Railway Traffic, the Directorate of Construction, and the Directorate of Light Railways, these and other technical troops during 1918 built or reconstructed 2,340 miles of broad-gauge and 1,348 miles of narrow-gauge railway. Throughout the whole period of their operation they guaranteed the smooth and efficient working of the railway system. In the six months, May to October 1918, a weekly average of 1,800 trains was run for British Army traffic, carrying a weekly average load of approximately 400,000 tons, while a further 130,000 tons were carried weekly by our light railways. The number of locomotives imported to deal with this traffic rose from 62 in 1916 to over 1,200 by the end of 1918, while the number of trucks rose from 3,840 to 52,600.

The Inland Water Transport section were organized under a separate Directorate for the working in France and Flanders of the canal and cross-Channel barge traffic. On inland waterways alone an average of 56,000 tons of material was carried weekly during 1918, the extent of waterways worked by us at the date of the Armistice being some 465 miles.

The wonderful development of all methods of transportation had an important influence upon the course of events. No war has been fought with such ample means of quick transportation as were available during the recent struggle. Despite the huge increase in the size of armies, it was possible to effect great concentrations of troops with a speed which, having regard to the numbers of men and bulk of material moved, has never before been equalled. Strategic and tactical mobility has been the guiding principle of our transportation arrangements; but this was itself at all times vitally affected by questions of supply, and by the necessity of providing for the evacuation and replacement on a vast scale of the sick and wounded.

The successful co-ordination and economic use of all the various kinds of transportation require most systematic management, based on deep thought and previous experience. So great was the work entailed in the handling of the vast quantities of which some few examples are given above, so complex did the machinery of transport become, and so important was it that the highest state of efficiency should be maintained, that in the autumn of 1916 I was forced to adopt an entirely new system for running our Lines of Communication. The appointment of Inspector-General of Communications was abolished, and the services previously directed by that Officer were brought under the immediate control of the Adjutant-General, the Quartermaster-General, and the Director-General of Transportation. The last mentioned was a new office, created with a separate Staff, composed for the greater part of civilian experts, to deal specifically with transportation questions. At the same time, the command and administration of the troops on the Lines of Communication were vested in a "General Officer Commanding the Lines of Communication Area."

The huge bulk of the supplies to be handled was due not merely to the size of our Army. It arose also from the introduction of new weapons and methods of war, and from the establishment of a higher standard of comfort for the troops. The incessant demands of the fighting forces for munitions were supplied by the Directorate of Ordnance Services, combined with a great expansion of Ordnance Workshops; while the Directorate of Engineering Stores provided on a vast scale the materials required for the construction of trench defences and kindred purposes. For the comfort and well-being of the troops, the Directorate of Supplies stored and distributed in sound condition fresh food, to take the place as far as possible of tinned rations. Through the agency of an Inspectorate of Messing and Economics, regular schools of cookery gave instruction to nearly 25,000 cooks, and careful measures were taken for the recovery of kitchen by-products. In August 1918, over 860,000 lb. of dripping were received from Armies and consigned to England, while the cash value of the by-products disposed of from all sources has exceeded £60,000 in a single month. Provision was made for baths, and a new Inspectorate supervised the running of Army laundries on up-to-date lines.

The Expeditionary Force Canteens made it possible to obtain additional comforts close up to the front. During 1918 the value of the weekly sales in the different canteens averaged 8½ million francs. These canteens were valuably supplemented by the various voluntary institutions ministering to the comfort and recreation of our troops, such as the Y.M.C.A., the Church Army, the Scottish Churches Huts, the Salvation Army, the Soldiers' Christian Association, the Catholic Women's League and Club Huts, the United Army and Navy Board, the Wesleyan Soldiers' Institute, and the British Soldiers' Institute. In many cases these organizations carried on their work almost in the actual fighting line, and did much to maintain the high *moral* of our Armies. To permit the troops to avail themselves of the opportunities so offered, methods devised by the Paymaster-in-Chief enabled soldiers to obtain money anywhere in the Field. Parcels and letters from home have been delivered by the Army Postal Service with remarkable regularity.

As the effects of the enemy submarine warfare began to be felt and the shortage of shipping became more and more acute, so it became increasingly necessary for the Army in France to be more self-supporting. To meet this emergency vast hospitals and convalescent depôts capable of accommodating over 22,000 men were erected west of the Seine at Trouville. Additional General Hospitals with accommodation for over 7,000 patients were established in the neighbourhood of Boulogne, Etaples, and elsewhere. Between January 1916 and November 1918 the total capacity of hospitals and convalescent depôts in France grew from under 44,000 to over 157,000 persons.

Great installations were set up for the manufacture of gun parts and articles of like nature, for the repair of damaged material, as well as for the utilization of the vast quantities of articles of all kinds collected from the battlefields by the organization working under the direction of the Controller of Salvage. The Forestry Directorate, controlling over 70 Canadian and other Forestry Companies, worked forests all over France, in the North-West, Central, and South-West Departments, the Vosges, Jura, and Bordeaux country. As the result of its work our Armies were made practically independent of overseas imported timber. The Directorate of Agricultural Production organized farm and garden enterprises for the local supply of vegetables, harvested the crops abandoned by the enemy in his retreat, and commenced the reclamation of the devastated area.

At the same time, a great saving of shipping was effected by the speeding up of work at the docks. The average tonnage discharged per hour in port rose from 12½ tons in January 1917 to 34½ tons in July 1918; while the average number of days lost by ships waiting berth at the ports fell from some 90 ship days per week at the beginning of 1917 to about 9 ship days per week in 1918.

For the accommodation of so wide a range of services, installations of all kinds, hutments, factories, workshops, storage for ammunition, clothing, meat and petrol, power houses and pumping stations, camps and hospitals, had to be planned and constructed by the Directorate of Works. Our business relations with the French, the obtaining of sites and buildings, called for the establishment of a Directorate of Hirings and Requisitions; while my Financial Adviser in France assisted in the adjustment of financial questions connected with the use of French railways and harbours, the exploitation of French forests, and similar matters. The safeguarding from fire of the great number of buildings erected or taken over by us and of the masses of accumulated stores was entrusted to a definite Staff under the supervision of a Fire Expert.

The creation and maintenance of the great organization briefly outlined above made big demands upon our available supply of personnel. Though these demands as far as possible were met, under the supervision of the Controller of Labour, by imported labour or prisoners of war, it was not practicable at any time to supply more than a proportion of our needs in this manner. Many fit men who might otherwise have reinforced the fighting line had also to be employed, especially during the earlier stages of the war.

As, however, our organization arrived at a greater state of completion and its working became smooth, so it began to be possible to withdraw considerable numbers of fit men from the rearward services. In many cases it was possible, where replacement was necessary, to fill the places of the fit men so withdrawn by women or unfit men. In this way when the man-power situation became acute a considerable saving was effected. During the great British attacks of 1918, of a total male feeding strength of a little over 2¼ millions, 1½ millions were in front of railhead. Even so, as has been found to be the case in the Armies of all other belligerents, so in our Army the number of fit men employed in the rearward services has at all times been large, and necessarily so.

It is hardly too much to assert that, however seemingly extravagant in men amd money, no system of supply except the most perfect should ever be contemplated. To give a single example, unless our supply services had been fully efficient the great advance carried out by our Armies during the autumn of last year could not have been achieved.

Wars may be won or lost by the standard of health and *moral* of the opposing forces. *Moral* depends to a very large extent upon the feeding and general well-being of the troops. Badly supplied troops will invariably be low in *moral*, and an army ravaged by disease ceases to be a fighting force. The feeding and health of the fighting forces are dependent upon the rearward services, and so it may be argued that with the rearward services rests victory or defeat. In our case we can justly say that our supply system has been developed into one of the most perfect in the world.

Replacement, Discipline, and Welfare of the Troops.

(20) The preceding paragraph illustrates the demands which the conduct of operations made on the Staff and Directorates controlled by the Quartermaster-General. The parallel development of the Adjutant-General's Branch, while concerned with matters less patent to the casual observer, has been no less remarkable. The problem of ensuring the supply of reinforcements at the times and places at which they will be required to replace casualties is present in all warfare, and is difficult in any circumstances. In operations conducted on the scale reached in this war it is exceedingly intricate.

The successful solution of this problem alone entitles the Adjutant-General and his Staff to the greatest credit. It has formed, however, but a small part of their work.

Owing to the impossibility of foretelling what claims would be made on man power by industry or by other theatres of war, it was necessary to prepare elaborate forecasts of the personnel likely to be required at various future dates, and to work out in advance the best manner of utilizing reinforcements in the event of their being available in greater or less numbers. We were faced with an unexpected contraction in man power in the winter of 1917 and an unexpected expansion in the summer of 1918. Both these developments were encountered with a success which could only have been attained by the greatest forethought and application on the part of the Staff concerned.

To reduce to cadre a depleted Division, to fill it up when men became available, to break up a battalion and redistribute its personnel, to comb out a certain number of fit men from the rearward services, all sound simple operations. In reality each requires an immense amount of sympathetic treatment and clerical labour, the extent of the work involved being instanced by the fact that in the month of April 1918 over 200,000 reinforcements were sent up to the fighting forces. The carrying out of measures of this nature was made more difficult by the continual formation of new types of unit to meet new requirements. It was necessary to find the personnel for those units with the least possible dislocation elsewhere, and with an eye to the most advantageous employment of the individual in regard to his medical category and special qualifications. The following figures will give some indication of the magnitude of the task. The Adjutant-General's Office at the Base has prepared over 8 million records containing the military history of individual soldiers in France, and has received and dispatched over 22 million letters.

Whatever the quality of the troops, a just and efficient

administration of military law is an indispensable adjunct to a high standard of discipline. I gratefully acknowledge the care with which officers of the Adjutant-General's Branch in all formations have ensured the observation of every safeguard which our law provides against injustice. They have seen to it that every plea which an accused or convicted soldier wishes to bring forward is heard, and that Commanders are advised as to the suitability of sentences. I take this opportunity of recording my satisfaction at the success which has attended the operation of the Suspension of Sentences Act. The number of men under suspended sentence who by good conduct and gallant service in the field have earned remission of their sentence has been most encouraging.

Closely related to the administration of military law is the work of the military police under the Provost Marshal, and of the military prisons in the field. In the battle zone, where frequently they had to do duty in exposed positions under heavy fire and suffered severe casualties, the military police solved an important part of the problem of traffic control, by preventing the unavoidable congestion of troops and transport on roads in the vicinity of active operations from degenerating into confusion. In back areas, their vigilance and zeal have largely contributed to the good relations maintained between our troops and the civilian population.

Although the number of soldiers undergoing sentences of imprisonment in France has at no time amounted to 1 per thousand, the size of the Army has necessitated a considerable expansion of the Military Prisons in the field. The Director of Military Prisons, his Governors and warders, have sought, not retribution, but to build up the self-discipline of the prisoner. They have been rewarded by seeing a large percentage of the men committed to their charge subsequently recover their characters as good soldiers.

Under the general control of the Adjutant-General, the Base Stationery Depôt, which went to France in 1914 with a personnel of ten, has expanded into the Directorate of Army

Printing and Stationery Services, employing over 60 officers and 850 other ranks. In addition to the printing and distribution of orders and instructions, it undertook the reproduction on a vast scale of aerial and other photographs, the number of which grew from 25,000 in 1916 to two and a quarter million in 1918. Other examples of administrative success are the Prisoners of War Section and the Directorate of Graves Registration and Enquiries.

Of the care taken for the physical and moral welfare of the troops I cannot speak too highly.

In the former domain, the achievements of the Director-General of Medical Services and his subordinates have been so fully recorded by me in previous dispatches that they need no further emphasis. It is sufficient to say that, in spite of the numbers dealt with, there has been no war in which the resources of science have been utilized so generously and successfully for the prevention of disease, or for the quick evacuation and careful tending of the sick and wounded.

In the latter sphere, the devoted efforts of the Army Chaplains of all denominations have contributed incalculably to the building up of the indomitable spirit of the Army. As the result of their teaching, all ranks came to know and more fully understand the great and noble objects for which they were fighting.

Under the immediate direction of the Adjutant-General in matters concerning military administration, the Principal Chaplain for members of all churches except the Church of England, and the Deputy Chaplain-General for members of the Church of England, administer to the greatest harmony a very complete joint organization. Provided with a definite establishment for armies, corps, and divisions, as well as for the principal base ports, base camps, hospitals, and certain other units, they ensure that the benefit of religion is brought within the reach of every soldier.

In all the senior offices of this joint organization, down to divisions, the Principal Chaplain and Deputy Chaplain-General have each their representatives, the appointments to those offices in the Principal Chaplain's section being apportioned between the different Churches, Protestant and Roman Catholic, in proportion to the numbers of their following in the Army as a whole. This organization has worked for the common good in a manner wholly admirable and with a most noteworthy absence of friction. It has undoubtedly been much assisted, both in its internal economy and in its relations with commanders and troops, by being at all times in direct touch with the Adjutant-General's Branch.

No survey of the features of the war would be complete without some reference to the part played by women serving with the British Armies in France. Grouped also under the Adjutant-General's Branch of the General Staff, Queen Alexandra's Imperial Military Nursing Service, the Nursing Sisters of the Canadian Army Medical Corps, and of the Australian, New Zealand, South African, and Territorial Force Nursing Services and the British Red Cross Society have maintained and embellished a fine tradition of loyalty and efficiency. These services have been reinforced by members of Voluntary Aid Detachments from the British Isles, the Oversea Dominions, and the United States of America, who have vied with their professional sisters in cheerfully enduring fatigue in times of stress and gallantly facing danger and death.

Women in the British Red Cross Society and other organizations have driven ambulances throughout the war, undeterred by discomfort and hardship. Women have ministered to the comfort of the troops in huts and canteens. Finally, Queen Mary's Auxiliary Army Corps, recruited on a wider basis, responded with enthusiasm to the call for drafts, and by the aid they gave to our declining man power contributed materially to the success of our arms.

Training and Organization.

(21) The experience gained in this war alone, without the study and practice of lessons learned from other campaigns, could not have sufficed to meet the ever-changing tactics

which have characterized the fighting. There was required also the sound basis of military knowledge supplied by our Training Manuals and Staff Colleges.

The principles of command, Staff work, and organization elaborated before the war have stood the test imposed upon them, and are sound. The militarily educated officer has counted for much, and the good work done by our Staff Colleges during the past 30 years has had an important influence upon the successful issue of the war. In solving the various strategic and tactical problems with which we have been faced, in determining principles of training and handling of troops, and in the control and elaboration of Army organization generally, the knowledge acquired by previous study and application has been invaluable. Added to this have been the efficiency and smoothness of working resulting from standardization of principles, assisted in many cases by the previous personal acquaintance at the Staff College of those called upon to work together in the field.

The course of the war has brought out very clearly the value of an efficient and well-trained High Command, in which I include not merely commanders of higher formations, but their Staffs also.

This has been the first time in our history that commanders have had to be provided for such large forces. Before the war no one of our generals had commanded even an Army Corps such as has been used as a subsidiary formation in the battles of the last few years. In consequence, commanders have been faced with problems very different to those presented by the small units with which they had been accustomed to train in peace. That they exercised their commands with such success as most of them did, shows, I venture to think, that their prior training was based on sound principles and conducted on practical lines.

Similarly as regards the Staff, the magnitude of our operations introduced a situation for which no precedent existed. The Staff Colleges had only produced a reserve of Staff officers adequate to the needs of our Army on a peace footing, and for the mobilization of the Expeditionary Force of six divisions. Consequently, on the expansion of the Army during the war many officers had to be recruited for Staff appointments—from good regular officers chiefly, but also from officers of our new Armies—and trained for the new duties required of them. Though numbers of excellent Staff Officers were provided in this way, it was found, as a general rule, that the relative efficiency in Staff duties of men who had passed through the Staff Colleges, as compared with men who had not had that advantage, was unquestionably greater.

Good Staff work is an essential to success in all wars, and particularly in a struggle of such magnitude as that through which we had just passed. No small part of the difficulty of achieving it lies in the possibility that officers on the Staff of higher formations may get out of touch with the fighting forces, and so lose sense of proportion and become unpractical. Every endeavour was made to avoid this by maintaining a constant interchange of such officers with others from the front, so that all might keep abreast with the latest ideas and experience both in the fighting line and elsewhere. In pursuance of this principle, in addition to 18 officers from Army or Corps Staffs and other officers from the Intelligence Corps or General List, there were brought in during the period of my command some 50 officers direct from active duty with divisions or smaller units, to hold for longer or shorter periods appointments in the General Staff branch at G.H.Q.

It may be accepted as a general rule that previous organization should be upset as little as possible in war. As each war has certain special conditions, so some modification of existing ideas and practices will be necessary, but if our principles are sound these will be few and unimportant. In the present war, new organizations and establishments for dealing with the demands of both the fighting and the rearward services have been brought into being continually, and added to or absorbed by our existing organization and establishment.

The constant birth of new ideas has demanded the exercise of the greatest care, not only to ensure that no device or suggestion of real value should be overlooked or discouraged, but also to regulate the enthusiasm of the specialist and prevent each new development assuming dimensions out of proportion to its real value. As the result of our own experience and that of the French during the fighting of 1915, all kinds of trench weapons were invented—bombs, bomb throwers, mortars, and even such instruments as trench daggers. In those days, the opinion was freely expressed that the war would be finished in the trenches, and every effort was made to win victories in the trenches, themselves. In consequence, rifle shooting was forgotten, and was fast becoming a lost art. Similarly as regards artillery, the idea of dominating and defeating the hostile artillery before proceeding to the infantry attack was considered an impossibility.

Then followed the experience of the Battle of the Somme in 1916, which showed that the principles of our pre-war training were as sound as ever. That autumn, a revival of old methods was inaugurated. Musketry shooting was everywhere carried out, and bayonet fighting was taught as the really certain way of gaining supremacy in hand-to-hand fighting. At the same time, as pointed out in para. 17 above, the greatest care was devoted to artillery shooting, as well as to the training of all arms for open fighting. The events of the next two years fully confirmed the lessons drawn from the Battle of the Somme. In short, the longer the war has lasted the more emphatically has it been realized that our original organization and training were based on correct principles. The danger of altering them too much, to deal with some temporary phase, has been greater than the risk of adjusting them too little.

(22) Some idea of the extent of the organization built up during the war for the training of our Armies can be gathered from a survey of the different schools actually established.

In the Armies important schools were maintained for the

instruction of officers and non-commissioned officers of infantry and artillery in their several duties, for training in scouting, observation and sniping, in the use of trench mortars, in signalling, musketry and bayonet fighting, anti-gas precautions, mining and defence against tanks. The different Corps controlled a similar series of schools. Added to these were the special schools of the Cavalry Corps, including a School of Equitation; the Tank Corps Mechanical School; and the different courses instituted and managed by divisions, which were largely attended whenever the battle situation permitted.

Other schools under the direct supervision of General Headquarters provided instruction in the machine gun, Lewis gun, and light mortar, in anti-aircraft gunnery, in observation for artillery, in sound ranging and flash spotting, wireless, bridging and other engineering duties, in firing and bombing from aeroplanes, and in physical and recreational training. At the Base depôts, big training and reinforcement camps were set up for infantry, artillery, cavalry, engineers, machine gunners, cyclists, tank corps, signal and gas personnel. Further, a regular succession of Staff officers and others were sent home to take part in the various schools and courses established in England.

In the course of the past year it was found desirable to make provision for the more thorough co-ordination of effort among these various schools, and also for assisting commanders, especially during battle periods, in the training and instruction of such troops as might from time to time be in reserve. For this purpose an Inspectorate of Training was established. Training and organization must always go hand-in-hand; for while tactical considerations dictate the organization of units and methods of training, upon sound tactical organization and training depend the development and effective employment of good tactics.

In the early spring of 1918, the foundations were laid of an educational scheme which might give officers and men throughout the Army an opportunity to prepare themselves for their return to civil life. Delayed in its application by the German offensive and the crowded events of the summer and autumn of that year, since the conclusion of the Armistice the scheme has been developed with most excellent results under the general direction of the training sub-section of my General Staff branch, and generously supported in every possible way by the Educational Department at home. Divided into a general and a technical side, every effort has been made both to give opportunities for the improvement of general knowledge and to enable trained men to "get their hands in" before returning to civil life. In this way, between 400,000 and 500,000 persons have been brought under instruction, while the number of attendances at lectures has approached a million in the course of a month.

Our New Armies.

(23) The feature of the war which to the historian may well appear the most noteworthy is the creation of our new Armies.

To have built up successfully in the very midst of war a great new Army on a more than Continental scale, capable of beating the best troops of the strongest military nation of pre-war days, is an achievement of which the whole Empire may be proud. The total of over 327,000 German prisoners captured by us on the Western front is in striking contrast to the force of six divisions, comprising some 80,000 fighting men all told, with which we entered the war. That we should have been able to accomplish this stupendous task is due partly to the loyalty and devotion of our Allies and to the splendid work of the Royal Navy, but mainly to the wonderful spirit of the British race in all parts of the world.

Discipline has never had such a vindication in any war as in the present one, and it is their discipline which most distinguishes our new Armies from all similarly created armies of the past. At the outset the lack of deep-seated and instinctive discipline placed our new troops at a disadvantage compared with the methodically trained enemy. This disadvantage, however, was overcome, and during the last two years the discipline of all ranks of our new Armies, from whatever part of the Empire they have come, was excellent. Born from a widespread and intelligent appreciation of the magnitude of the issues at stake and a firm belief in the justice of our cause, it drew strength and permanence from a common-sense recognition of what discipline really means—from a general realization that true discipline demands as much from officers as from men, and that without mutual trust, understanding, and confidence on the part of all ranks the highest form of discipline is impossible.

Drawn from every sphere of life, from every profession, department, and industry of the British Empire, and thrust suddenly into a totally new situation full of unknown difficulties, all ranks have devoted their lives and energies to the service of their country in the whole-hearted manner which the magnitude of the issues warranted. The policy of putting complete trust in subordinate commanders and of allowing them a free hand in the choice of means to attain their object has proved most successful. Young officers, whatever their previous education may have been, have learnt their duties with enthusiasm and speed, and have accepted their responsibilities unflinchingly.

Our universities and public schools throughout the Empire have proved once more, as they have proved time and again in the past, that in the formation of character, which is the root of discipline, they have no rivals. Not that universities and public schools enjoy a monopoly of the qualities which make good officers. The life of the British Empire generally has proved sound under the severest tests, and while giving men whom it is an honour for any officer to command, has furnished officers of the highest standard from all ranks of society and all quarters of the world.

Promotion has been entirely by merit, and the highest appointments were open to the humblest, provided he had the necessary qualifications of character, skill, and knowledge. Many instances could be quoted of men who from civil or comparatively humble occupations have risen to important commands. A schoolmaster, a lawyer, a taxicab driver, and an ex-Sergeant-Major have commanded brigades; one editor has commanded a division, and another held successfully the position of Senior Staff Officer to a Regular division; the under-cook of a Cambridge College, a clerk to the Metropolitan Water Board, an insurance clerk, an architect's assistant, and a police inspector became efficient General Staff Officers; a Mess Sergeant, a railway signalman, a coal miner, a market gardener, an assistant secretary to a haberdasher's company, a Quartermaster-Sergeant, and many private soldiers have risen to command battalions; clerks have commanded batteries; a schoolmaster, a collier, the son of a blacksmith, an iron moulder, an instructor in tailoring, an assistant gas engineer, a grocer's assistant, as well as policemen, clerks, and privates, have commanded companies or acted as adjutants.

As a body, and with few exceptions, new officers have understood that the care of their men must be their first consideration, that their men's comforts and well-being should at all times come before their own, that without this they cannot expect to win the affection, confidence, loyalty, and obedience of those they are privileged to command, or to draw the best from them. Moreover, they have known how to profit by the experience of others, and in common with their men they have turned willingly to the members of the old Regular Army for instruction and guidance in all branches of their new way of life.

On their part, officers, non-commissioned officers, and men of the old Regular Army have risen to the demands made upon them in a manner equally marvellous. Their leaven has pervaded the whole of the mighty force which in 4½ years of war has gathered from all parts of the world round the small highly trained Army with which we entered the war. The general absence of jealousy and the readiness to learn, which in the Field has markedly characterized all ranks of our new Armies, is proof both of the quality of our old Army and of the soundness of our pre-war training. If further proof were needed, it is found in the wonderful conduct and achievements of our Armies new and old, and in the general pride with which they are universally regarded.

In the earlier stages of the war the Regular Army was called on to provide instructors and cadres round which the new Armies could be formed. All that was best in the old Regular Army, its discipline, based on force of character, leadership, and mutual respect, its traditions, and the spirit that never knows defeat, have been the foundations on which the new Armies have been built up. Heavy demands were necessarily made upon our establishment of trained regular officers, most regrettably depleted by the heavy sacrifices of the early days of the war. The way in which such demands have been met by those who survived those days have justified our belief in them.

Neither have the officers of the new Armies, whether drawn from the British Isles or the Dominions, risen with less spirit and success to the needs of the occasion. The great expansion of the Army, and the length of the war, necessitated an ever-increasing demand being made on them for filling responsible positions in command, staff, and administrative appointments. The call has been met most efficiently. The longer the war continued, the greater became the part played in it by the new Armies of the Empire.

PART III.

My Thanks to Commanders and Staffs.

(24) In the body of previous Dispatches I have found a welcome opportunity to mention by name many distinguished officers, Commanders of Corps and Divisions, whose high soldierly qualities, powers of leadership, and knowledge of men

have largely influenced the course of the operations with which those Dispatches have dealt. I have also been able to refer to some few of the many able and experienced Staff officers by whom I have at all times been so greatly assisted. It is not practicable, in the text of this Dispatch, to set out the full list of those to whom I am indebted. I would say, however, of all those already mentioned, as well as of those whose names appear below and the many others whom the limits of space compel me to exclude, that no Commander has ever had or ever could wish for more loyal assistance given more ungrudgingly, or with a more complete devotion to the noble cause for which we have worked in common.

My thanks are especially due to the five Army Commanders—General Sir Herbert Plumer, General Sir Henry Rawlinson, General Sir Henry Horne, General the Hon. Sir Julian Byng, and General Sir William Birdwood—whose names have become household words throughout the length and breadth of our Empire. I desire to associate with them the names of General Sir Charles Monro, who left the command of the First Army to assume the Chief Command in India; of General Sir Edmund Allenby, who, after conducting the operations of the Third Army in the Battle of Arras, 1917, has since led our arms to victory in Palestine; and General Sir Hubert Gough, who, after distinguished service as a Brigade, Divisional, and Corps Commander, commanded the Fifth Army (first known as the Reserve Army) during the Battles of the Somme and Ancre in 1916, east of Ypres in 1917, and finally in the great and gallant fight of March 1918, the story of which is fresh in the minds of all.

To the Heads of the Sections of my General Staff Branch at Headquarters, both past and present, I owe and readily acknowledge a great debt of gratitude for the energy, ability, and loyalty with which they have discharged their important duties. Throughout the long and difficult period of the wearing-out battles of 1916 and 1917, my former Chief of the General Staff, Lieut.-General Sir Lancelot Kiggell, gave his great abilities and deep military learning to the service of his country with a loyalty and devotion which never spared himself, and in the end made demands upon his health which compelled him to retire under medical advice from the responsible position he had so ably held. His successor, Lieut.-General the Hon. Sir Herbert Lawrence, has continued his work with a like ability and with an unfailing insight, calm resolution, and level judgment which neither ill fortune nor good was able to disturb. My grateful thanks are due also to Major-General Sir R. H. K. Butler, who acted as Deputy Chief of my General Staff until his appointment to the command of the III. Corps at the beginning of 1918.

Under the able, energetic, and successful directions of Brigadier-General J. Charteris, the Intelligence Section of my General Staff Branch was developed into a far-reaching and most efficient organization for the rapid collection, sifting, and dissemination of information concerning the disposition, movements, and intentions of the enemy. The activities of the Intelligence Section were incessant, and the knowledge obtained thereby of the utmost value. On the transfer of General Charteris to other duties, his work was carried on with great ability by Brig.-General E. W. Cox, and after the regrettable accident resulting in the death of that distinguished officer, by Brig.-General G. S. Clive.

Since the appointment of Lieut.-General Sir Nevil Macready to be Adjutant-General at home early in 1916, the work of my Adjutant-General's Branch has been most efficiently conducted under the direction of Lieut.-General Sir George Fowke. The problems of organizing the supply of reinforcements to meet the needs of our Armies while active operations were in progress, of dealing with casualties and matters of discipline, have been succeeded or supplemented since the conclusion of the Armistice by the scarcely less difficult question of demobilization. These different tasks have been performed by all ranks of the Adjutant-General's Branch with great ability and success, despite the fact that in each instance they were confronted by conditions without precedent in the history of our Army.

Throughout 1916 and 1917 the duties of the Quartermaster-General's Branch were ably directed during a period of constant expansion by Lieut.-General Sir Ronald Maxwell. Since his retirement the control of the vast organization, some of the broad outlines of which are described in paragraph 19 of this Dispatch, has been exercised by Lieut.-General Sir Travers Clarke, who has carried on the same task in the most efficient manner.

The Director-General ot Transportation's Branch was formed under the brilliant direction of Major-General Sir Eric Geddes during the autumn of 1916, as above stated. To the large number of skilled and experienced civilians included by him on his Staff, drawn from the railway companies of Great Britain and the Dominions, the Army is deeply indebted for the general excellence of our transportation services. Since the transfer of Sir Eric Geddes to other duties his work has been ably conducted by his successors, Major-Generals Sir F. A. M. Nash and S. D'A. Crookshank.

The important work of the Military Secretary's Branch has been admirably carried out under the direction of Major-General Sir W. E. Peyton and his successor, Major-General H. G. Ruggles-Brice.

The steady increase of our strength in artillery and the development of the use of that important arm upon sound and successful lines has been due in great measure to the efforts of my artillery adviser, Lieut.-General Sir J. F. N. Birch and the able Staff working under him, among them Colonel J. T. Dreyer and Colonel S. W. H. Rawlins.

The wide range of services performed by the Royal Engineers were successfully directed during the battles of 1916 and 1917 by Major-General Sir S. R. Rice. Since that date they have been controlled with great efficiency by his successor in the post of Engineer-in-Chief, Major-General Sir G. M. Heath, formerly Chief Engineer of the First Army, assisted by my Deputy Engineers-in-Chief, Brig.-Generals J. E. Edmonds and H. Biddulph.

As indicated in a preceding paragraph, the activities of the Signal Service have expanded greatly during the period of my command. Under the direction of my Signal Officer-in-Chief, Major-General Sir J. S. Fowler, and my Deputy Signal Officer-in-Chief, Colonel E. V. Turner, the growing needs of the Army have been fully met.

The office of the Inspector-General of Training, established in the latter half of 1918, has been ably filled by Lieut.-General Sir Ivor Maxse, assisted by my Deputy Inspector-General of Training, Major-General H. C. C. Uniacke, formerly commanding the artillery of the Fifth Army, as hereinafter mentioned.

Second only to the work of the Army Commanders and heads of Branches at General Headquarters in their influence upon the conduct of operations have been the parts played by the Senior General Staff officers of the several Armies. In their responsible and arduous tasks they have been most ably seconded by the general efficiency of the Army Staffs working with them, and in particular by the heads of the "A" and "Q" Branches of Army Staffs, the General Officers Commanding Royal Artillery within the Armies, and the Chief Engineers of Armies.

From the commencement of the preparations for the first Battle of the Somme and throughout all subsequent operations the General Staff work of the Fourth Army Staff has been directed with great ability and success by Major-General Sir A. A. Montgomery. The admirable work done by the head of the Administrative Branch of the Staff, Major-General H. C. Holman, by Major-General C. E. D. Budworth, who has controlled the work of the artillery of that Army with conspicuous success, and by the Chief Engineer of the Army, Major-General R. U. H. Buckland, has also contributed very materially to the success of the many brilliant operations undertaken by the Fourth Army.

The General Staff of the Army known during the Somme battle as the Reserve Army and later as the Fifth Army was well directed by Major-General N. Malcolm until the close of 1917. Major-General H. N. Sargent, Head of the "A" and "Q" Branch of the Fifth Army Staff, Major-General Uniacke while commanding the artillery of the Army, and Major-Generals R. P. Lee and P. G. Grant, successively Chief-Engineers of the Army, have also filled their important and responsible positions with distinction and success. Subsequent to the appointment of Major-General Malcolm to the command of a division, the duties of senior General Staff Officer of the Fifth Army were efficiently discharged by Major-General J. S. J. Percy until his transfer to the Second Army, and thereafter by Major-General Sir C. B. B. White, with whom have been associated as Head of the "A" and "Q" Branch and commander of the artillery of the Army respectively, Major-General P. O. Hambro and Major-General C. C. Van Straubenzee.

During the Battle of Arras the office of senior General Staff Officer of the Third Army was held by Major-General L. J. Bols. This able officer, who at a later date accompanied his Army Commander to Palestine, was succeeded by Major-General L. R. Vaughan (Indian Army), who has directed the work of the Third Army General Staff with great efficiency throughout the whole of the subsequent operations of that Army. The able manner in which have been performed the arduous duties devolving upon the Head of the "A" and "Q" Branch, Major-General A. F. Sillem, upon Major-Generals R. St. C. Lecky and A. E. Wardrop, successively commanding the artillery of the Army, and Major-Generals E. R. Kenyon and W. A. Liddell, successive Chief Engineers of the Army, is also deserving of the highest commendation.

The work of the General Staff of the First Army in the attack and capture of the Vimy Ridge in 1917 and in all subsequent operations has been most ably directed by Major-General W. H. Anderson. Major-Generals P. G. Twining and

A. W. Peck, the successive Heads of the "A" and "Q" Branch of the Army Staff, Major-Generals Sir H. F. Mercer and E. W. Alexander, successively commanding the artillery of the Army, and Major-Generals G. M. Heath and E. H. de V. Atkinson, successively Chief Engineers of the Army, have also carried out their duties in a distinguished manner.

Throughout the operations of the Second Army at Messines and east of Ypres during the summer and autumn of 1917, the elaborate General Staff arrangements for that successful fighting were admirably directed by Major-General C. H. Harington. When at a later date General Harington was appointed Deputy Chief of the Imperial General Staff at the War Office his work was undertaken by Major-General J. S. J. Percy, the present senior General Staff Officer of the Second Army. Major-General A. A. Chichester, Head of the "A" and "Q" Branch, Major-General G. Mc. K. Franks and Major-General C. R. Buckle, successively commanding the artillery of the Army, and Major-General Sir F. M. Glubb, Chief Engineer of the Army, have also accomplished the arduous and responsible tasks associated with their respective appointments with great ability and success.

I recall with gratitude the magnificent work done during the fighting of 1916 and 1917 by Major-General Sir H. M. Trenchard, at that time commanding the Royal Flying Corps. The influence exerted by this able and distinguished officer upon the *moral* and the development of the British Air Service and in the creation of its splendid traditions can scarcely be exaggerated. Since his transfer to another but kindred field of activity, his work has been most ably and successfully carried on by Major-General Sir J. M. Salmond, commander of the Royal Air Force on the Western front.

The rapid development of the tank as a most potent instrument of war and the creation of the high traditions of the Tank Corps have been due in great measure to the energy and inspiration of their commander, Major-General H. J. Elles.

The steady increase in the effectiveness of Gas as a weapon

of offence is largely to be attributed to the able work of my Director of Gas Services, Brigadier-General C. H. Foulkes.

Since the formation of the Machine Gun Corps and the creation of the office of Inspector of Machine Gun Units, held successively by Brigadier-Generals C. H. T. Lucas and L. F. Renny, the use of the Machine Gun has received a new impulse. Very gallant and efficient service has been rendered by all Machine Gun units, and not least by the battalions of the Guards Machine Gun Regiment, lately formed from personnel of the Household Cavalry Brigade and the Guards Division.

The development of bayonet fighting, and the high standard generally attained by the troops in the use of this essential weapon are due in great measure to the teaching and enthusiasm of Col. R. B. Campbell, formerly Deputy Inspector of Physical and Bayonet Training.

The general efficiency of our Mining Services, and in particular the great success of the extensive mining operations carried out by us preparatory to the Battle of Messines, is largely owed to the work of my former Inspector of Mines, Brigadier-General R. N. Harvey.

During the rapid and extensive troop movements of 1918 in particular, the constant work of the Auxiliary (Omnibus) Park was controlled with great ability by its commander, Lieut.-Col. G. L. H. Howell.

Among others responsible for the efficient work of the various rearward services and Administrative Services and Departments, my thanks are especially due to Lieut.-Gen. Sir J. J. Asser, under whose command a vast organization with a numerous Staff has been built up on the Lines of Communication, involving the control and administration of a wide extent of France, including the administrative areas of Abbeville, Etaples, Trouville, and other places, and important bases at Dunkirk, Calais, Boulogne, Dieppe, Havre, Rouen, Cherbourg, Brest, and Marseilles ; to my Directors of Medical Services past and present, namely, Surgeon-General Sir A. T. Sloggett and Lieut.-General C. H. Burtchaell, with their deputies, Surgeon-General Sir W. G. Macpherson and Major-General J. Thomson; my Deputy Adjutant-Generals, Major-Generals J. T. Burnett-Stuart and Sir E. R. C. Graham; my Deputy Quartermaster-Generals, Major-Generals R. Ford and R. S. May; the General Officer Commanding the Canadian Section at General Headquarters, Brigadier-General J. F. L. Embury; Lieut.-General Sir E. Locke Elliot, Commanding the Indian Contingent; my Provost-Marshal, Brigadier-General H. S. Rogers; my Director of Supplies, Major-General Sir E. E. Carter; my Director of Ordnance Services, Major-General Sir C. M. Mathew; my Director of Transport, Major-General Sir W. G. B. Boyce; my Director of Railway Traffic, Brigadier-General V. Murray; the Officer Commanding the Railway Operating Division, Lieut.-Colonel C. W. Paget; my Director of Light Railways, Brigadier-General G. H. Harrison; my Director of Roads, Brigadier-General H. P. Maybury; my Director of Inland Water Transport, Brigadier-General C. M. Luck; my Director of Docks, Brigadier-General R. L. Wedgwood; my Director of Works, Major-General Sir A. M. Stuart; my Director of Engineering Stores, Brigadier-General J. W. S. Sewell; my Director of Remounts, Brigadier-General Sir F. S. Garratt; my Director of Veterinary Services, Major-General J. Moore; my Director of Army Postal Services, Brigadier-General W. Price; my Controller of Labour, Brigadier-General E. G. Wace; my Director of Military Prisons, Brigadier-General P. Umfreville, who with his Staff has performed very exacting duties with great firmness and tact; my Director of Agricultural Production, Brigadier-General J., Earl of Radnor; my Controller of Salvage, Brigadier-General E. Gibb; my Inspector of Quartermaster-General's Services, Horse Feeding, and Economies, Major-General J. Vaughan; my Inspector of Quartermaster-General's Services, Messing, and Economies, Lieut.-Colonel E. Larken; my Director of Forestry, Brigadier-General Lord Lovat; my Director of Army Printing and Stationery Services, Colonel S. G. Partridge; my Director of Graves Registration and Enquiries, Major-General Fabian

Ware; my Financial Adviser, Brigadier-General H. G. Goligher; my Paymaster-in-Chief, Major-General Sir C. A. Bray; my Directors of Hirings and Requisitions, Major-General the Right Hon. L. B. Friend; and my Deputy Controller of Expeditionary Force Canteens, Colonel E. Benson.

The duties of the Principal Chaplain and Deputy Chaplain-General have been discharged by the Reverend J. M. Simms and the Right Reverend Bishop L. H. Gwynne with a zeal and devotion for which I wish to express to them my sincere gratitude. My thanks are due also to Miss Lila Davy, the Chief Controller of the Women's Auxiliary Army Corps in France, for the very valuable assistance given by her and all ranks serving under her, and to Colonel the Hon. Sir Arthur Lawley, who as Commissioner has supervised the wonderful work done by the British Red Cross Society in France.

I desire also to take this last opportunity to record my personal appreciation of the very valuable help rendered, during the great events described in my Dispatches, by other officers of my General Staff Branch at Headquarters, and in particular by Major-General Sir John Davidson, Head of the Operations Section, and those who worked under him, among them Brigadier-General J. G. Dill, Brigadier-General (at that time Lieut.-Colonel) E. Napper Tandy, Lieut.-Colonel W. G. S. Dobbie, and Major J. H. Boraston; by Major-General G. P. Dawnay, Head of the Staff Duties Section; Brigadier-General K. Wigram, formerly Head of the Operations (B) Section; Brigadier-General C. Bonham-Carter and Colonel H. F. Baillie for their work in connection with the formation and development of the Scheme for General and Technical Education within the Army; and Lieut.-Colonel E. M. Jack, under whose direction the work of the Field Surveying battalions in the preparation and supply of maps and the fixing of hostile battery positions has been of the greatest value to our artillery and other arms and services.

My relations with the Allied and Associated Armies, the co-ordination of our operations, and the good feeling existing between all ranks of our Armies and the civil population of France and Belgium have been greatly assisted by the work of the different Inter-Allied Missions. In this connection I desire to refer gratefully to the help long given to me by Brigadier-General Clive in my dealings with French General Headquarters; to the valuable work done by Lieut.-General Sir J. P. Du Cane, the Senior British Military Representative at Marshal Foch's Headquarters; by the Head of the British Mission with Belgian Headquarters, Brigadier-General the Earl of Athlone; by my present Representative at French General Headquarters, Brigadier-General F. W. L. S. H. Cavendish; by the Head of the British Mission with the American Expeditionary Force, Brigadier-General C. M. Wagstaff; and by Brigadier-General C. A. Ker, Head of the British Mission with the Portuguese Expeditionary Force.

I desire to refer also with deep gratitude to the invaluable assistance given to me by the able and gallant officers who in turn acted as Chief of the French Mission attached to my Headquarters, General des Vallières, who has since met a soldier's death, and his successors, Colonel de Bellaigue de Bughas and General de Laguiche. My thanks are due equally to Lieut.-General A. L. E. Orth, who as Chief of the Belgian Mission attached to my Headquarters has spared no pains to further the interests of our common cause; to Colonel C. Capello, Chief of the Italian Mission, and to Lieut.-Colonel Robert Bacon, who as Chief of the American Mission attached to my Headquarters has been able to give me advice and assistance of the greatest value on many occasions.

Finally, my thanks are due to the officers of my Personal Staff, and in particular to my Assistant Military Secretary, Lieut.-Colonel A. F. Fletcher; my Private Secretary, Major Sir Philip Sassoon, and Commandant E. A. Gemeau, by whose loyal and devoted assistance a great burden of work has been lifted from my shoulders.

(25) I desire to conclude this dispatch with a very warm and sincere acknowledgment of the great debt owed by all

ranks of the Armies in France to our kinsmen and kinswomen of the British Empire for the unfailing support they have given us by their thoughts, their prayers, and their work throughout the long years of war. In all those years their trust and confidence never wavered, their labours never ceased, and no sacrifices, hardships, or privations were too great to be borne, provided that thereby the needs of the troops might adequately be supplied. The dauntless spirit of the people at home strengthened and sustained the invincible spirit of the Army, the while their incessant toil on land and sea, in the mine, factory, and shipyard, placed in our hands the means with which to fight.

Neither do we forget the gratitude due from us to the various Home Authorities, and especially to the Ministry of Munitions, by whose efforts, in conjunction with those of the Governments of the Dominions, the working power and resources of the whole Empire were so rapidly developed and co-ordinated for the more vigorous prosecution of the war. The record of what they accomplished in the space of four and a half years is indeed stupendous. If the Army may justly be proud of a great victory, gallantly won at the end of an uphill fight, we have good reason to be thankful, too, for their devoted and patriotic work, which alone made it possible to continue the struggle until a successful conclusion had been reached.

I have the honour to be,

Sir,

Your most obedient Servant,

D. HAIG, Field-Marshal,

Commanding-in-Chief, British Armies in France.

THE END.

PRINTED IN GREAT BRITAIN AT
THE PRESS OF THE PUBLISHERS.

Gulf of Riga
Tukkum
Riga
Main line to Petrograd
Mitau
R. Duina (Duna)
Libau
BALTIC SEA
Shavli
Dvinsk (Dunaburg)
Memel
Tilsit
R. Niemen
Kovno
Koenigsberg
Vilna
Suwalki
Masurian Lake Region
Allenstein
Tannenberg
Grodno
Minsk
To Moscow
Ossowietz